A Few Perfect Hours

... and Other Stories from Southeast Asia & Central Europe

by Josh Neufeld

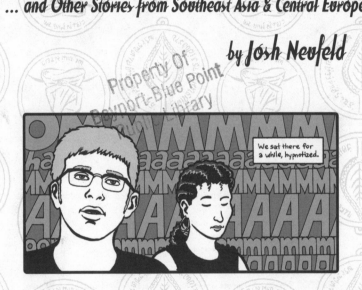

We sat there for a while, hypnotized.

Portions of this collection previously appeared in The Vagabonds, Alternative Comics #2,
SPX 2003, Maxine: A Literate Companion for Churlish Girls and Rakish Women,
In These Times, and Keyhole.

JOSH NEUFELD
www.JoshComix.com
joshcomix@mindspring.com

Designed by Danielle Nguyen and Josh Neufeld.
Production by Josh Neufeld.
Published through a generous grant from
The Xeric Foundation, www.XericFoundation.com.
Distributed in association with
Alternative Comics, www.indyworld.com/altcomics.

First printing: September 2004.
ISBN: 1-891867-79-2.
Printed in The United States.

For Sari,
my traveling companion,
my life companion, my love.

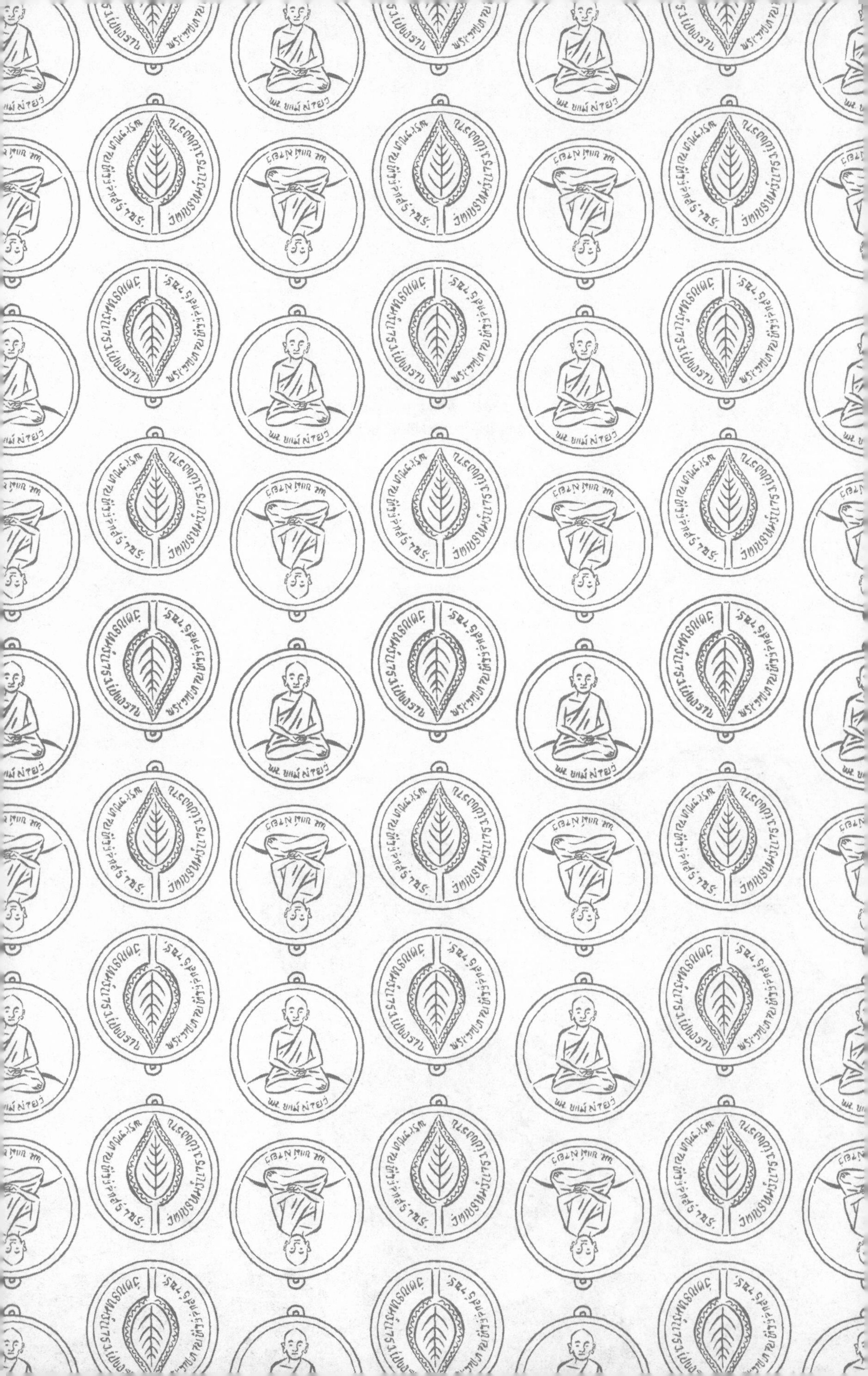

Contents

A Few Perfect Hours   1
BANGKOK, THAILAND -- Chaos and confusion . . . sanctuary in a Buddhist temple.

Travel Tip #6: How to Squat   15
Travel Tip #13: Bathing in the Tropics   16

The Cave of Fear   19
SOPPONG, THAILAND -- Eight hours in a dark, water-filled cave.

Tribal Rituals, Part I: On a Mission   31
NAKHON PHANOM, THAILAND -- Stranded . . . salvation . . . new perspectives . . .
Baptists and Buddhists.

Travel Tip #3: Less Weight in the Bag   45

Mr. Ong's Organic Farm   47
PENANG, MALAYSIA -- Sustainable agriculture versus the forces of
industrialization . . . a day's work.

How to Star in a Singaporean Soap Opera   59
SINGAPORE -- Extras on Chinese-language TV . . . how Singaporeans view
the West.

Travel Tip #45: Gynecology on the Go   69

The Balkan Express, Part I: The Serbian Bear   73
SERBIA -- Traveling from Istanbul to Prague . . . trampled by wartime
nationalism . . . peach schnapps.

The Balkan Express, Part II: The Ice Cream Man   81
BELGRADE, SERBIA -- Practicing English on two travelers in a train station.

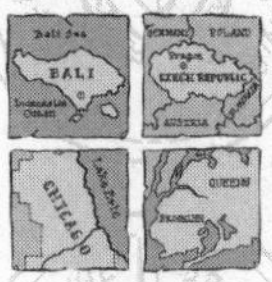

Tribal Rituals, Part II: Cremations, Cubicles, and Cant   89
PRAGUE, CHICAGO, BALI, AND NEW YORK -- Death, religion, and ritual . . .
saying farewell.

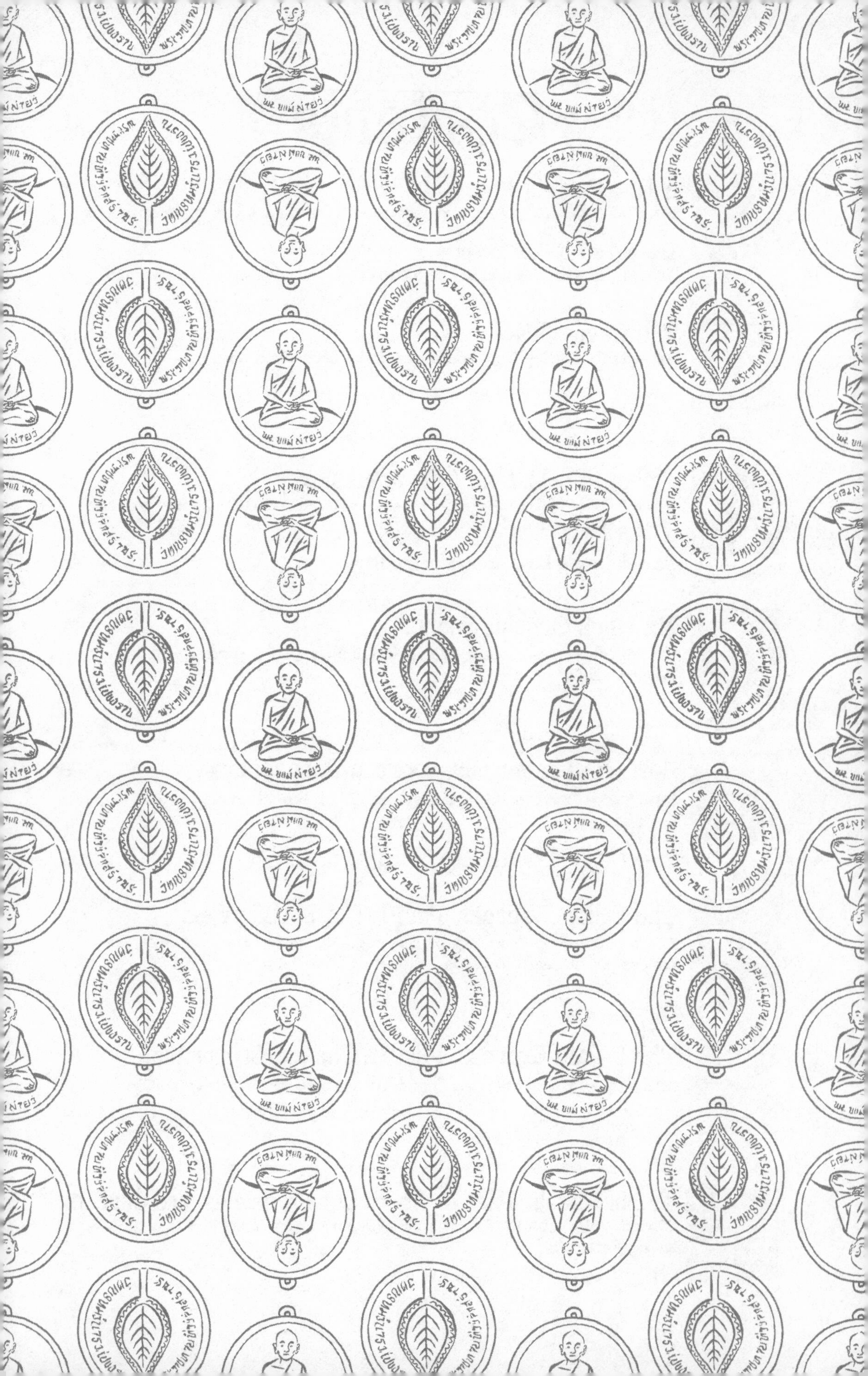

Foreword

By Sari Wilson

First, a word about my hair. When Josh presented me with the first comic-book rendition of myself, I was not pleased. Hair too puffy, nose too pointy. The hair has evolved (he's getting it, I think), the nose has stayed the same. I guess my nose really is that pointy.

On our early dates, when we leaned over our meals so far that our shirts kept getting stained, I told Josh stories of my backpacking adventures in Egypt, Israel, and Turkey. Just out of college, we squirmed in our jobs, we scoffed at money; we agreed that we hungered only for experience. Soon, Josh began to draw pictures, images from the stories I told him. Thus, I fell in love with him and my love was -- and is -- bound up in his sensitivity and curiosity.

So we went on a trip together. We started in Hong Kong and ended in Prague. Along the way, we traveled in Thailand, Malaysia, Indonesia, and Singapore and by train from the Czech Republic to Turkey -- and back. In Prague, we got jobs and dropped anchor for a year. In all, we were gone almost a year and a half. This book springs from that journey. The stories in *A Few Perfect Hours* have been labored over for many months and, in some cases, years. In the intervening period -- more than a decade -- they have gained the aura of personal myth. From fleeting moments in our travels, Josh has constructed a unique reading experience.

A Few Perfect Hours is travel literature in the tradition of Pico Iyer and Paul Theroux but with a twist: The stories are told in words and pictures. Actually, I think the comics form is uniquely suited to this genre. A sense of place is crucial to travel writing and Josh's lovingly rendered art -- his attention to the details of his environment -- is a great gift. As my eyes move from panel to panel, Josh brings me back to the ramshackle hilltop organic farm, the Dr. Seussian rock formations in the underground cave, the time-warped Baptist missionaries' bungalow. When he shows the re-creation of New York City's Chinatown on a set for a Singaporean soap opera, I remember the little ironies and absurdities: the Pacific Bell (?) phone booths, the sanitized graffiti, the spanking-clean streets.

To me, *A Few Perfect Hours* is a testament to the expansion of the mind and spirit that occurs when one throws oneself unbidden into the world. Time and again in these stories, Josh is faced with his inability to apprehend his own experience. In "The Cave of Fear," while crawling through a cave flooded with spring rains, Josh must confront his romantic notions of adventure. While acting on the set of the Singaporean TV soap, Josh experiences a role reversal when the non-Asian extras are crudely stereotyped as beggars, car thieves, and drug addicts. In one of my favorite stories, "The Ice Cream Man," Josh shifts the narrative perspective to a Serbian ice cream vendor trolling for customers in a Belgrade train station. In the process, Josh imbues a chance encounter with a stranger -- one of countless such encounters we all have that are generally soon forgotten -- with a remarkable dignity and grace. Tucked between these stories, you will find the occasional "Travel Tip," lighthearted how-to features on backpackers' hygiene and health care. (Check out my contribution, "Gynecology on the Go," which takes on challenges specific to the female traveler.) Josh ties together his themes in the final story, "Cremation, Cubicles, and Cant." This ambitious piece sees memory, desire, and experience merge into a dreamlike meditation on boundary-crossings -- cultural and anthropological -- including that final threshold, mortality.

The challenge of the backpacking odyssey is unique. Stripped of the normal scaffolding of life, we must narrate our own adventures to give them weight and to give ourselves form. When we travel, we become both actor and storyteller, hero and scribe. The stories Josh tells about himself as he encounters the world are striking in that they are so curious, gentle, and honest. In fact, I am always pushing him to spring into make-believe. ("Make us fight more," I say. "Conflict is interesting." "No," he says, "That's not how it happened.")

While the cartoon version of myself has evolved into something that looks more like me, Josh and I have with time moved farther from our incredulous, wide-eyed comic-book selves. This is at least partly because the world has changed around us. I write this in the summer of 2004, three years after 9/11, when it is no longer safe to traipse blithely about the world as young Josh and Sari did. Of course people are still doing it. They always will, thankfully. But there now must be in the minds of backpackers a specter of depersonalized violence. On our trip, Josh and I worried about communicating, understanding, connecting. We never truly feared for our survival.

The absence of this threat gives ***A Few Perfect Hours*** the air of a letter from the past. One that tells us, in its loving attention to the moment, something important about where the journey has taken us.

-- Sari Wilson, Brooklyn, July 2004

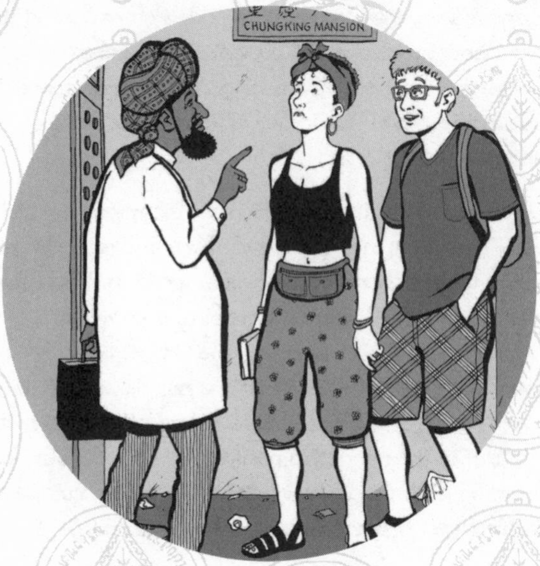
CHUNGKING MANSION

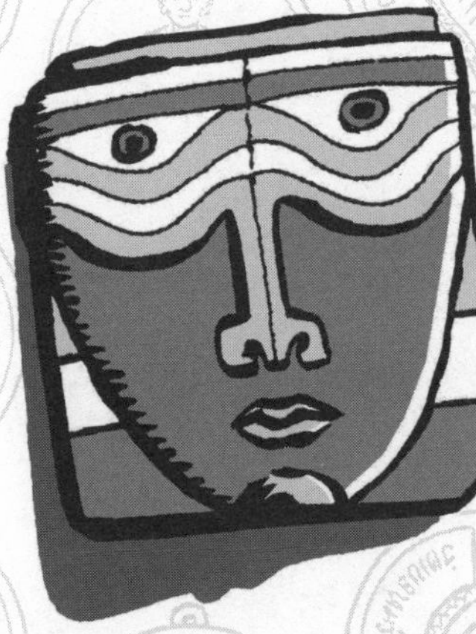

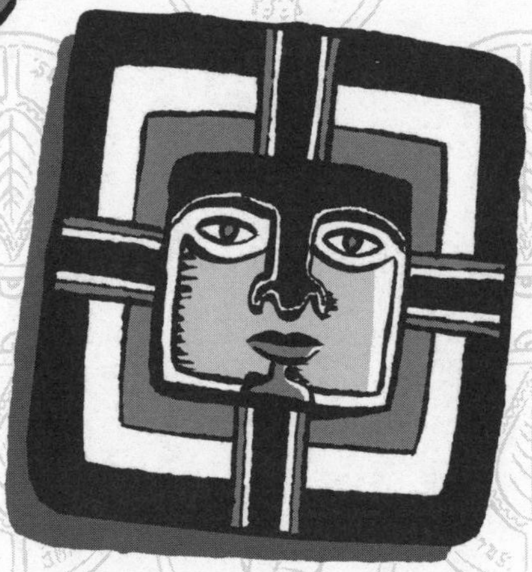

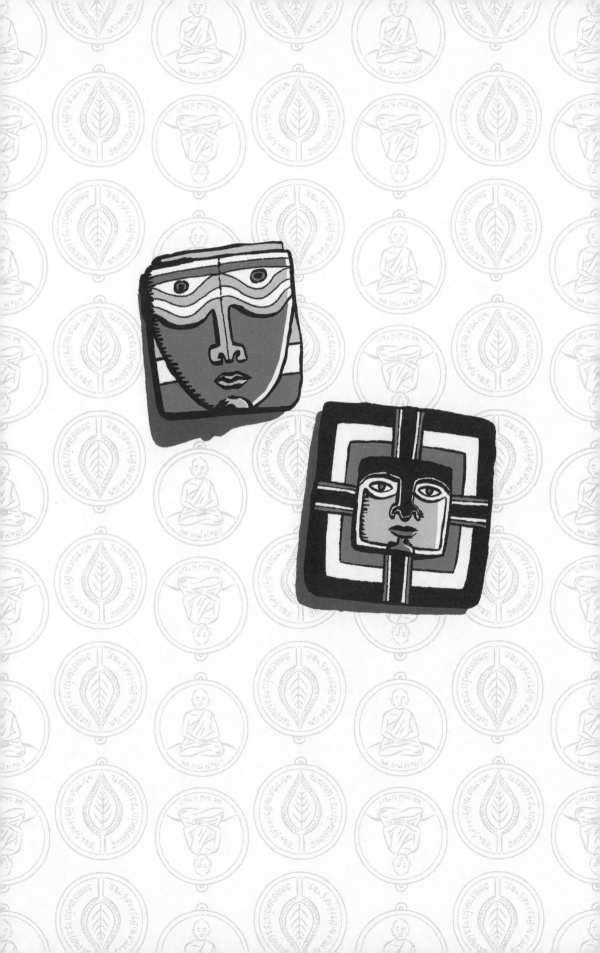

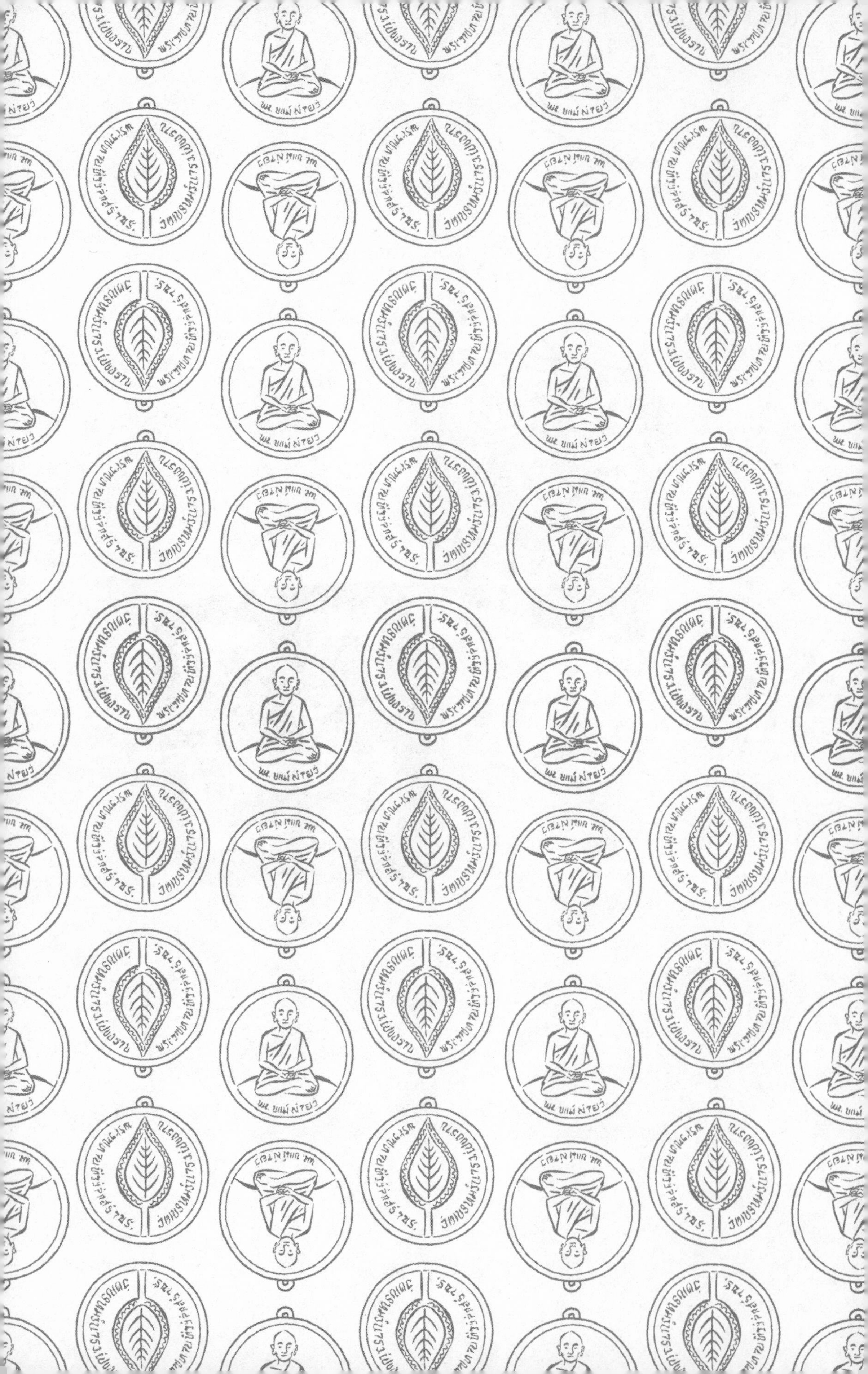

Home-keeping youth have ever homely wits....
I rather would entreat thy company
To see the wonders of the world abroad,
Than, living dully sluggardized at home,
Wear out thy youth with shapeless idleness.

– William Shakespeare
The Two Gentlemen of Verona I, 1

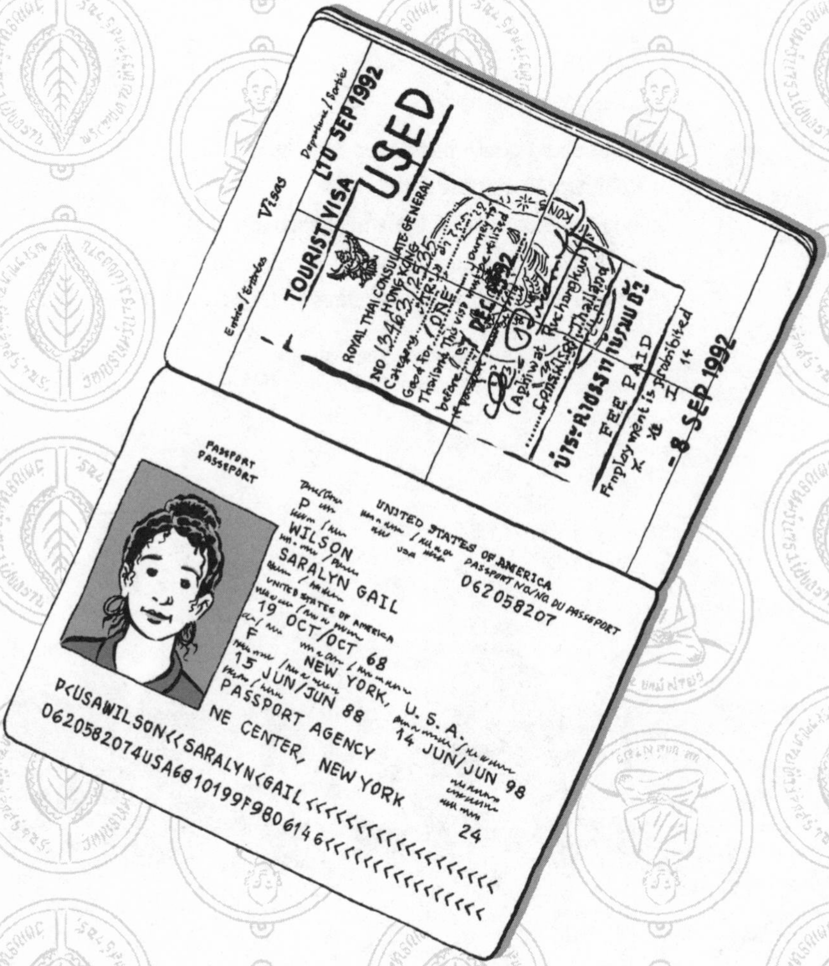

Visas
TOURIST VISA
LTU SEP 1992
USED
ROYAL THAI CONSULATE GENERAL
HONG KONG
FEE PAID
-8 SEP 1992
PASSPORT
PASSEPORT
UNITED STATES OF AMERICA
P
WILSON
SARALYN GAIL
062058207
UNITED STATES OF AMERICA
19 OCT/OCT 68
F
NEW YORK, U.S.A.
15 JUN/JUN 88
14 JUN/JUN 98
PASSPORT AGENCY
NE CENTER, NEW YORK
24
P<USAWILSON<<SARALYN<GAIL<<<<<<<<<<<<<<<<<<<<
0620582074USA6810199F9806146<<<<<<<<<<<<<<<<<

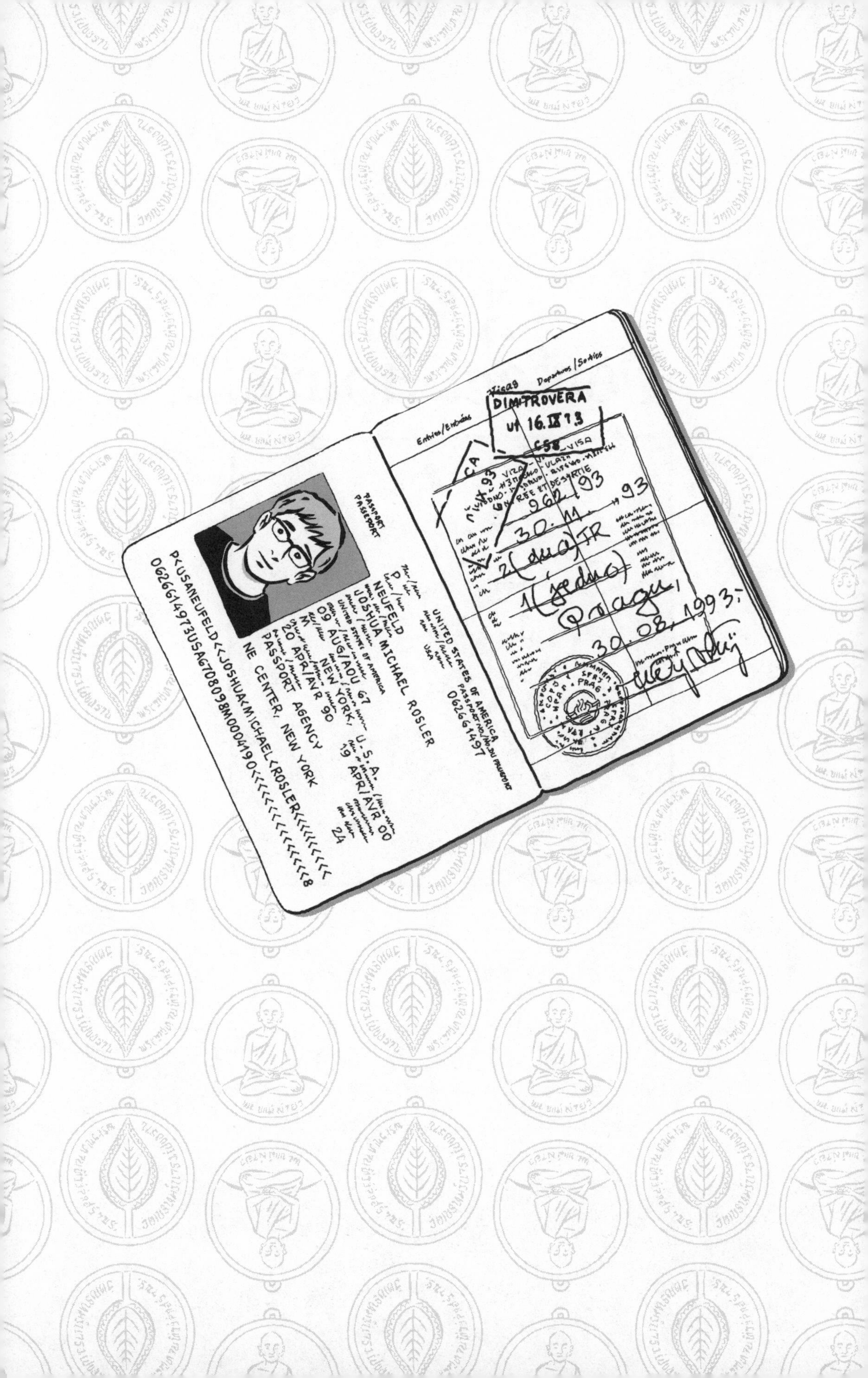
PASSPORT
PASSEPORT
UNITED STATES OF AMERICA
062661497
P
NEUFELD
JOSHUA MICHAEL ROSLER
UNITED STATES OF AMERICA
09 AUG/AOU 67
M
NEW YORK, U.S.A.
20 APR/AVR 90
19 APR/AVR 00
PASSPORT AGENCY
NE CENTER, NEW YORK
P<USANEUFELD<<JOSHUA<MICHAEL<ROSLER<<<<<<<<<<<
0626614973USA6708098M0004190<<<<<<<<<<<<<<8
Visas
Departures/Sorties
Entries/Entrées
DIMITROVERA
VISA
Prague
30.08.1993

A Few Perfect Hours

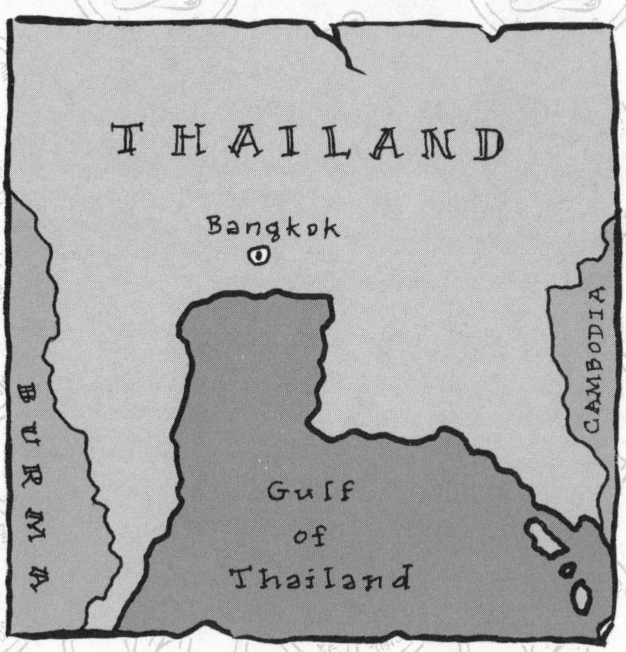
THAILAND
Bangkok
BURMA
CAMBODIA
Gulf of Thailand

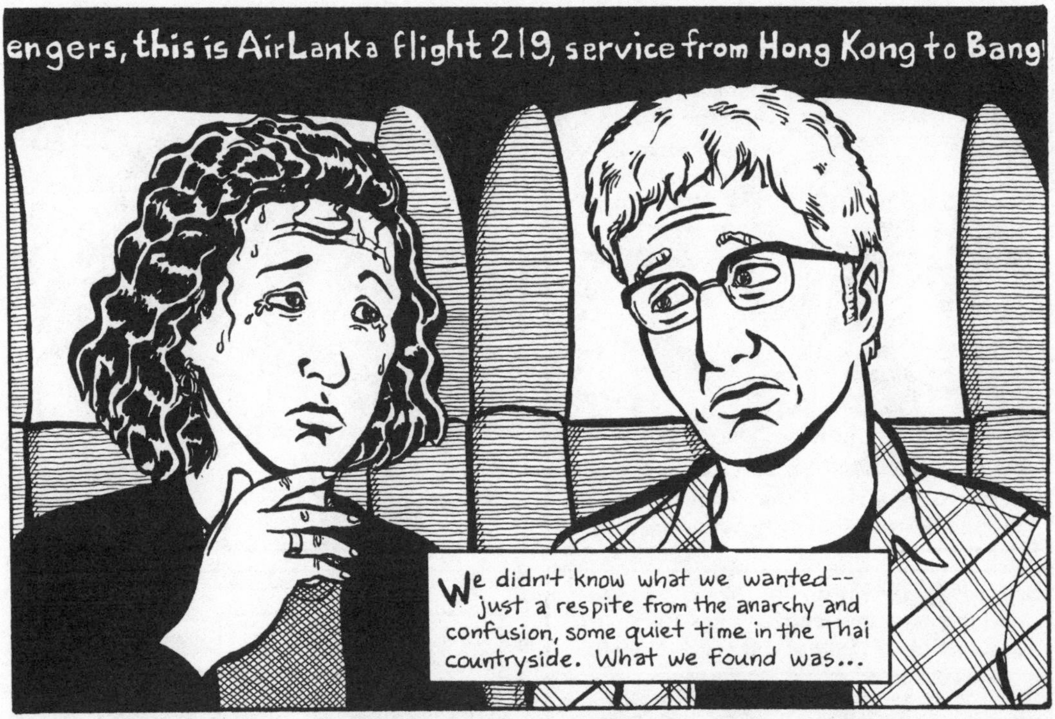
engers, this is AirLanka flight 219, service from Hong Kong to Bang
We didn't know what we wanted-- just a respite from the anarchy and confusion, some quiet time in the Thai countryside. What we found was...

A Few PERFECT Hours

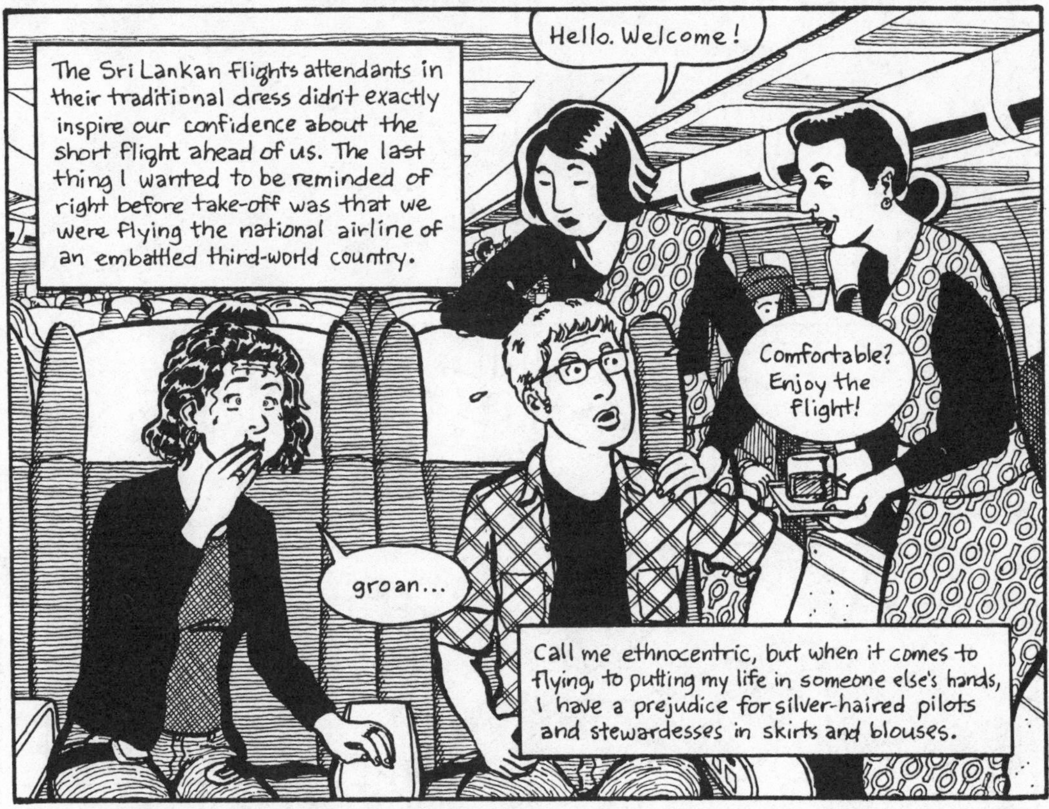
Hello. Welcome!
The Sri Lankan flights attendants in their traditional dress didn't exactly inspire our confidence about the short flight ahead of us. The last thing I wanted to be reminded of right before take-off was that we were flying the national airline of an embattled third-world country.
Comfortable? Enjoy the flight!
groan...
Call me ethnocentric, but when it comes to flying, to putting my life in someone else's hands, I have a prejudice for silver-haired pilots and stewardesses in skirts and blouses.

The combination of malaria pills, jet lag and Hong Kong's devastating humidity had transformed Sari into a giant airsick bag. She felt awful.

Why do we have to fly in circles like this?

huh?

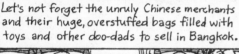
Everything about the flight seemed weird and threatening.

And of course we had a choice neighbor...

Off for some fun in Phat Phong, eh, Yanks?

Let's not forget the unruly Chinese merchants and their huge, overstuffed bags filled with toys and other doo-dads to sell in Bangkok.

Sari spent the entire flight with her head on the food tray or dragging herself to the bathroom to throw up.

tsk

COMIX TRIPS

A trip to the toilet meant pushing through a dense cloud of smoke emitted from the ad hoc businessman's club forming at the back of the plane.

cough! hack!

What had brought us to this pitch of desperation?!

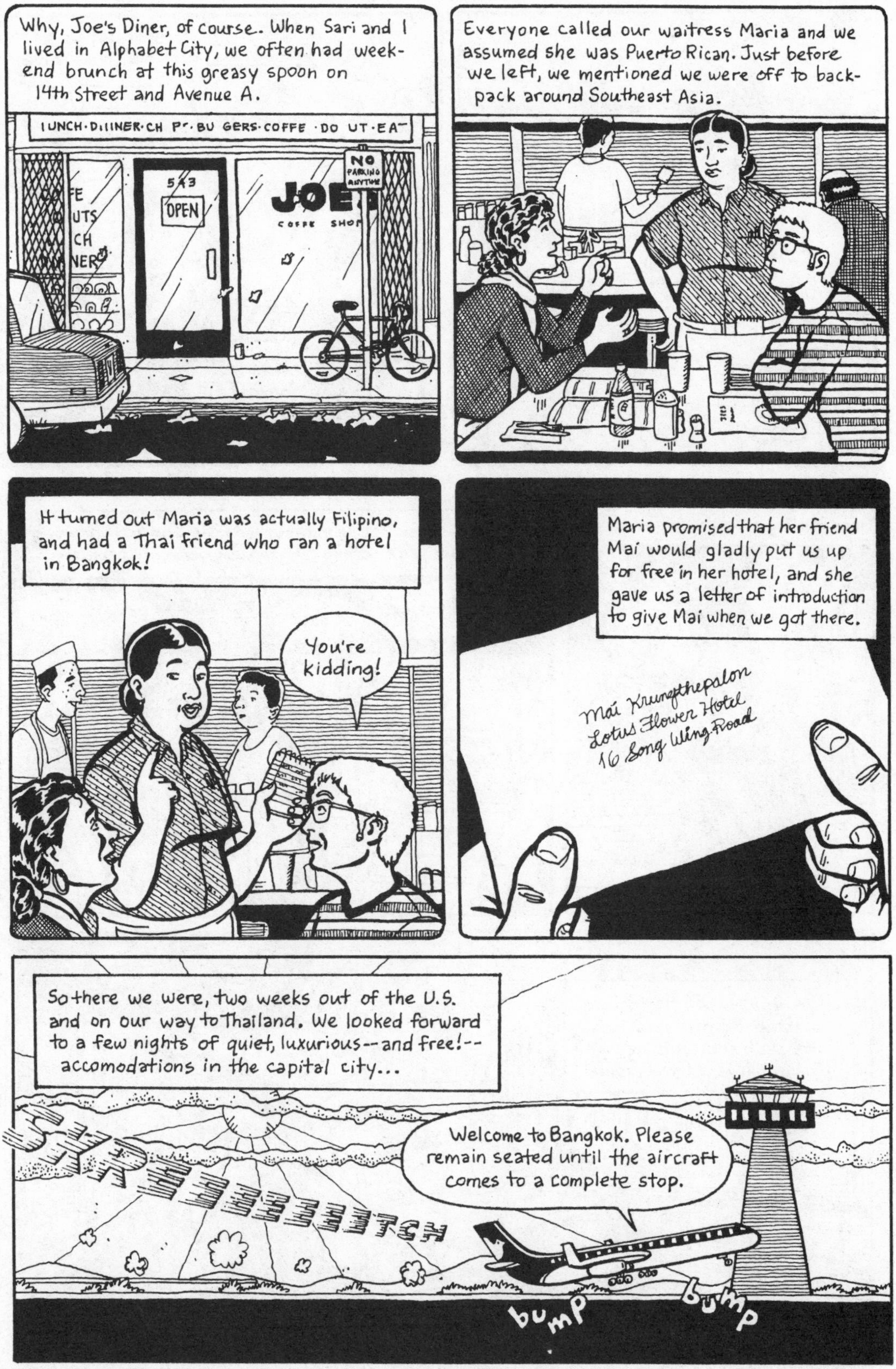

Why, Joe's Diner, of course. When Sari and I lived in Alphabet City, we often had weekend brunch at this greasy spoon on 14th Street and Avenue A.
543
OPEN
NO PARKING ANYTIME
Everyone called our waitress Maria and we assumed she was Puerto Rican. Just before we left, we mentioned we were off to backpack around Southeast Asia.
It turned out Maria was actually Filipino, and had a Thai friend who ran a hotel in Bangkok!
You're kidding!
Maria promised that her friend Mai would gladly put us up for free in her hotel, and she gave us a letter of introduction to give Mai when we got there.
Mai Krungthepalon
Lotus Flower Hotel
16 Song Wing Road
So there we were, two weeks out of the U.S. and on our way to Thailand. We looked forward to a few nights of quiet, luxurious--and free!--accomodations in the capital city...
Welcome to Bangkok. Please remain seated until the aircraft comes to a complete stop.
bump
bump

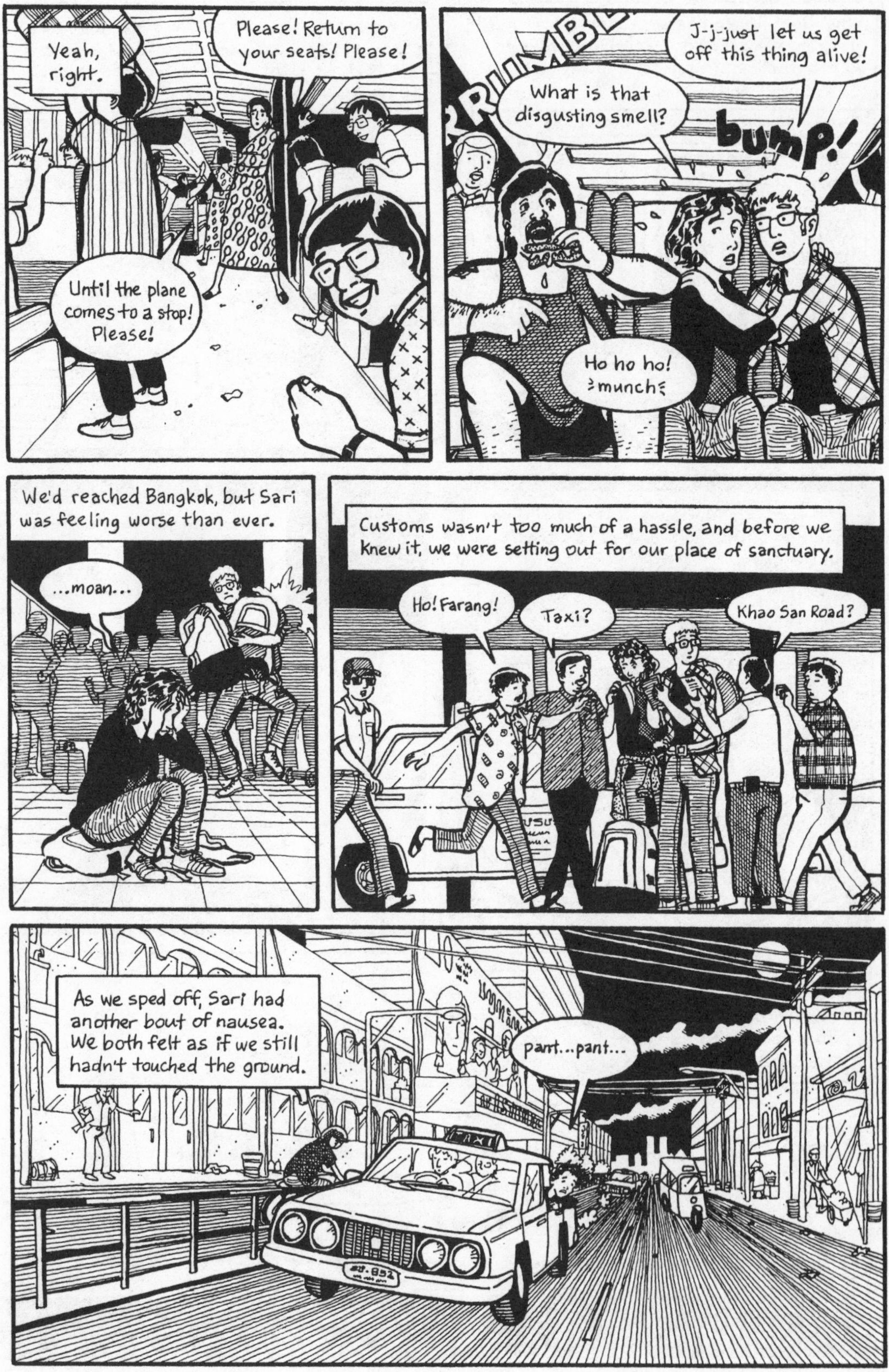
Yeah, right.
Please! Return to your seats! Please!
Until the plane comes to a stop! Please!
RRUMBLE
What is that disgusting smell?
J-j-just let us get off this thing alive!
bump!
Ho ho ho! munch
We'd reached Bangkok, but Sari was feeling worse than ever.
...moan...
Customs wasn't too much of a hassle, and before we knew it, we were setting out for our place of sanctuary.
Ho! Farang!
Taxi?
Khao San Road?
As we sped off, Sari had another bout of nausea. We both felt as if we still hadn't touched the ground.
pant...pant...

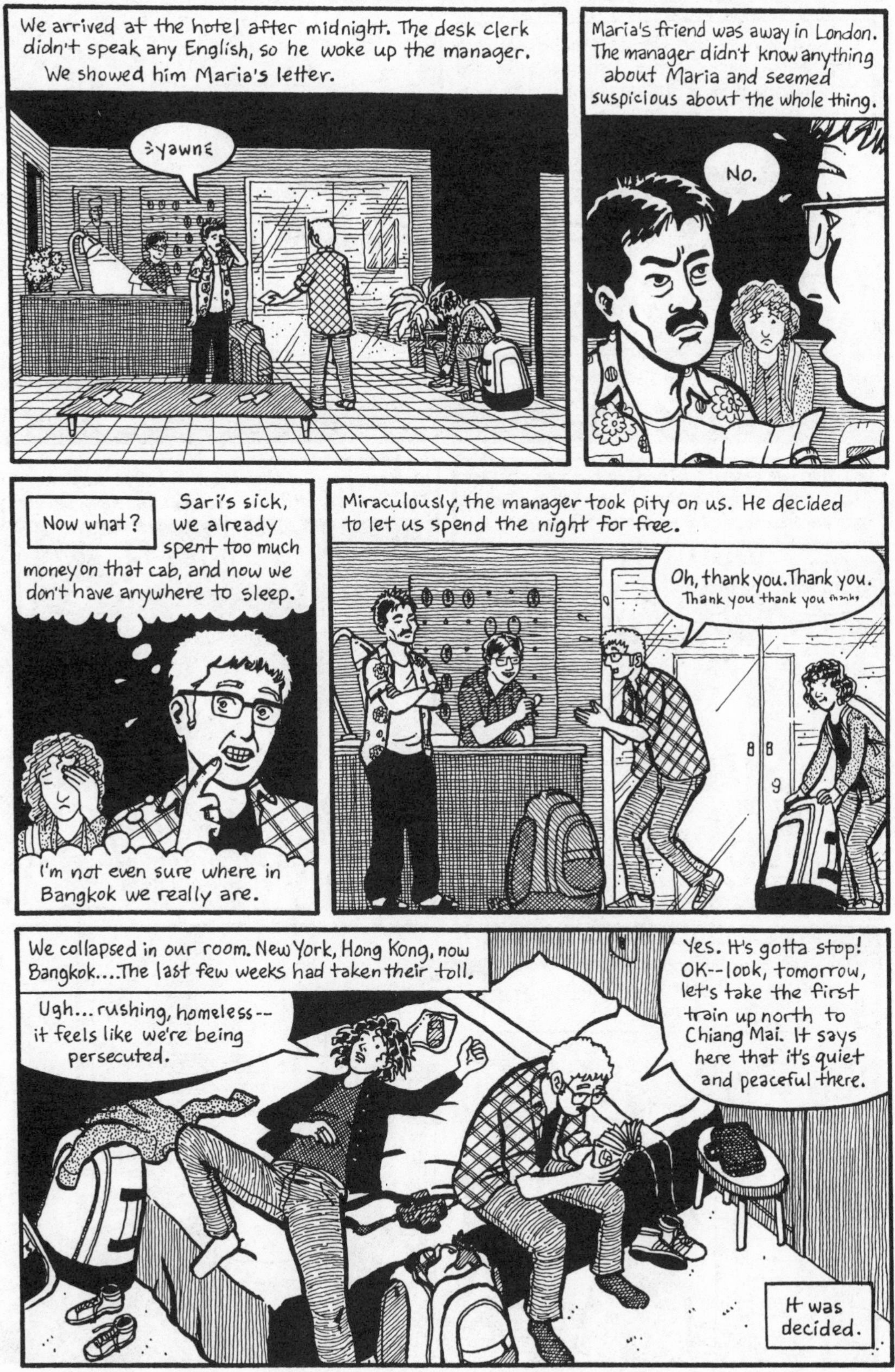
We arrived at the hotel after midnight. The desk clerk didn't speak any English, so he woke up the manager. We showed him Maria's letter.
yawn
Maria's friend was away in London. The manager didn't know anything about Maria and seemed suspicious about the whole thing.
No.
Now what?
Sari's sick, we already spent too much money on that cab, and now we don't have anywhere to sleep.
I'm not even sure where in Bangkok we really are.
Miraculously, the manager took pity on us. He decided to let us spend the night for free.
Oh, thank you. Thank you.
Thank you thank you
We collapsed in our room. New York, Hong Kong, now Bangkok.... The last few weeks had taken their toll.
Ugh... rushing, homeless -- it feels like we're being persecuted.
Yes. It's gotta stop! OK--look, tomorrow, let's take the first train up north to Chiang Mai. It says here that it's quiet and peaceful there.
It was decided.

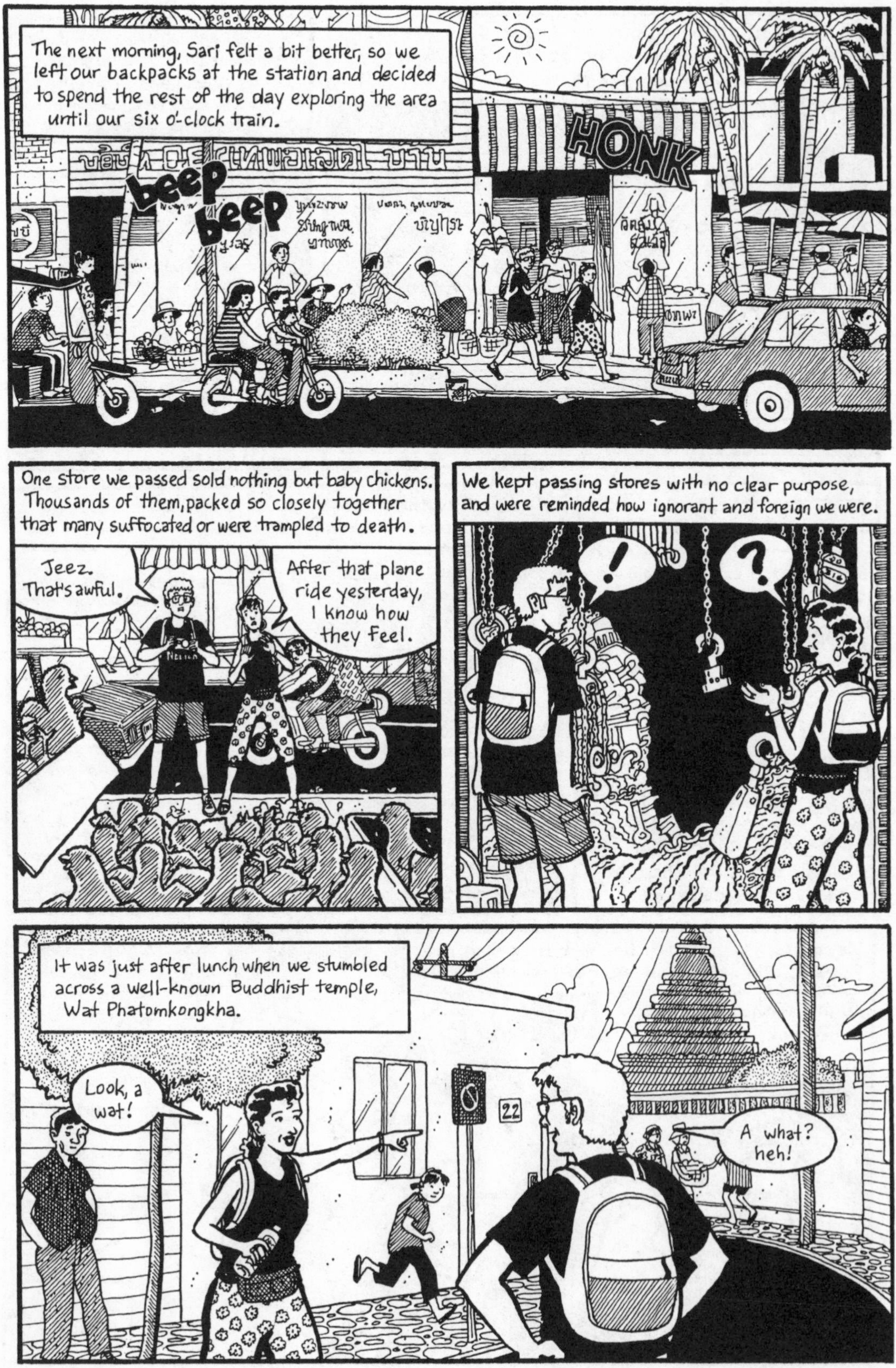
The next morning, Sari felt a bit better, so we left our backpacks at the station and decided to spend the rest of the day exploring the area until our six o'-clock train.
beep
beep
HONK
One store we passed sold nothing but baby chickens. Thousands of them, packed so closely together that many suffocated or were trampled to death.
Jeez. That's awful.
After that plane ride yesterday, I know how they feel.
We kept passing stores with no clear purpose, and were reminded how ignorant and foreign we were.
!
?
It was just after lunch when we stumbled across a well-known Buddhist temple, Wat Phatomkongkha.
Look, a wat!
22
A what? heh!

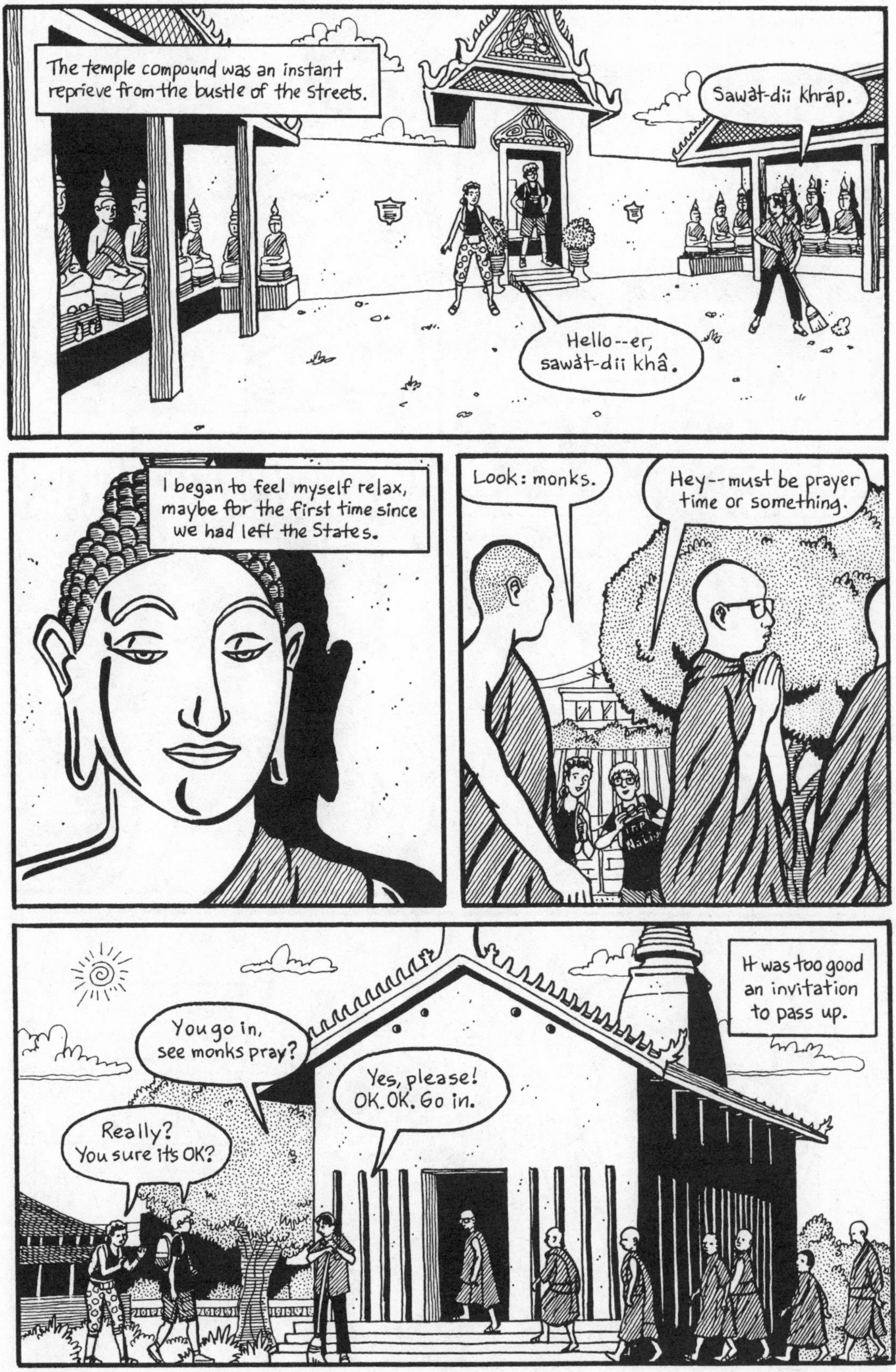

The temple compound was an instant reprieve from the bustle of the streets.
Sawàt-dii Khráp.
Hello--er, sawàt-dii khâ.
I began to feel myself relax, maybe for the first time since we had left the States.
Look: monks.
Hey--must be prayer time or something.
It was too good an invitation to pass up.
You go in, see monks pray?
Really? You sure it's OK?
Yes, please! OK. OK. Go in.

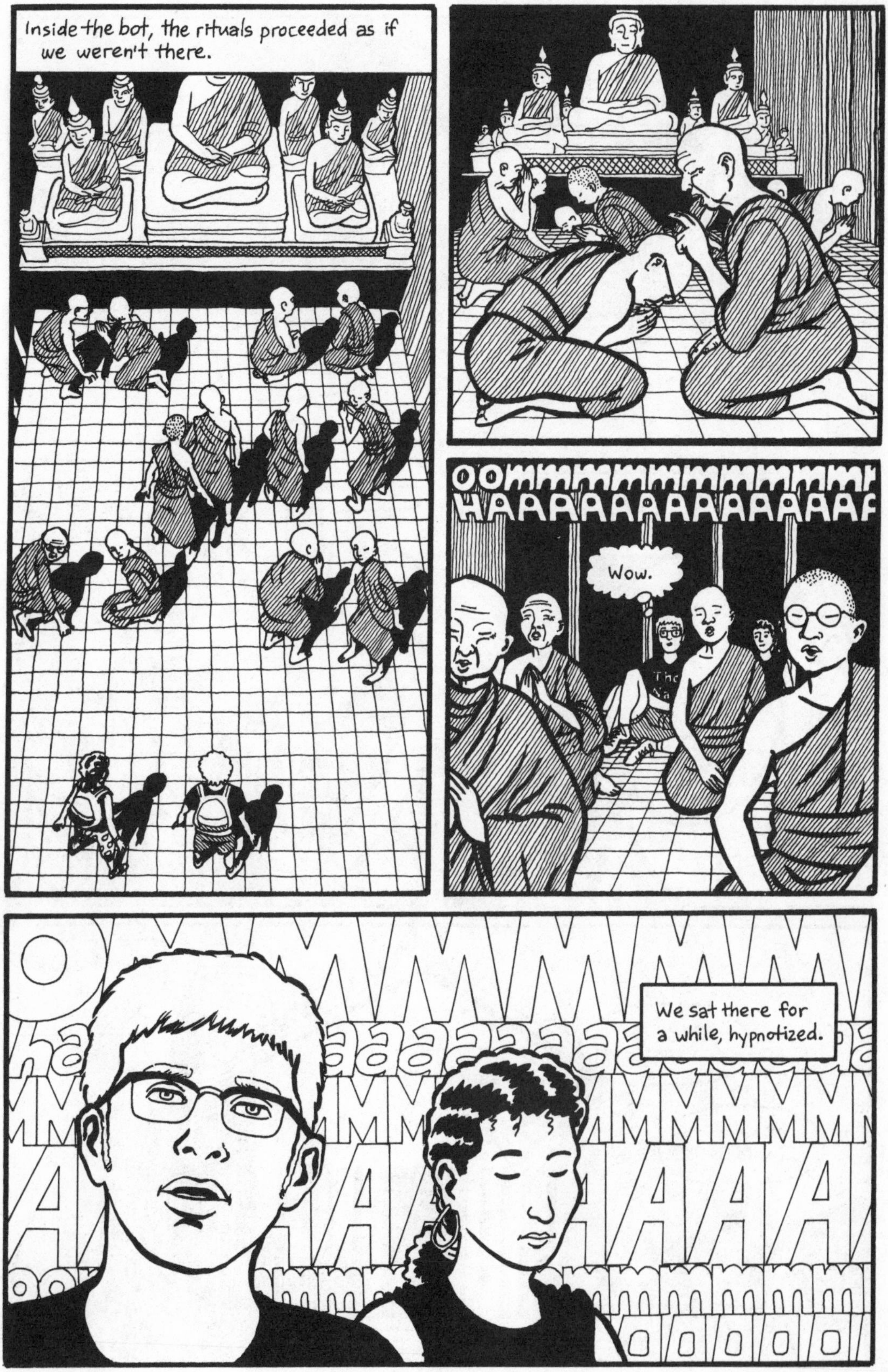
Inside the bot, the rituals proceeded as if we weren't there.
OOmmmmmmmmmmmm
HAAAAAAAAAAAAAA
Wow.
We sat there for a while, hypnotized.

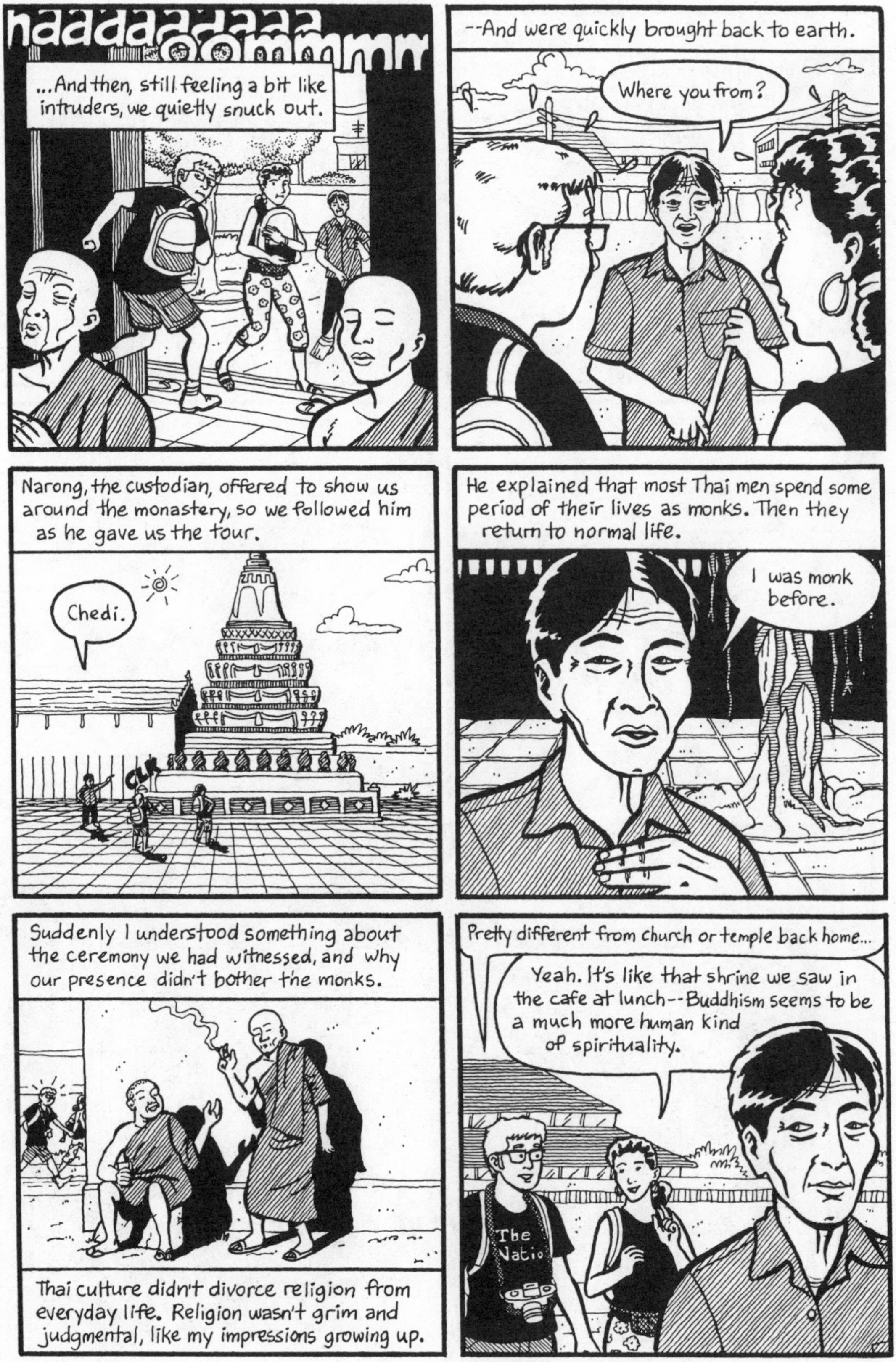
naaaaaaaaaaOOmmmmmm
...And then, still feeling a bit like intruders, we quietly snuck out.
--And were quickly brought back to earth.
Where you from?
Narong, the custodian, offered to show us around the monastery, so we followed him as he gave us the tour.
Chedi.
CLK
He explained that most Thai men spend some period of their lives as monks. Then they return to normal life.
I was monk before.
Suddenly I understood something about the ceremony we had witnessed, and why our presence didn't bother the monks.
Thai culture didn't divorce religion from everyday life. Religion wasn't grim and judgmental, like my impressions growing up.
Pretty different from church or temple back home...
Yeah. It's like that shrine we saw in the cafe at lunch--Buddhism seems to be a much more human kind of spirituality.
The Natio

Narong continued the tour...

Chao Phraya River.

...Until we were back at the courtyard, where we prepared to say good-bye.

Thank you, Narong!

Thank you, yes.

You want blessing from monk?

The day was getting curiouser and curiouser. It was difficult to process the sudden transformation from being harried anonymous tourists to welcome guests. Was all this friendliness and hospitality for real?

huh?

Is this whole "tour" just some complex scam? I've heard the horror stories of tourists being drugged and robbed in situations like this.

Josh?

Come. OK, OK!

All right, OK...

My ingrained urban paranoia made it difficult to accept good fortune, to trust the unexpected.

Ha ha. Heh.

Ptht

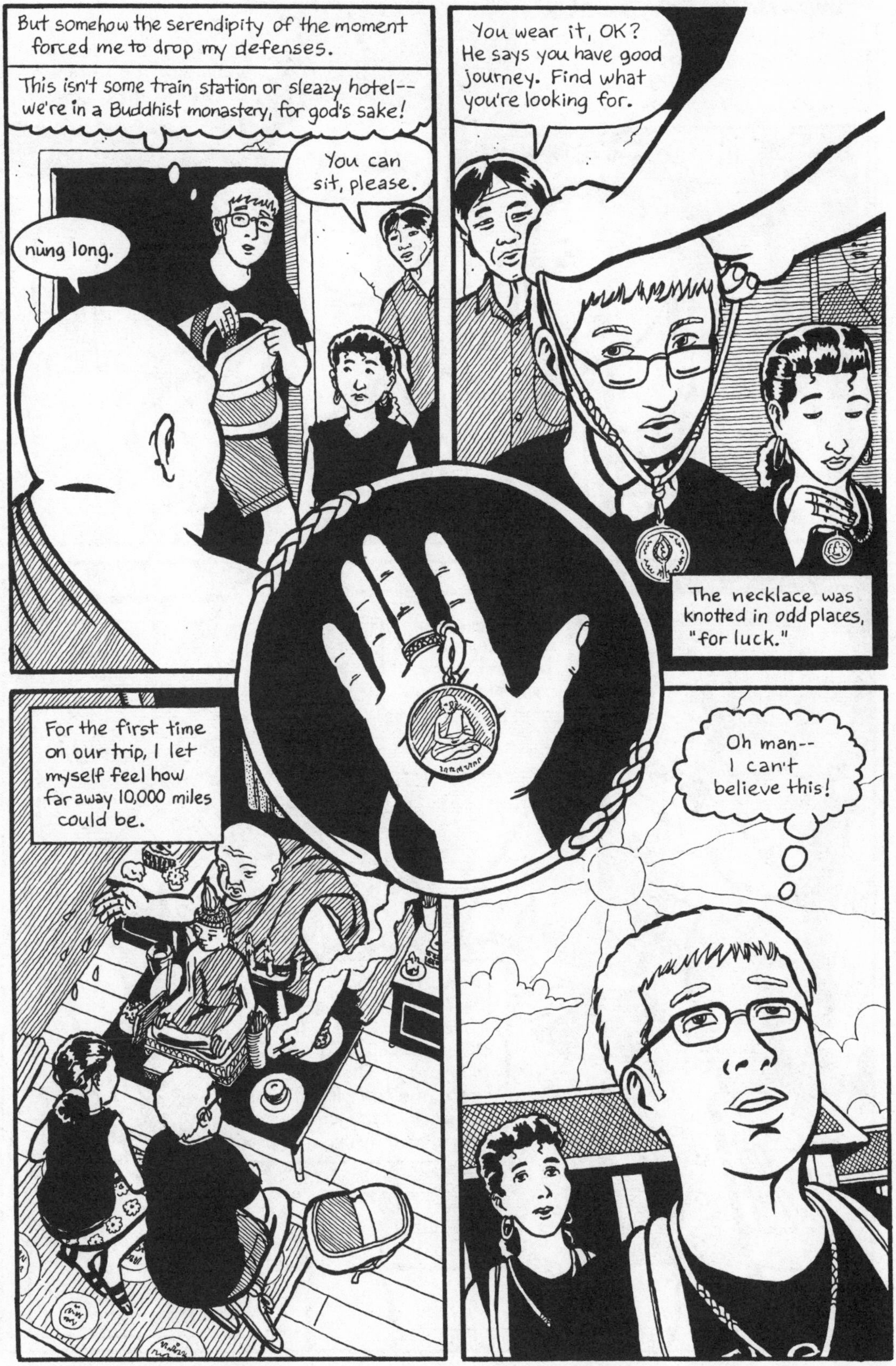

But somehow the serendipity of the moment forced me to drop my defenses.
This isn't some train station or sleazy hotel--we're in a Buddhist monastery, for god's sake!
You can sit, please.
nùng long.
You wear it, OK? He says you have good journey. Find what you're looking for.
The necklace was knotted in odd places, "for luck."
For the first time on our trip, I let myself feel how far away 10,000 miles could be.
Oh man--I can't believe this!

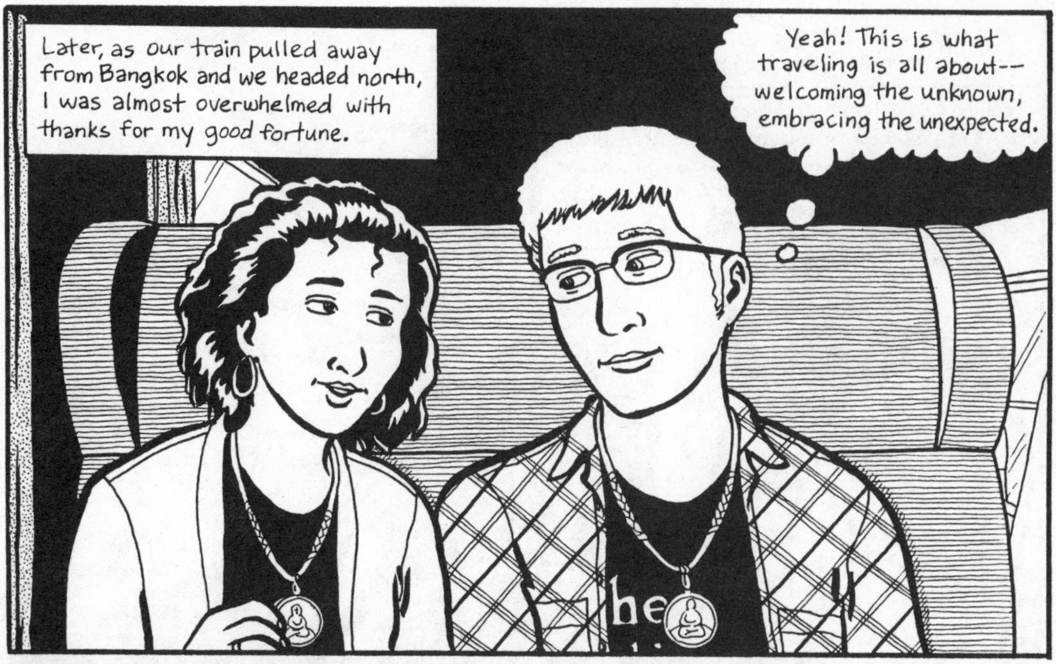
Later, as our train pulled away from Bangkok and we headed north, I was almost overwhelmed with thanks for my good fortune.
Yeah! This is what traveling is all about--welcoming the unknown, embracing the unexpected.

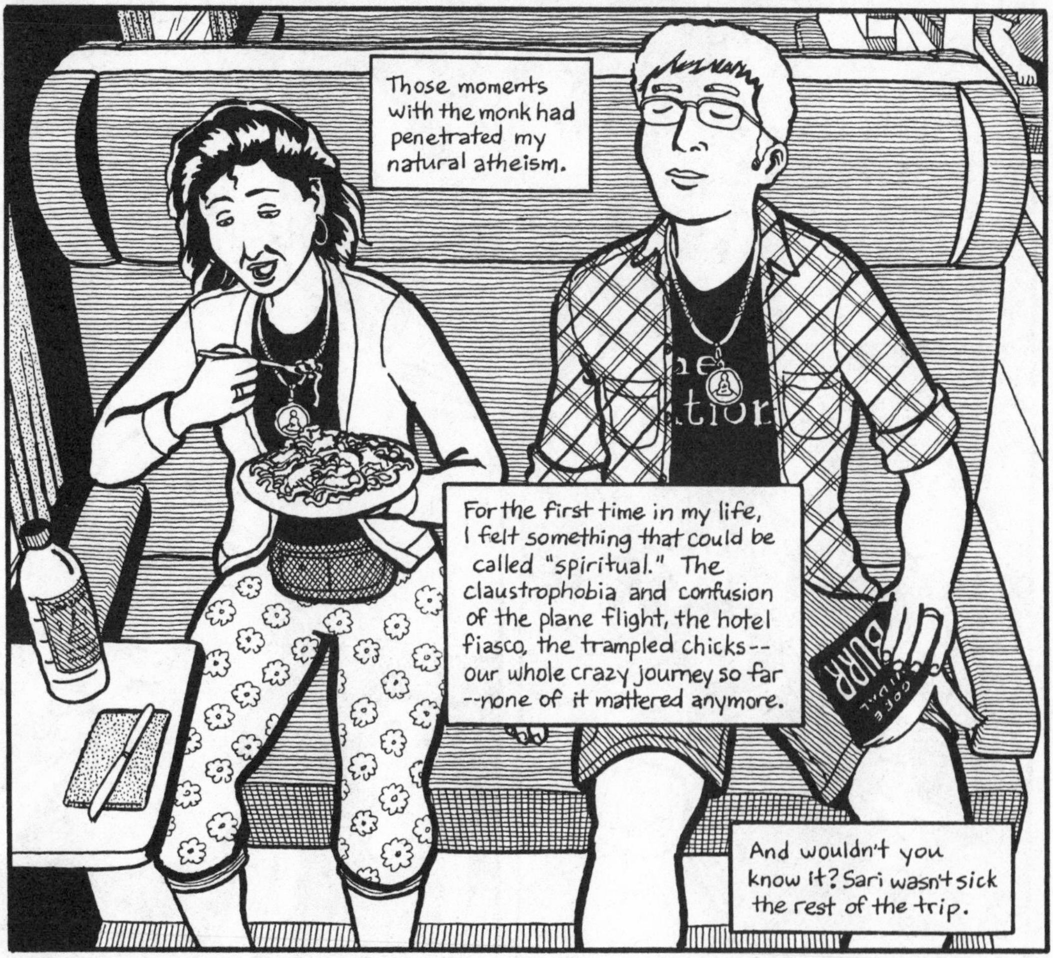
Those moments with the monk had penetrated my natural atheism.
For the first time in my life, I felt something that could be called "spiritual." The claustrophobia and confusion of the plane flight, the hotel fiasco, the trampled chicks--our whole crazy journey so far --none of it mattered anymore.
BURR
And wouldn't you know it? Sari wasn't sick the rest of the trip.

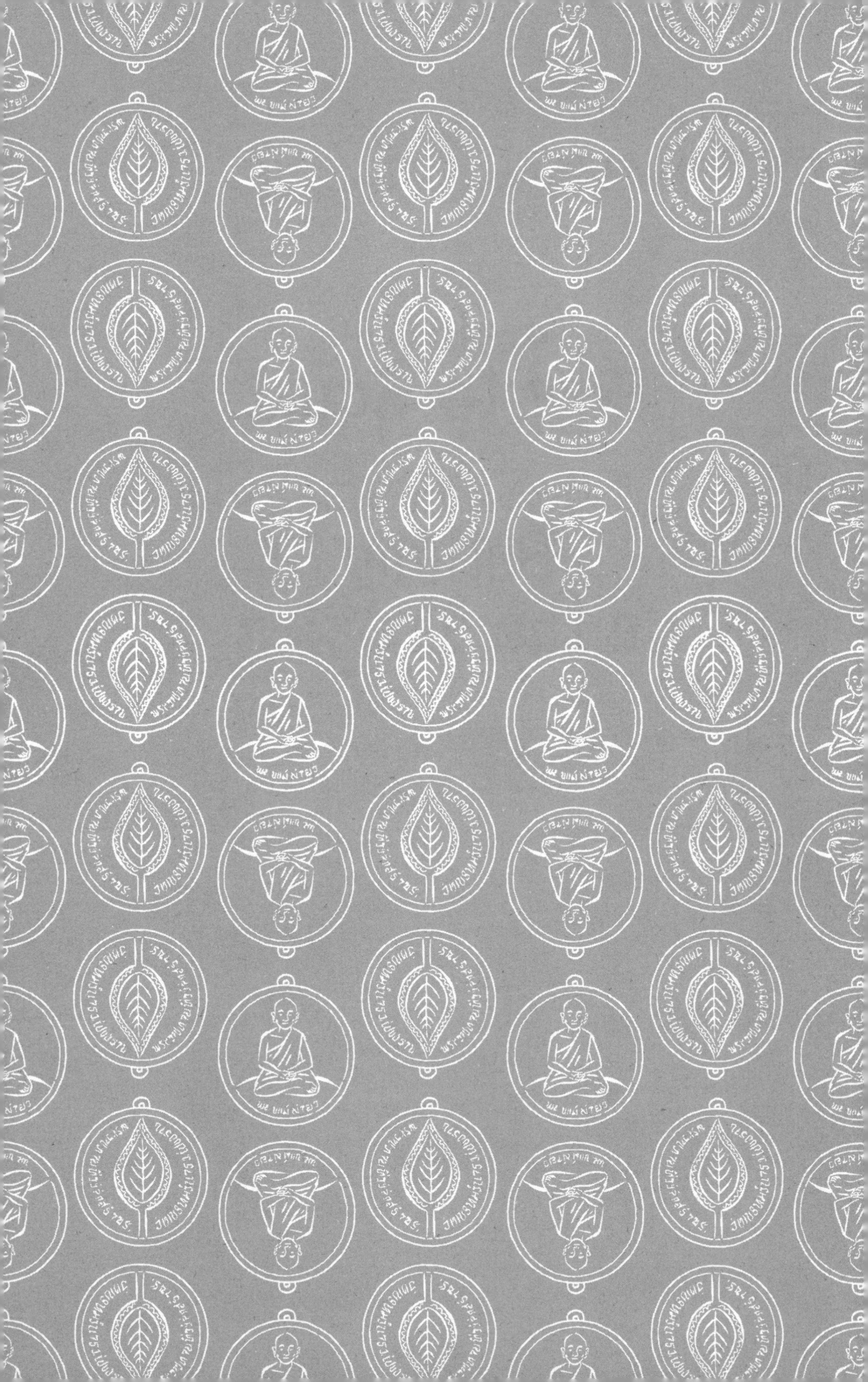

Travel Tip #6:
How to Squat

Travel Tip #13:
Bathing in the Tropics

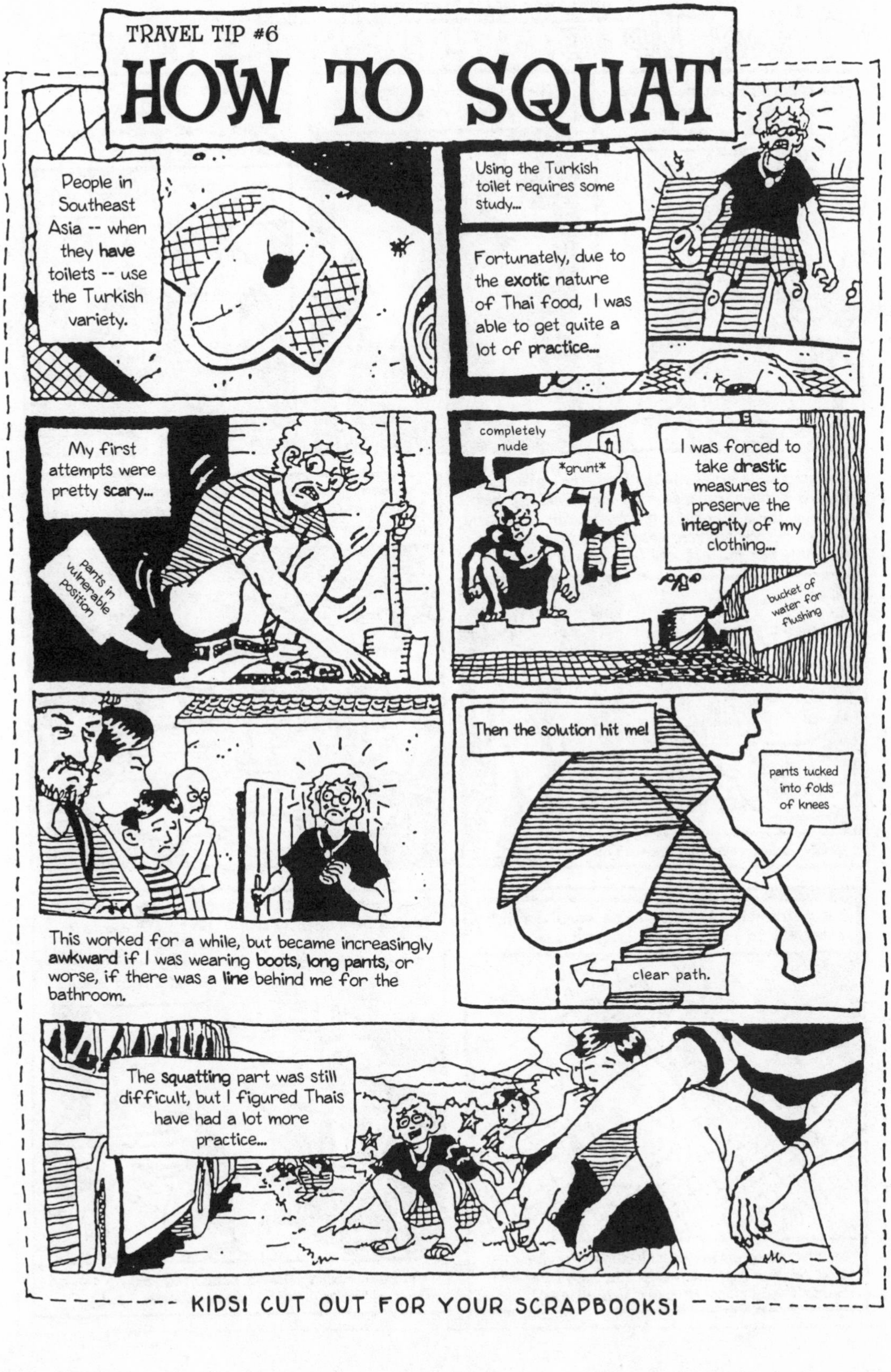
TRAVEL TIP #6
HOW TO SQUAT
People in Southeast Asia -- when they have toilets -- use the Turkish variety.
Using the Turkish toilet requires some study...
Fortunately, due to the exotic nature of Thai food, I was able to get quite a lot of practice...
My first attempts were pretty scary...
pants in vulnerable position
completely nude
grunt
I was forced to take drastic measures to preserve the integrity of my clothing...
bucket of water for flushing
This worked for a while, but became increasingly awkward if I was wearing boots, long pants, or worse, if there was a line behind me for the bathroom.
Then the solution hit me!
pants tucked into folds of knees
clear path.
The squatting part was still difficult, but I figured Thais have had a lot more practice...
KIDS! CUT OUT FOR YOUR SCRAPBOOKS!

Hey, l'il buddies! Clip out this priceless info and hoard it for future use!

Travel Tip #13: BATHING IN THE TROPICS

Backpackers in Southeast Asia know that a nice hot shower is a foreign concept.

There is, of course, the Hong Kong version...

hot water on timer

But many people find it too stressful, especially since you start sweating again even as you're drying off!

Why bother? I'm not moving!

air-con on meter

In the places we stayed in Thailand, the water came in only one temperature-- fine for drinking,* but requiring some fortitude to step under. Especially during monsoon season, when it can go from being incredibly hot to quite chilly in minutes...

Go ahead.

You can go first

No--be my guest

* Never drink the tap water in Thailand!

The mandi is the closest you'll get to a shower in Indonesia. Balinese people enjoy their mandis in the many streams that wind through the island.

But the romance of a Balinese mandi doesn't translate to your typical guest house.

Yes, the same water for flushing the toilet is used for bathing. Dip the cup, brace yourself and pour it over your head!

That and the fact that the humidity kept our towels permanently damp gave us a certain Bohemian attitude about bathing...

Ah, this is the life!

What's that smell?

And remember: Always keep your mouth closed from all those pesky water parasites!

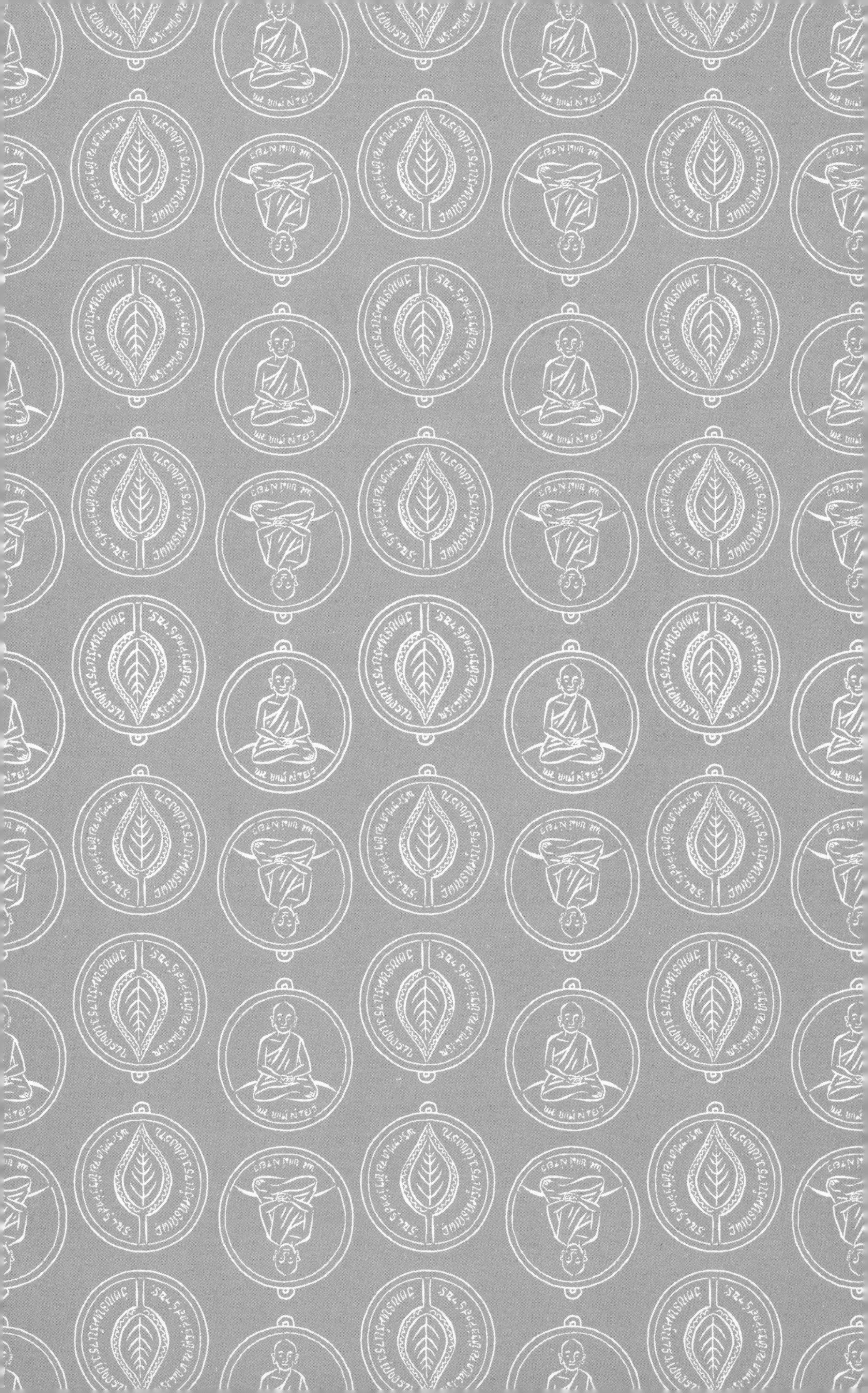

The Cave
of Fear

BURMA

Soppong

⊙ Chiang Mai

THAILAND

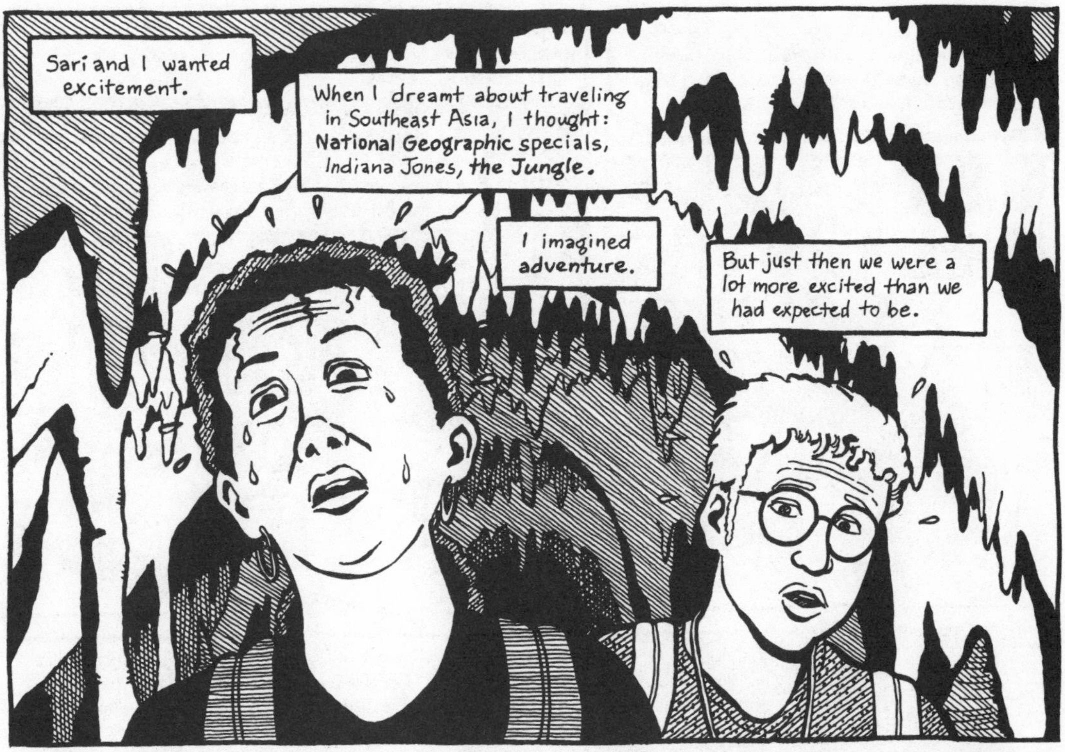
Sari and I wanted excitement.
When I dreamt about traveling in Southeast Asia, I thought: National Geographic specials, Indiana Jones, the Jungle.
I imagined adventure.
But just then we were a lot more excited than we had expected to be.

JOSH and SARI in

THE CAVE OF FEAR

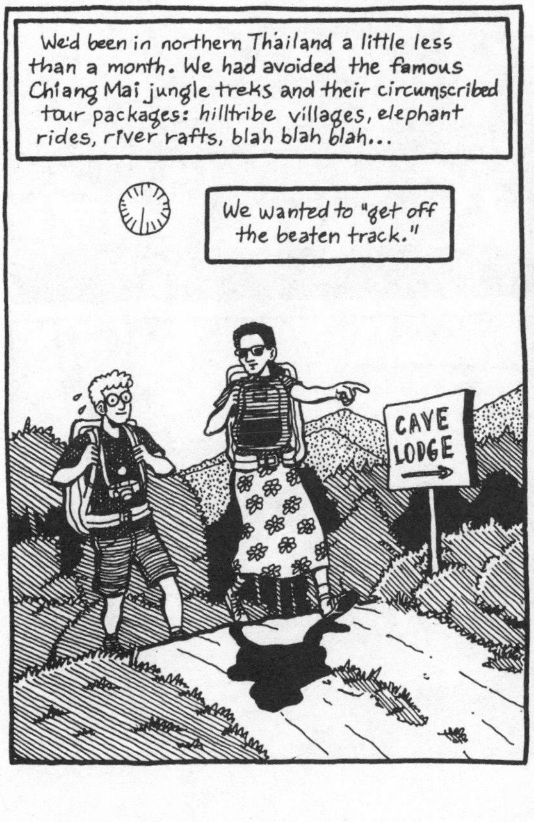
We'd been in northern Thailand a little less than a month. We had avoided the famous Chiang Mai jungle treks and their circumscribed tour packages: hilltribe villages, elephant rides, river rafts, blah blah blah...
We wanted to "get off the beaten track."
CAVE LODGE

Tips from other backpackers led us to the Cave Lodge, a campsite about an hour from the Burmese border. It was so off the track it wasn't even mentioned in our Lonely Planet guidebook.

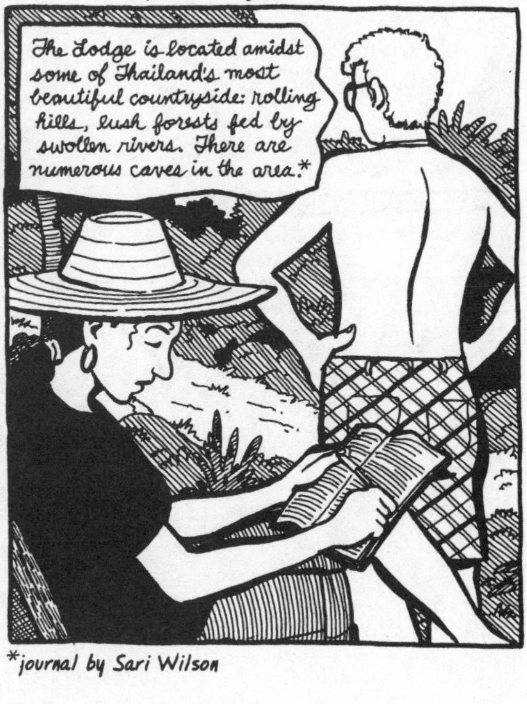
The Lodge is located amidst some of Thailand's most beautiful countryside: rolling hills, lush forests fed by swollen rivers. There are numerous caves in the area.*

*journal by Sari Wilson

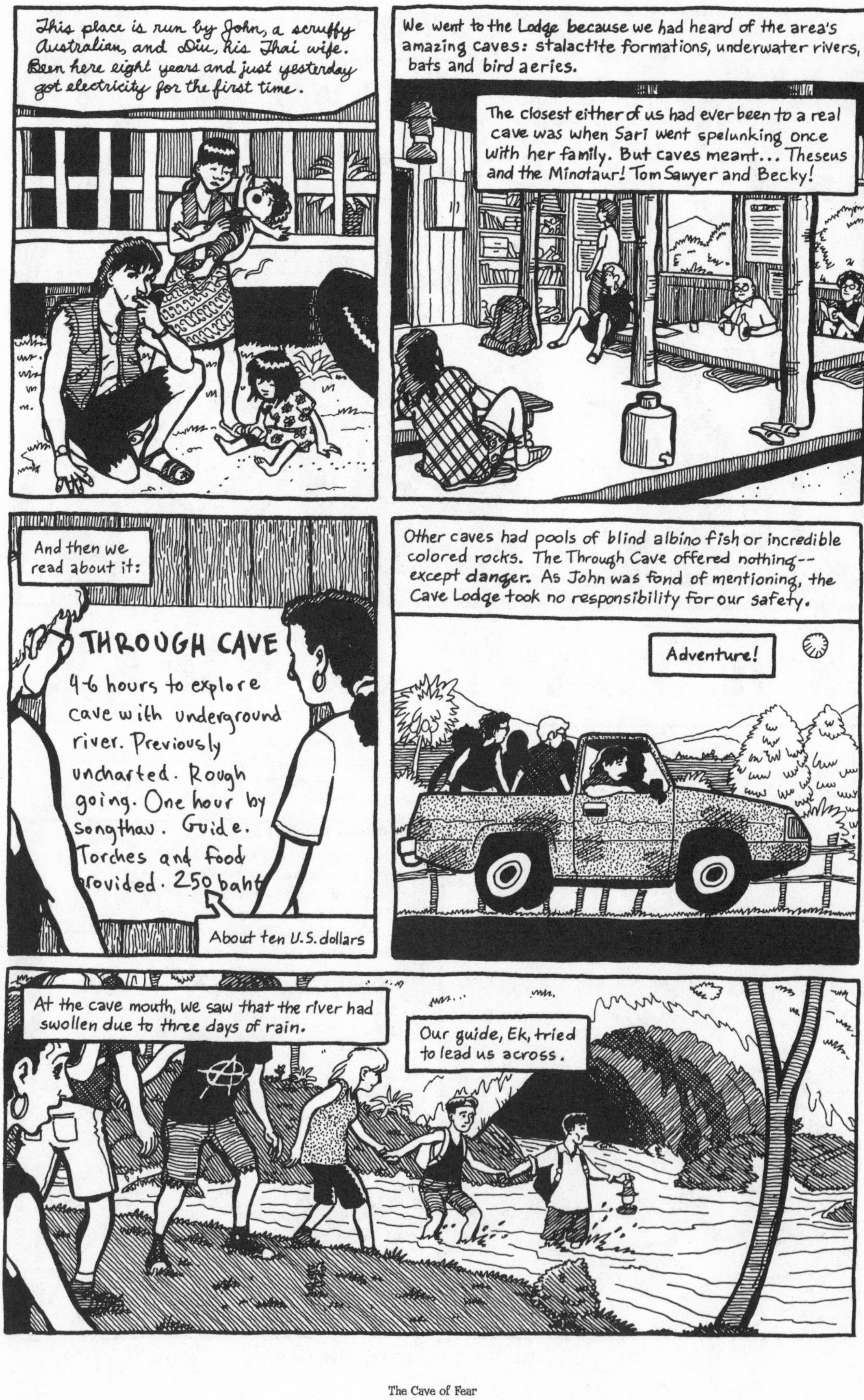
This place is run by John, a scruffy Australian, and Diu, his Thai wife. Been here eight years and just yesterday got electricity for the first time.
We went to the Lodge because we had heard of the area's amazing caves: stalactite formations, underwater rivers, bats and bird aeries.
The closest either of us had ever been to a real cave was when Sari went spelunking once with her family. But caves meant... Theseus and the Minotaur! Tom Sawyer and Becky!
And then we read about it:
THROUGH CAVE
4-6 hours to explore cave with underground river. Previously uncharted. Rough going. One hour by songthau. Guide. Torches and food provided. 250 baht
About ten U.S. dollars
Other caves had pools of blind albino fish or incredible colored rocks. The Through Cave offered nothing-- except danger. As John was fond of mentioning, the Cave Lodge took no responsibility for our safety.
Adventure!
At the cave mouth, we saw that the river had swollen due to three days of rain.
Our guide, Ek, tried to lead us across.

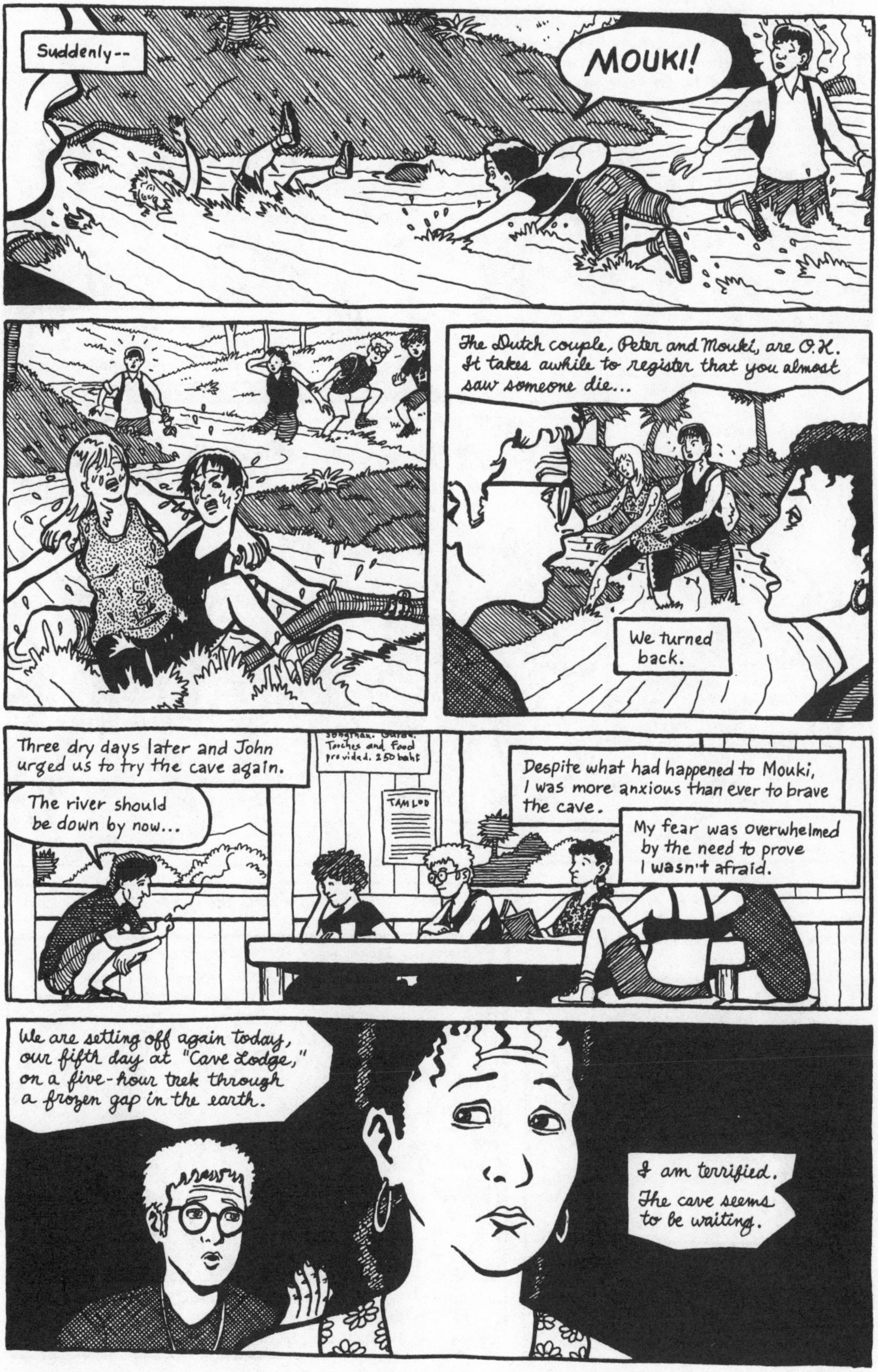
Suddenly--
MOUKI!
The Dutch couple, Peter and Mouki, are O.K. It takes awhile to register that you almost saw someone die...
We turned back.
Three dry days later and John urged us to try the cave again.
Torches and Food provided. 250 baht
The river should be down by now...
TAMLOD
Despite what had happened to Mouki, I was more anxious than ever to brave the cave.
My fear was overwhelmed by the need to prove I wasn't afraid.
We are setting off again today, our fifth day at "Cave Lodge," on a five-hour trek through a frozen gap in the earth.
I am terrified. The cave seems to be waiting.

We set out with a new group. Peter and Mouki--and a few others who'd gone with us the first time--decided not to risk their necks twice...

Lek, our new guide, was taciturn, not full of smiles like many Thais. But he seemed capable enough.

This time we entered the cave via the "skylight," a deep crevice which led down into darkness.

We were in the cave!

Fear and adrenaline. Just the need to survive the next five hours-- this is what I think.

Our route would take us downstream. The water was swift, but it was nothing like the torrent which had almost swept Mouki away forever.

I am surprised at how the fear accumulates, wraps itself around me like a blanket.

Sari was still nervous about the water and often warned me to be careful.

I have many fears; most of the time they stay safe in my dreams. Navigating daytime life, I encounter few. But here, deep under the earth, they come out to haunt me.

I couldn't believe anything bad could happen. Far from The City and its muggers and dark streets, I felt somehow invulnerable, immortal.

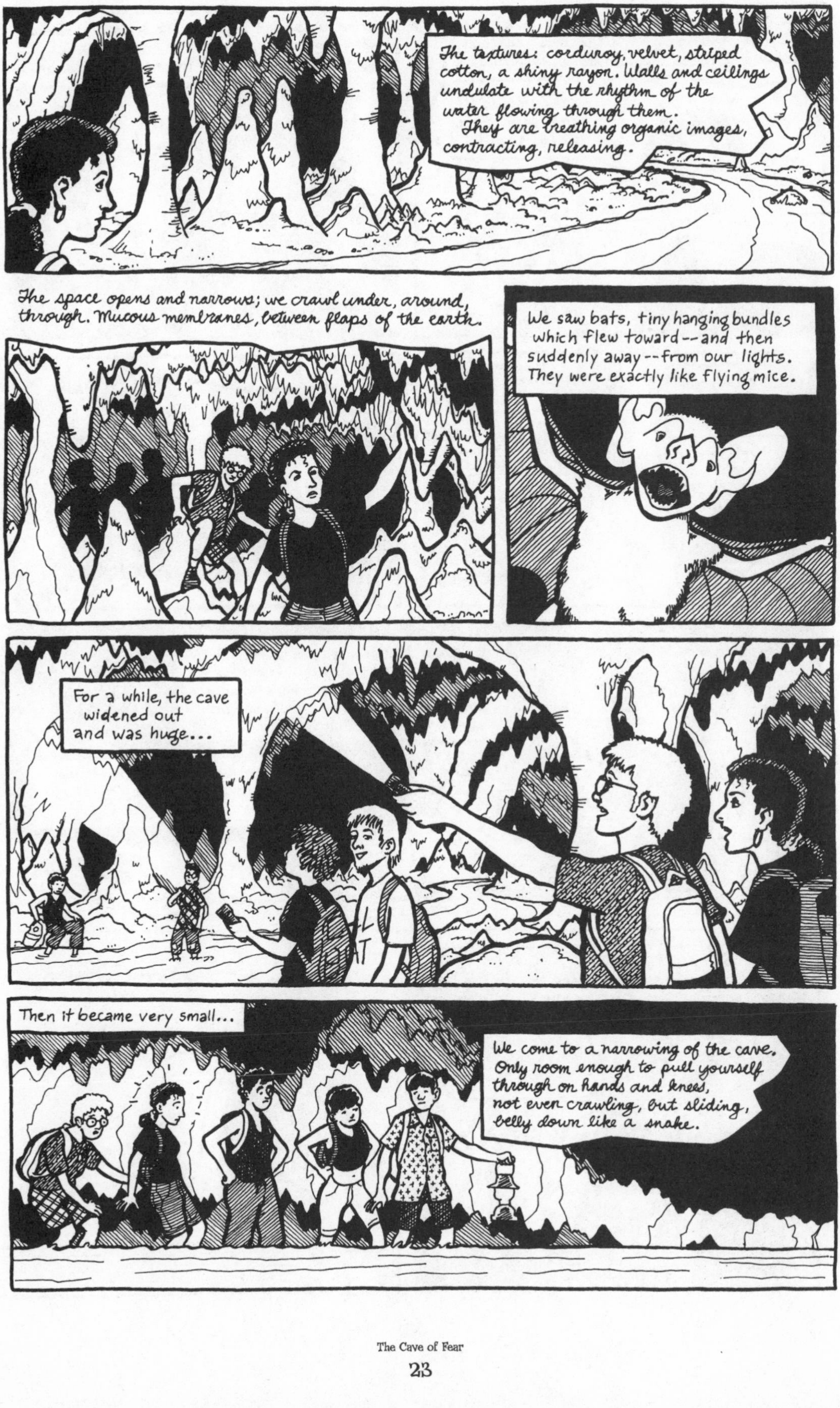
The textures: corduroy, velvet, striped cotton, a shiny rayon. Walls and ceilings undulate with the rhythm of the water flowing through them.
They are breathing organic images, contracting, releasing.
The space opens and narrows; we crawl under, around, through. Mucous membranes, between flaps of the earth.
We saw bats, tiny hanging bundles which flew toward--and then suddenly away--from our lights. They were exactly like flying mice.
For a while, the cave widened out and was huge...
Then it became very small...
We come to a narrowing of the cave. Only room enough to pull yourself through on hands and knees, not even crawling, but sliding, belly down like a snake.

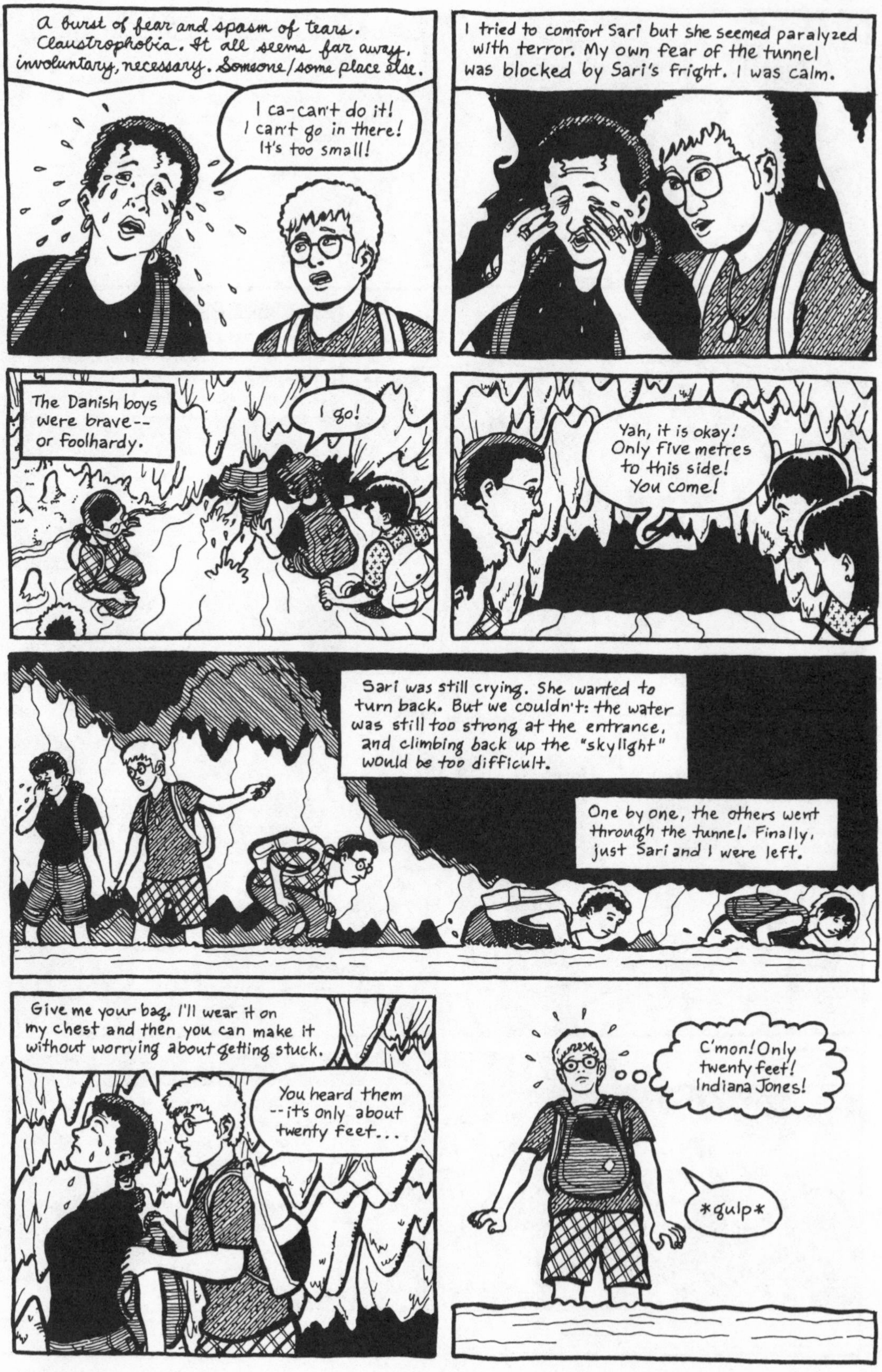
A burst of fear and spasm of tears. Claustrophobia. It all seems far away, involuntary, necessary. Someone/some place else.
I ca-can't do it! I can't go in there! It's too small!
I tried to comfort Sari but she seemed paralyzed with terror. My own fear of the tunnel was blocked by Sari's fright. I was calm.
The Danish boys were brave-- or foolhardy.
I go!
Yah, it is okay! Only five metres to this side! You come!
Sari was still crying. She wanted to turn back. But we couldn't: the water was still too strong at the entrance, and climbing back up the "skylight" would be too difficult.
One by one, the others went through the tunnel. Finally, just Sari and I were left.
Give me your bag. I'll wear it on my chest and then you can make it without worrying about getting stuck.
You heard them --it's only about twenty feet...
C'mon! Only twenty feet! Indiana Jones!
gulp

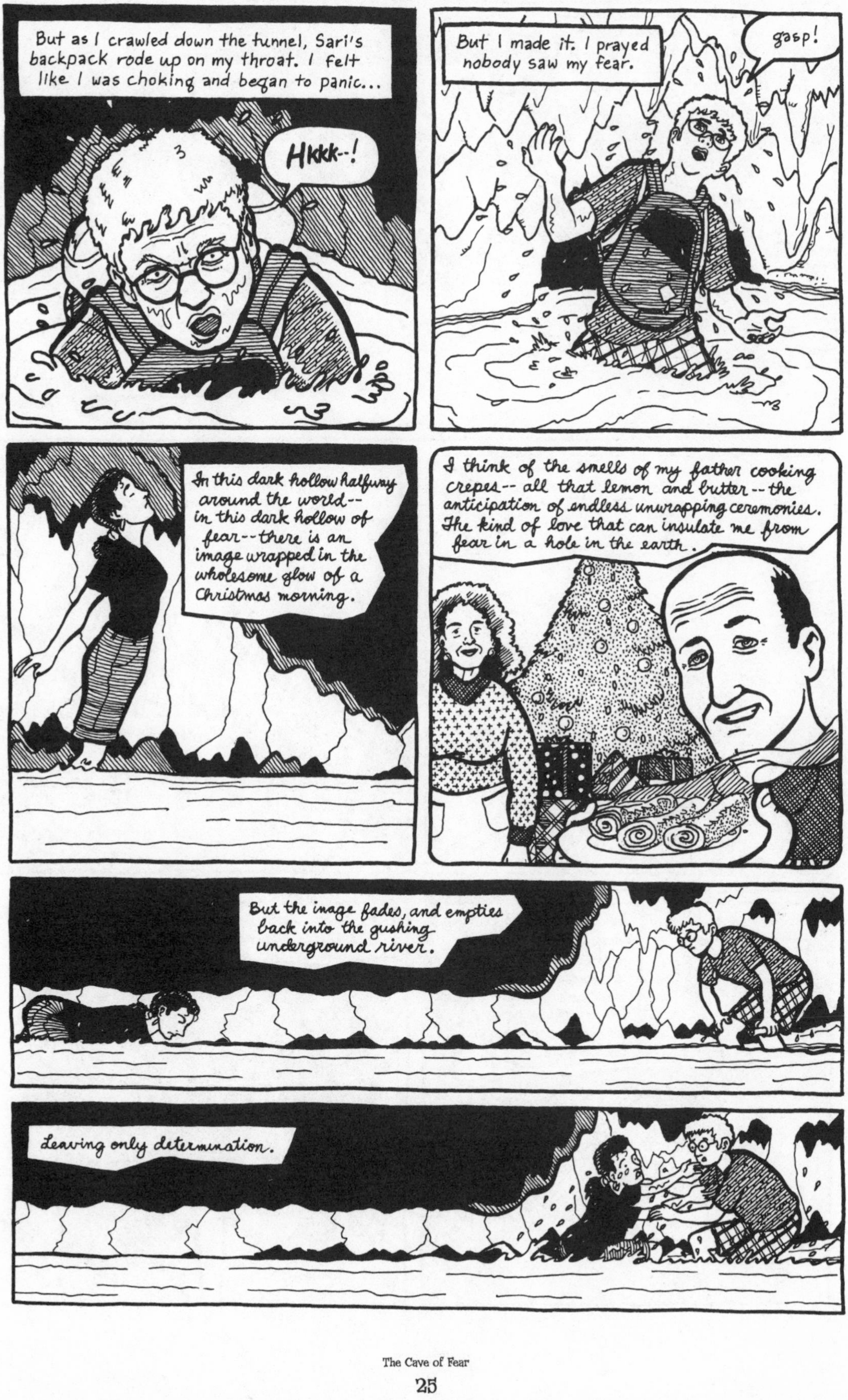
But as I crawled down the tunnel, Sari's backpack rode up on my throat. I felt like I was choking and began to panic...
HKKK--!
But I made it. I prayed nobody saw my fear.
gasp!
In this dark hollow halfway around the world-- in this dark hollow of fear--there is an image wrapped in the wholesome glow of a Christmas morning.
I think of the smells of my father cooking crepes-- all that lemon and butter--the anticipation of endless unwrapping ceremonies. The kind of love that can insulate me from fear in a hole in the earth.
But the image fades, and empties back into the gushing underground river.
Leaving only determination.

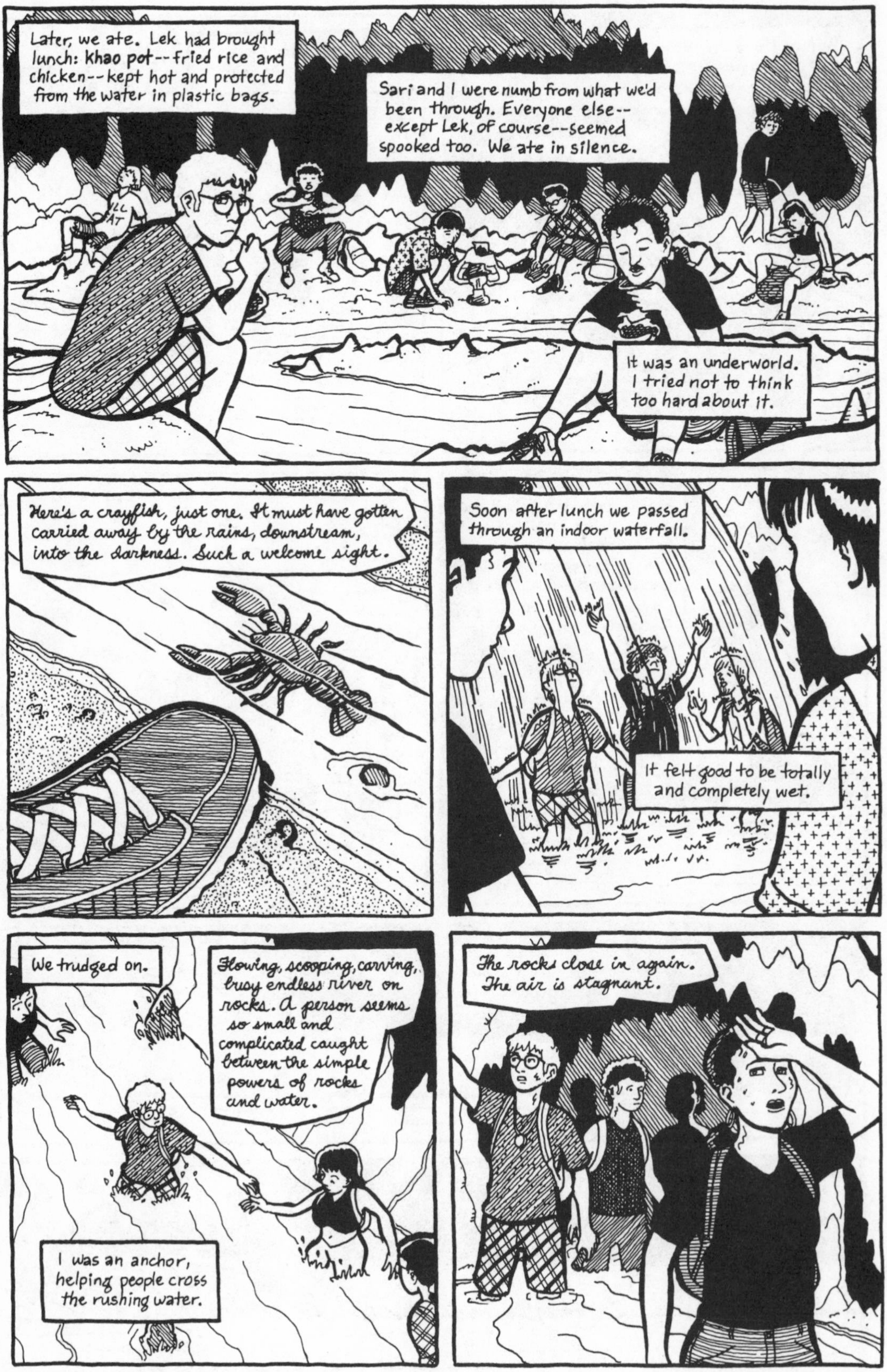
Later, we ate. Lek had brought lunch: khao pot--fried rice and chicken--kept hot and protected from the water in plastic bags.
Sari and I were numb from what we'd been through. Everyone else--except Lek, of course--seemed spooked too. We ate in silence.
It was an underworld. I tried not to think too hard about it.
Here's a crayfish, just one. It must have gotten carried away by the rains, downstream, into the darkness. Such a welcome sight.
Soon after lunch we passed through an indoor waterfall.
It felt good to be totally and completely wet.
We trudged on.
Flowing, scooping, carving, busy endless river on rocks. A person seems so small and complicated caught between the simple powers of rocks and water.
I was an anchor, helping people cross the rushing water.
The rocks close in again. The air is stagnant.

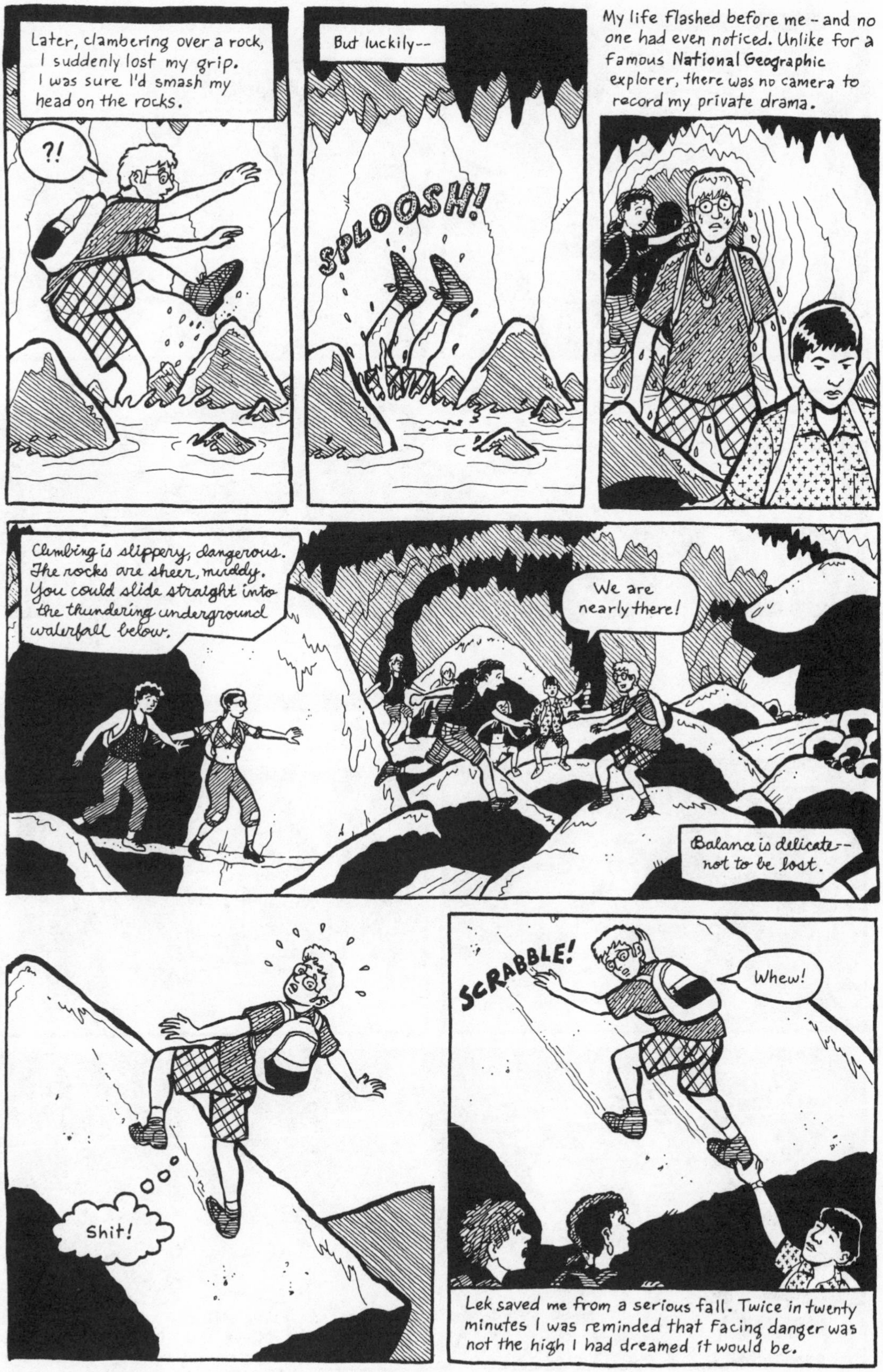
Later, clambering over a rock, I suddenly lost my grip. I was sure I'd smash my head on the rocks.
?!
But luckily--
SPLOOSH!
My life flashed before me - and no one had even noticed. Unlike for a famous National Geographic explorer, there was no camera to record my private drama.
Climbing is slippery, dangerous. The rocks are sheer, muddy. You could slide straight into the thundering underground waterfall below.
We are nearly there!
Balance is delicate - not to be lost.
Shit!
SCRABBLE!
Whew!
Lek saved me from a serious fall. Twice in twenty minutes I was reminded that facing danger was not the high I had dreamed it would be.

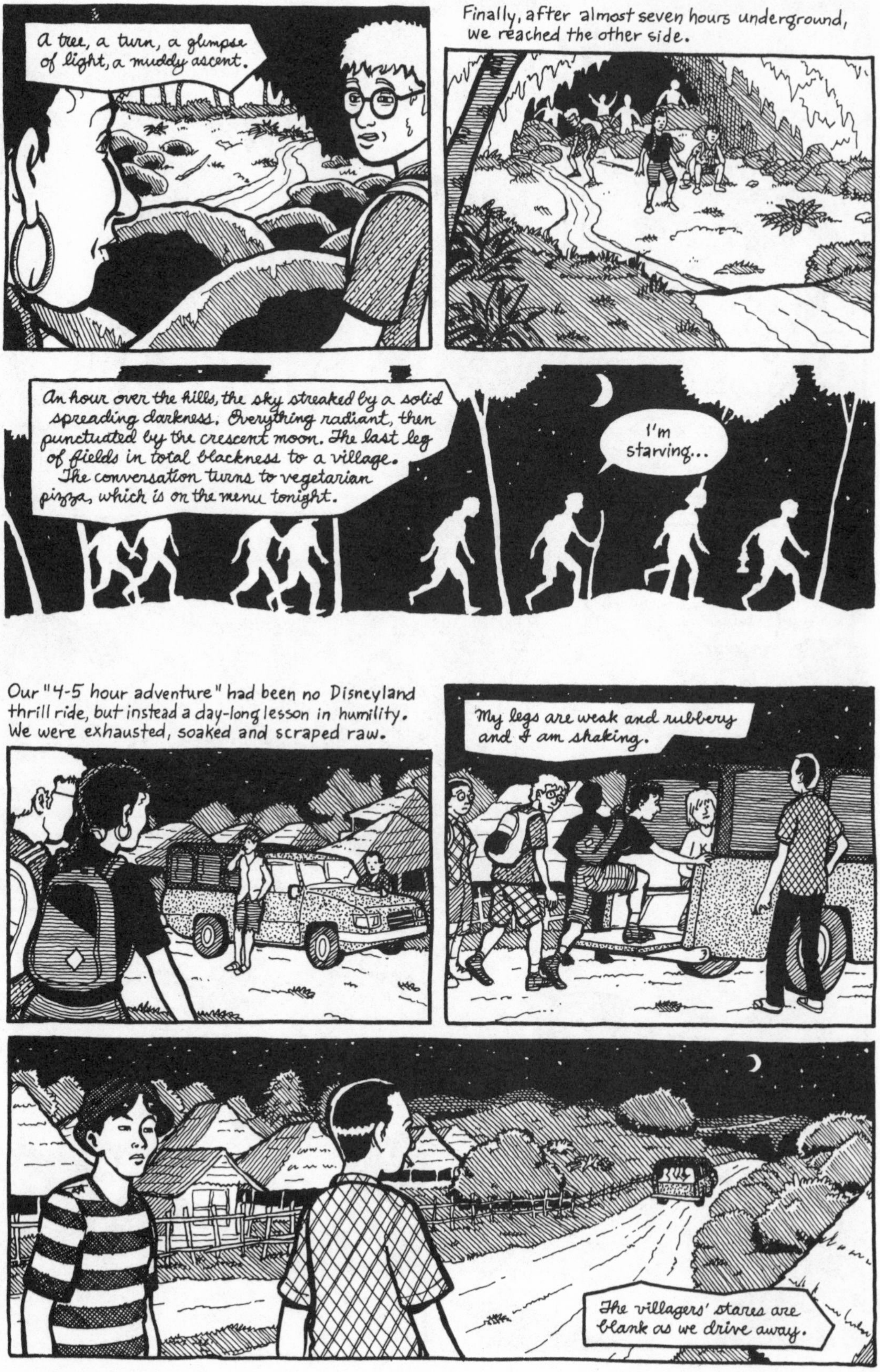
A tree, a turn, a glimpse of light, a muddy ascent.
Finally, after almost seven hours underground, we reached the other side.
An hour over the hills, the sky streaked by a solid spreading darkness. Everything radiant, then punctuated by the crescent moon. The last leg of fields in total blackness to a village. The conversation turns to vegetarian pizza, which is on the menu tonight.
I'm starving...
Our "4-5 hour adventure" had been no Disneyland thrill ride, but instead a day-long lesson in humility. We were exhausted, soaked and scraped raw.
My legs are weak and rubbery and I am shaking.
The villagers' stares are blank as we drive away.

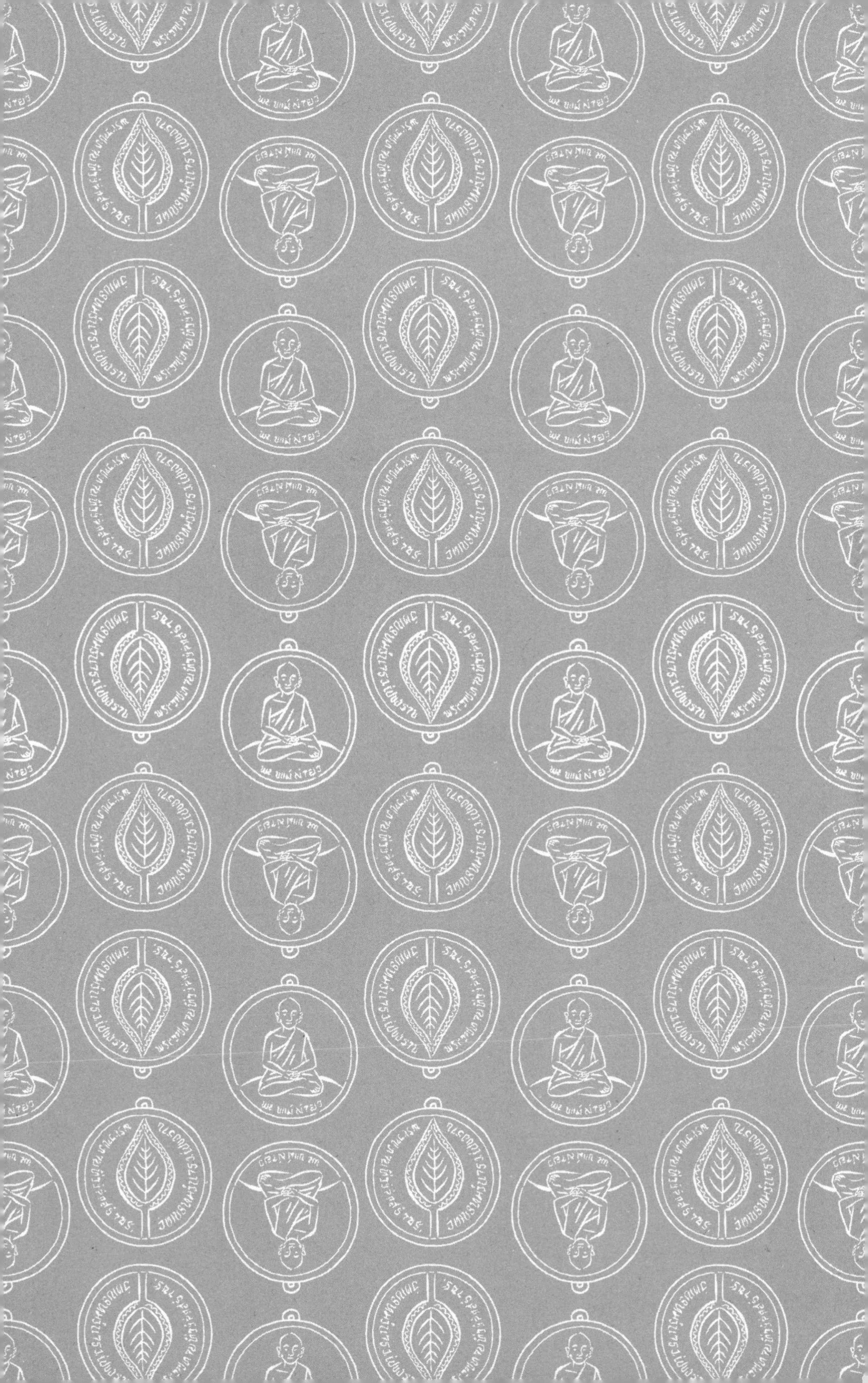

Tribal Rituals, Part I: On a Mission

South China Sea
VIETNAM
Nakhon Phanom
LAOS
THAILAND

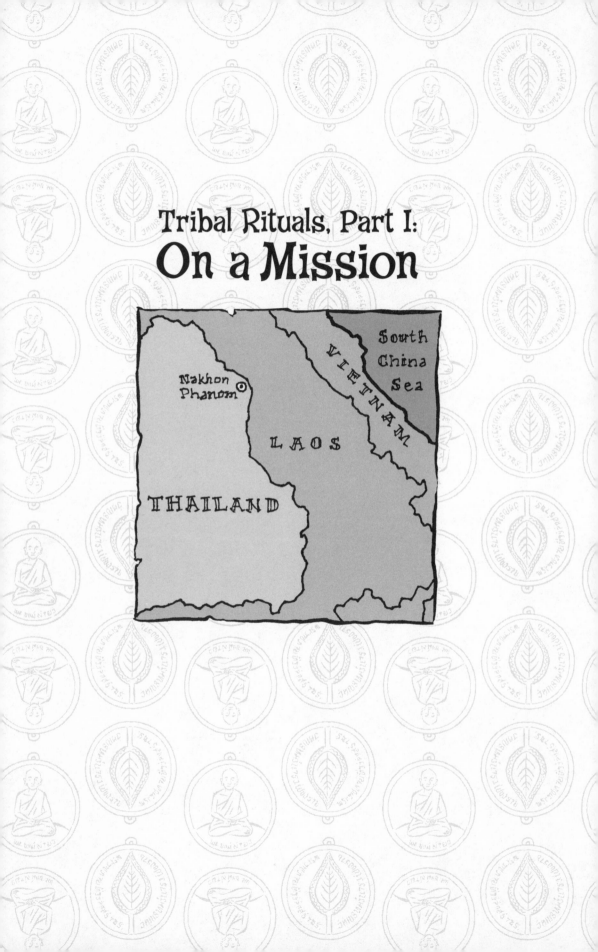

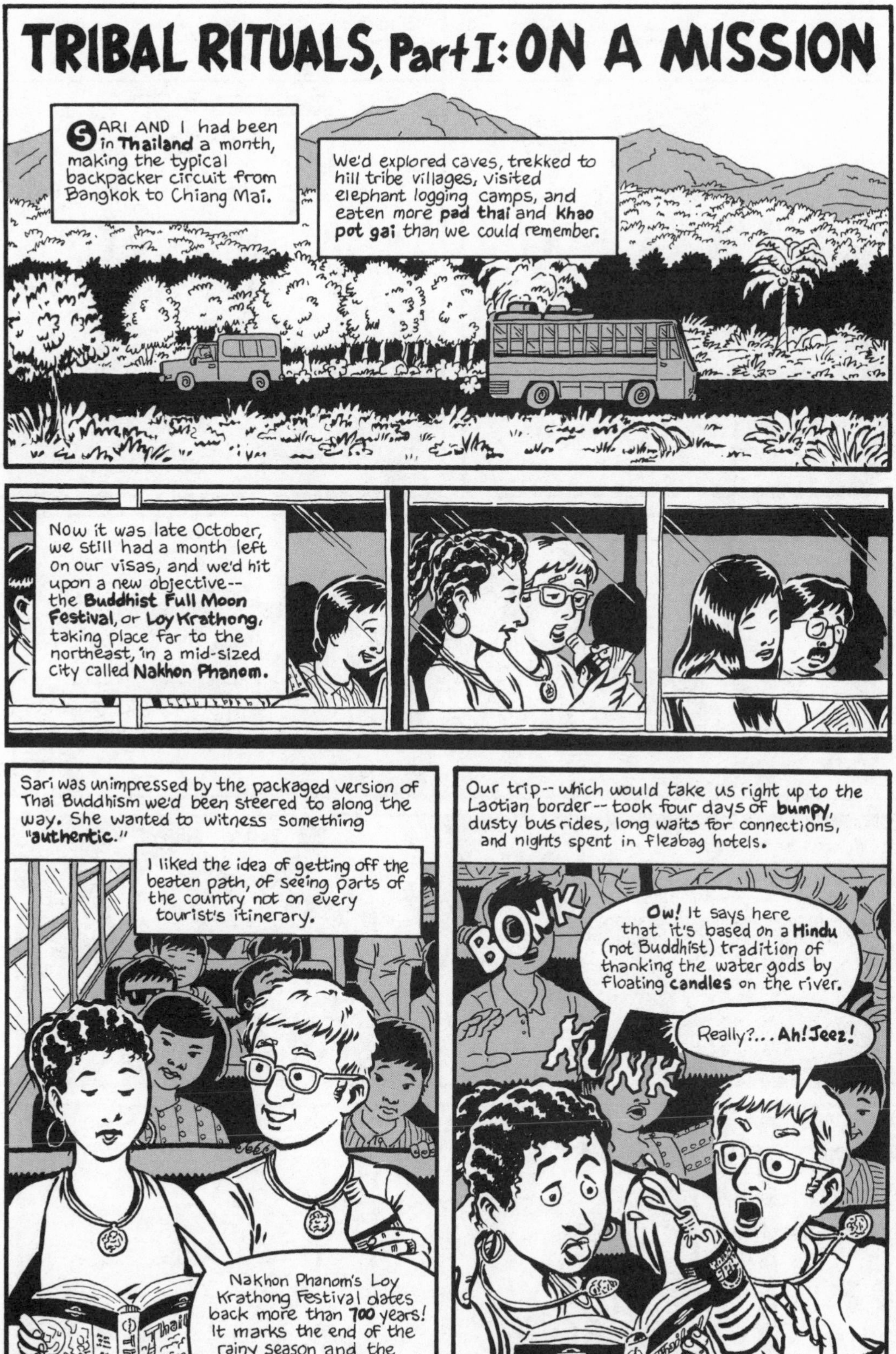
TRIBAL RITUALS, Part I: ON A MISSION
SARI AND I had been in Thailand a month, making the typical backpacker circuit from Bangkok to Chiang Mai.
We'd explored caves, trekked to hill tribe villages, visited elephant logging camps, and eaten more pad thai and khao pot gai than we could remember.
Now it was late October, we still had a month left on our visas, and we'd hit upon a new objective-- the Buddhist Full Moon Festival, or Loy Krathong, taking place far to the northeast, in a mid-sized city called Nakhon Phanom.
Sari was unimpressed by the packaged version of Thai Buddhism we'd been steered to along the way. She wanted to witness something "authentic."
I liked the idea of getting off the beaten path, of seeing parts of the country not on every tourist's itinerary.
Nakhon Phanom's Loy Krathong Festival dates back more than 700 years! It marks the end of the rainy season and the main rice harvest.
Our trip-- which would take us right up to the Laotian border-- took four days of bumpy, dusty bus rides, long waits for connections, and nights spent in fleabag hotels.
BONK
Ow! It says here that it's based on a Hindu (not Buddhist) tradition of thanking the water gods by floating candles on the river.
KLUNK
Really?... Ah! Jeez!

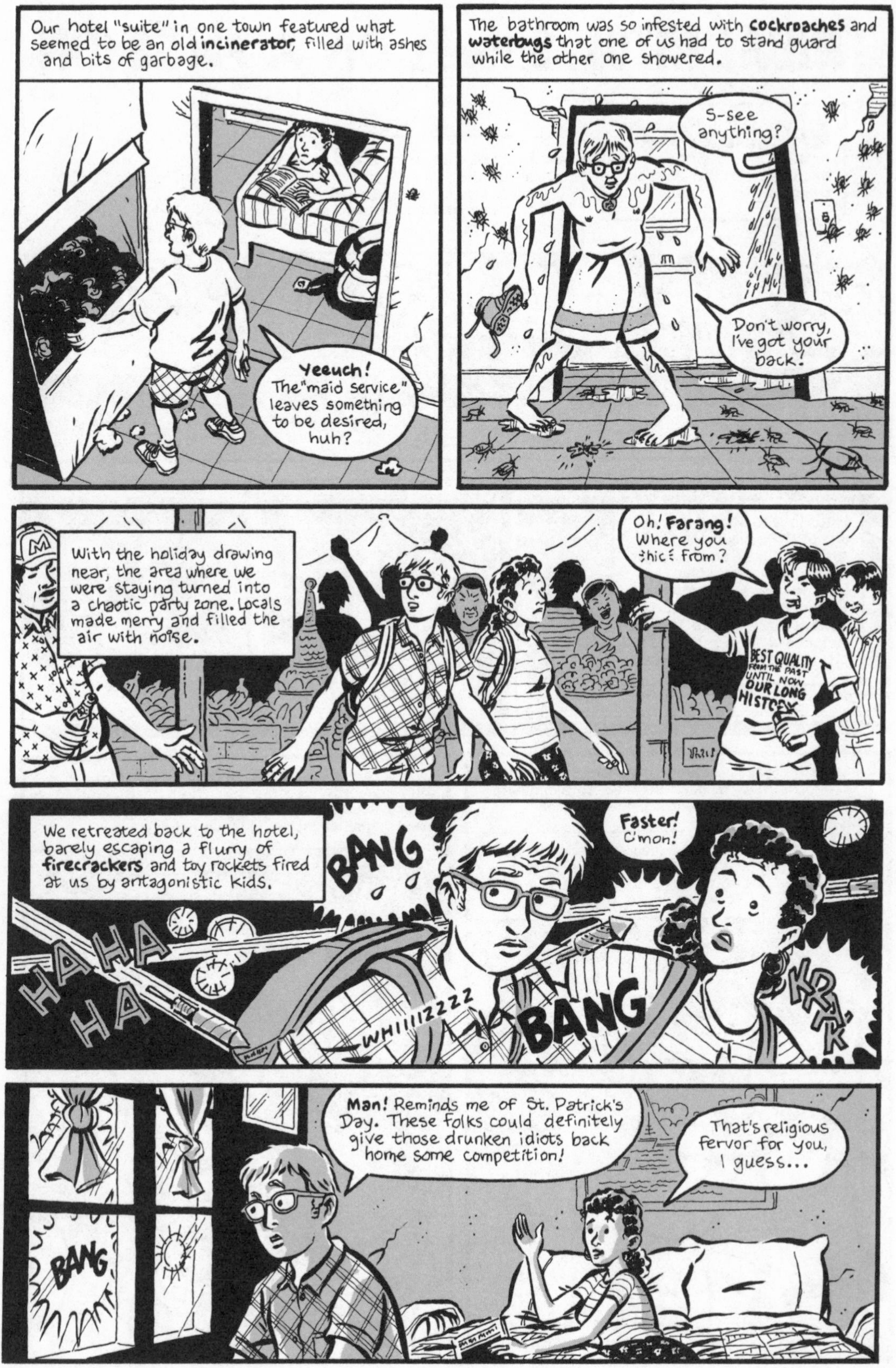

Our hotel "suite" in one town featured what seemed to be an old incinerator, filled with ashes and bits of garbage.
Yeeuch! The "maid service" leaves something to be desired, huh?
The bathroom was so infested with cockroaches and waterbugs that one of us had to stand guard while the other one showered.
S-see anything?
Don't worry, I've got your back!
With the holiday drawing near, the area where we were staying turned into a chaotic party zone. Locals made merry and filled the air with noise.
Oh! Farang! Where you hic from?
BEST QUALITY FROM THE PAST UNTIL NOW OUR LONG HISTORY
We retreated back to the hotel, barely escaping a flurry of firecrackers and toy rockets fired at us by antagonistic kids.
BANG
Faster! C'mon!
HAHA HA HA
WHIIIIZZZZ
BANG
KRAK
Man! Reminds me of St. Patrick's Day. These folks could definitely give those drunken idiots back home some competition!
That's religious fervor for you, I guess...
BANG

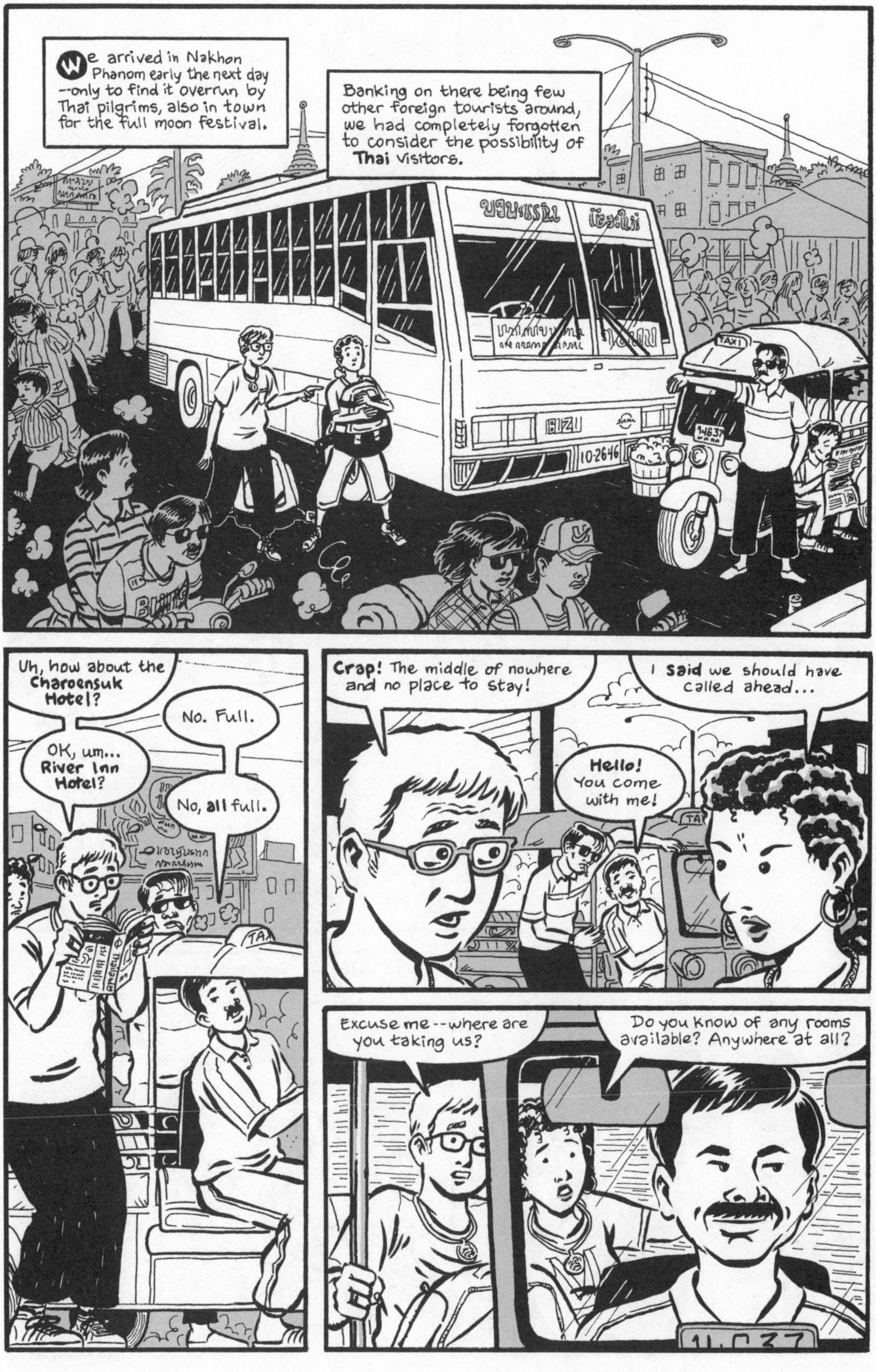
We arrived in Nakhon Phanom early the next day --only to find it overrun by Thai pilgrims, also in town for the full moon festival.
Banking on there being few other foreign tourists around, we had completely forgotten to consider the possibility of **Thai** visitors.
Uh, how about the **Charoensuk Hotel**?
No. Full.
OK, um... **River Inn Hotel**?
No, **all** full.
Crap! The middle of nowhere and no place to stay!
I **said** we should have called ahead...
Hello! You come with me!
Excuse me--where are you taking us?
Do you know of any rooms available? Anywhere at all?

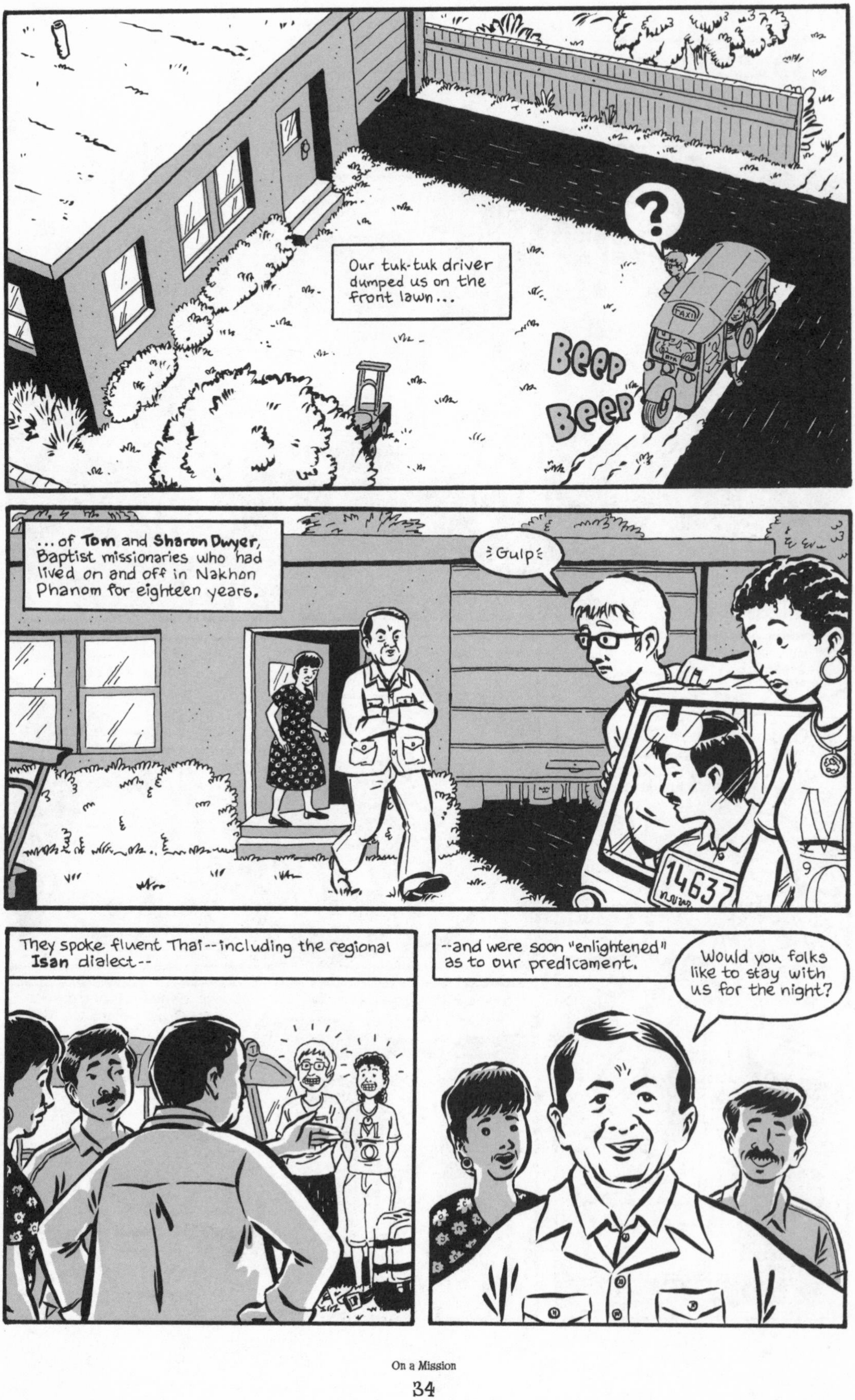
Our tuk-tuk driver dumped us on the front lawn...
?
Beep Beep
...of Tom and Sharon Dwyer, Baptist missionaries who had lived on and off in Nakhon Phanom for eighteen years.
Gulp
14637
They spoke fluent Thai--including the regional Isan dialect--
--and were soon "enlightened" as to our predicament.
Would you folks like to stay with us for the night?

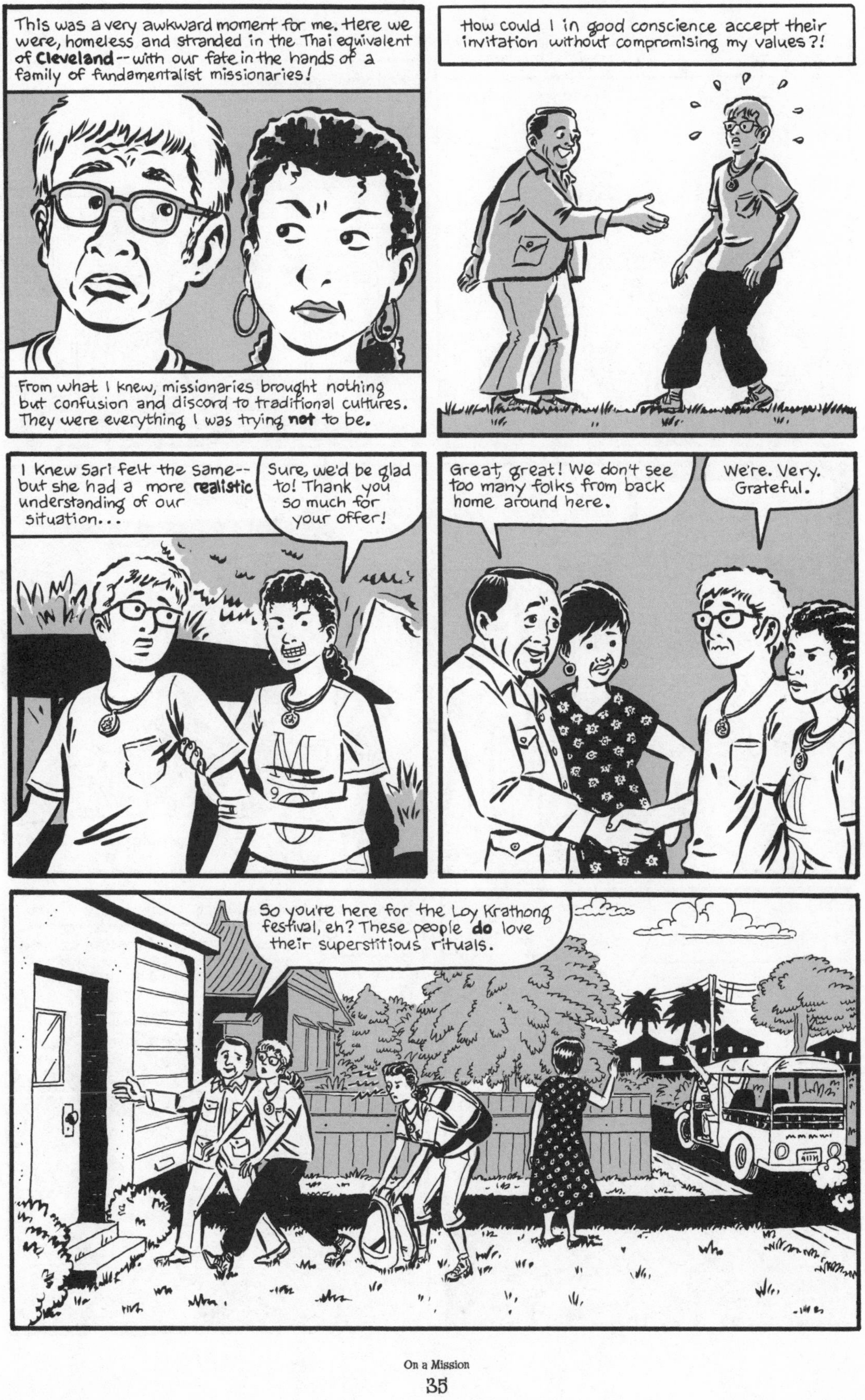
This was a very awkward moment for me. Here we were, homeless and stranded in the Thai equivalent of **Cleveland**--with our fate in the hands of a family of fundamentalist missionaries!
From what I knew, missionaries brought nothing but confusion and discord to traditional cultures. They were everything I was trying **not** to be.
How could I in good conscience accept their invitation without compromising my values?!
I knew Sari felt the same--but she had a more **realistic** understanding of our situation...
Sure, we'd be glad to! Thank you so much for your offer!
Great, great! We don't see too many folks from back home around here.
We're. Very. Grateful.
So you're here for the Loy Krathong festival, eh? These people **do** love their superstitious rituals.

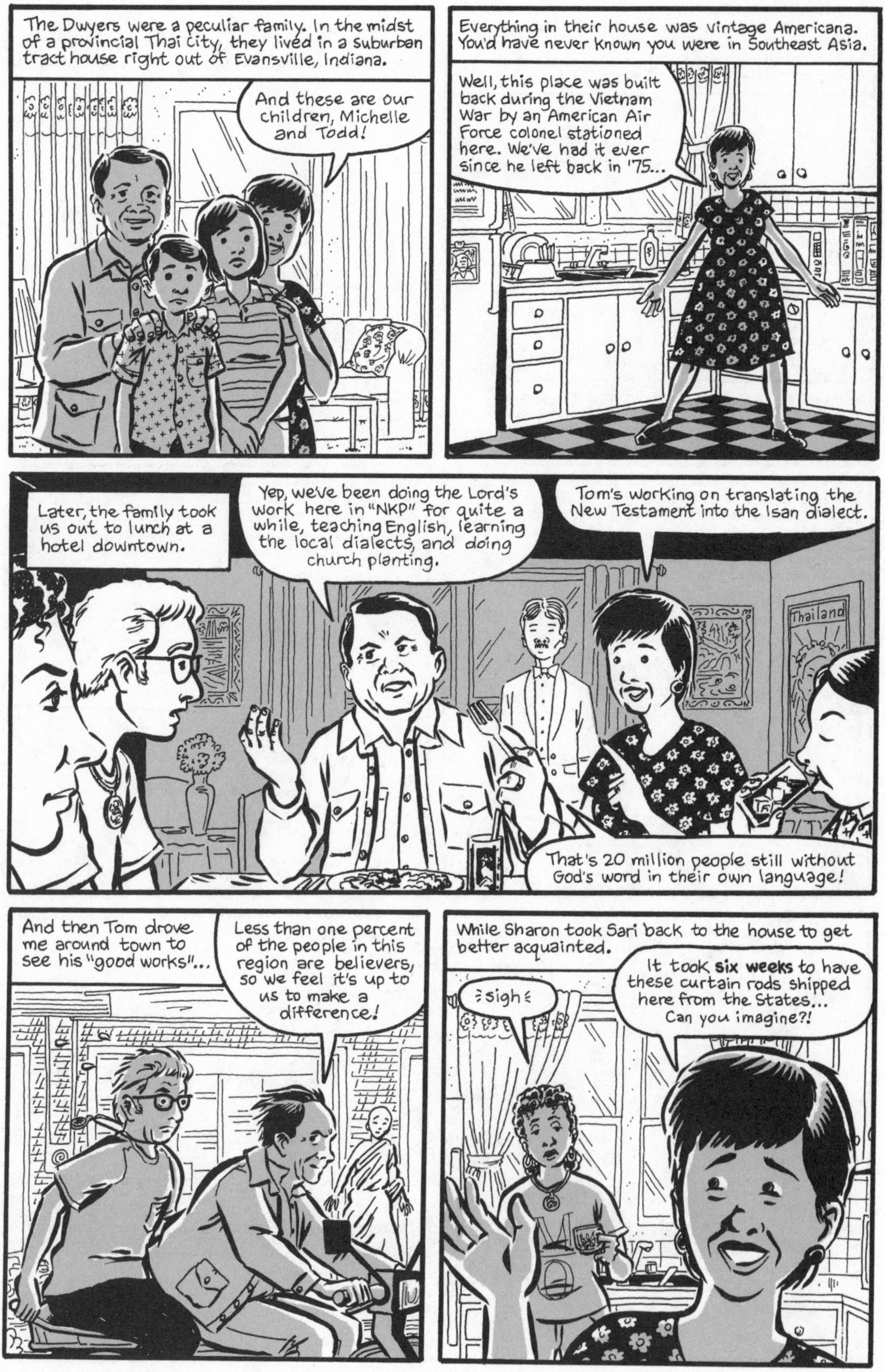
The Dwyers were a peculiar family. In the midst of a provincial Thai city, they lived in a suburban tract house right out of Evansville, Indiana.
And these are our children, Michelle and Todd!
Everything in their house was vintage Americana. You'd have never known you were in Southeast Asia.
Well, this place was built back during the Vietnam War by an American Air Force colonel stationed here. We've had it ever since he left back in '75...
Later, the family took us out to lunch at a hotel downtown.
Yep, we've been doing the Lord's work here in "NKP" for quite a while, teaching English, learning the local dialects, and doing church planting.
Tom's working on translating the New Testament into the Isan dialect.
Thailand
That's 20 million people still without God's word in their own language!
And then Tom drove me around town to see his "good works"...
Less than one percent of the people in this region are believers, so we feel it's up to us to make a difference!
While Sharon took Sari back to the house to get better acquainted.
sigh
It took **six weeks** to have these curtain rods shipped here from the States... Can you imagine?!

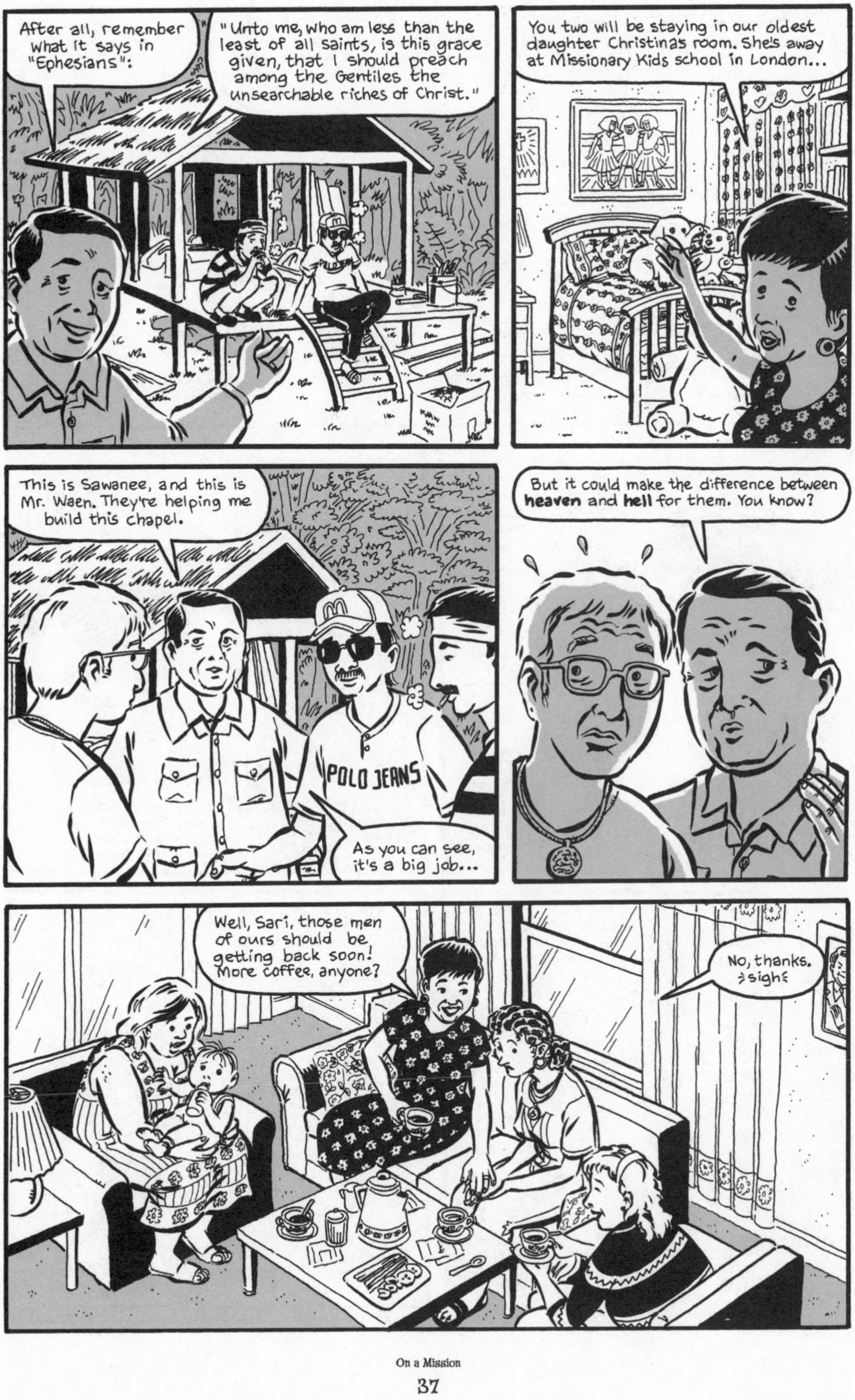
After all, remember what it says in "Ephesians":
"Unto me, who am less than the least of all saints, is this grace given, that I should preach among the Gentiles the unsearchable riches of Christ."
You two will be staying in our oldest daughter Christina's room. She's away at Missionary Kids school in London...
This is Sawanee, and this is Mr. Waen. They're helping me build this chapel.
POLO JEANS
As you can see, it's a big job...
But it could make the difference between **heaven** and **hell** for them. You know?
Well, Sari, those men of ours should be getting back soon! More coffee, anyone?
No, thanks. ≯sigh≮

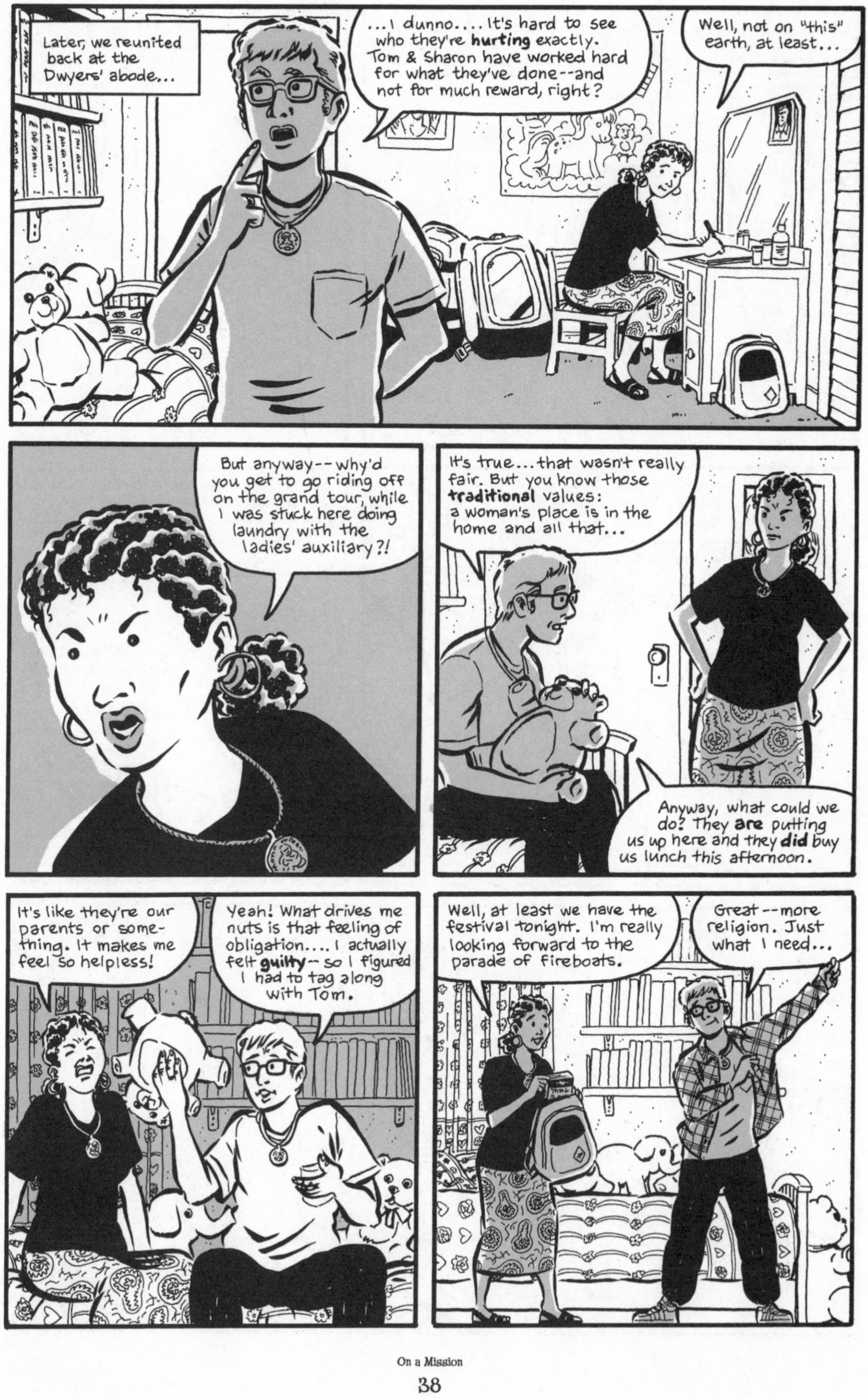
Later, we reunited back at the Dwyers' abode...
...I dunno.... It's hard to see who they're **hurting** exactly. Tom & Sharon have worked hard for what they've done--and not for much reward, right?
Well, not on "this" earth, at least...
But anyway--why'd you get to go riding off on the grand tour, while I was stuck here doing laundry with the ladies' auxiliary?!
It's true...that wasn't really fair. But you know those **traditional** values: a woman's place is in the home and all that...
Anyway, what could we do? They **are** putting us up here and they **did** buy us lunch this afternoon.
It's like they're our parents or something. It makes me feel so helpless!
Yeah! What drives me nuts is that feeling of obligation.... I actually felt **guilty**--so I figured I had to tag along with Tom.
Well, at least we have the festival tonight. I'm really looking forward to the parade of fireboats.
Great--more religion. Just what I need...

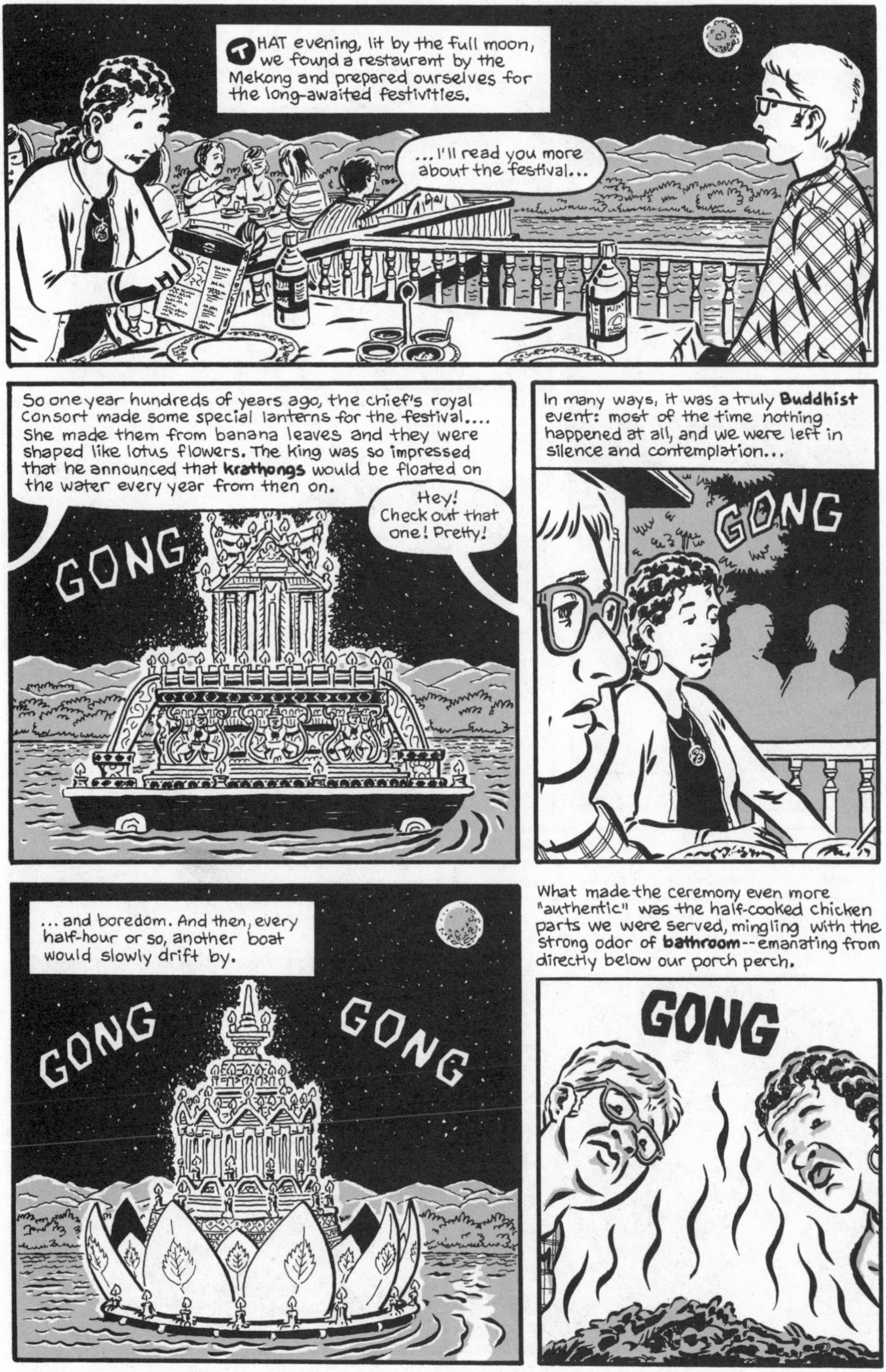
THAT evening, lit by the full moon, we found a restaurant by the Mekong and prepared ourselves for the long-awaited festivities.
...I'll read you more about the festival...
So one year hundreds of years ago, the chief's royal consort made some special lanterns for the festival.... She made them from banana leaves and they were shaped like lotus flowers. The king was so impressed that he announced that **krathongs** would be floated on the water every year from then on.
Hey! Check out that one! Pretty!
GONG
In many ways, it was a truly **Buddhist** event: most of the time nothing happened at all, and we were left in silence and contemplation...
GONG
...and boredom. And then, every half-hour or so, another boat would slowly drift by.
GONG
GONG
What made the ceremony even more "authentic" was the half-cooked chicken parts we were served, mingling with the strong odor of **bathroom**--emanating from directly below our porch perch.
GONG

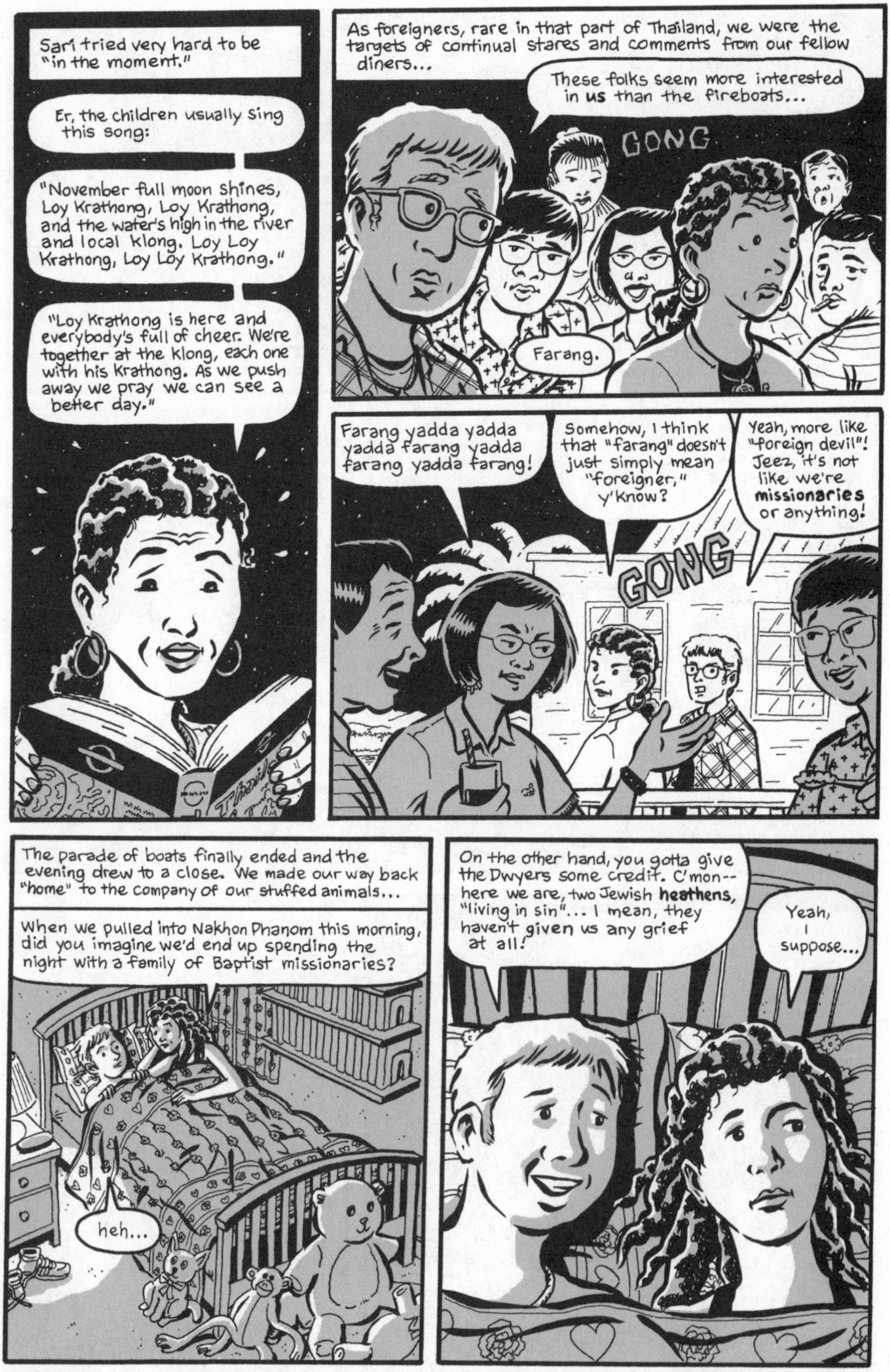
Sari tried very hard to be "in the moment."
Er, the children usually sing this song:
"November full moon shines, Loy Krathong, Loy Krathong, and the water's high in the river and local klong. Loy Loy Krathong, Loy Loy Krathong."
"Loy Krathong is here and everybody's full of cheer. We're together at the klong, each one with his Krathong. As we push away we pray we can see a better day."
As foreigners, rare in that part of Thailand, we were the targets of continual stares and comments from our fellow diners...
These folks seem more interested in **us** than the fireboats...
GONG
Farang.
Farang yadda yadda yadda farang yadda farang yadda farang!
Somehow, I think that "farang" doesn't just simply mean "foreigner," y'know?
Yeah, more like "foreign devil"! Jeez, it's not like we're **missionaries** or anything!
GONG
The parade of boats finally ended and the evening drew to a close. We made our way back "home" to the company of our stuffed animals...
When we pulled into Nakhon Phanom this morning, did you imagine we'd end up spending the night with a family of Baptist missionaries?
heh...
On the other hand, you gotta give the Dwyers some credit. C'mon-- here we are, two Jewish **heathens**, "living in sin"... I mean, they haven't **given** us any grief at all!
Yeah, I suppose...

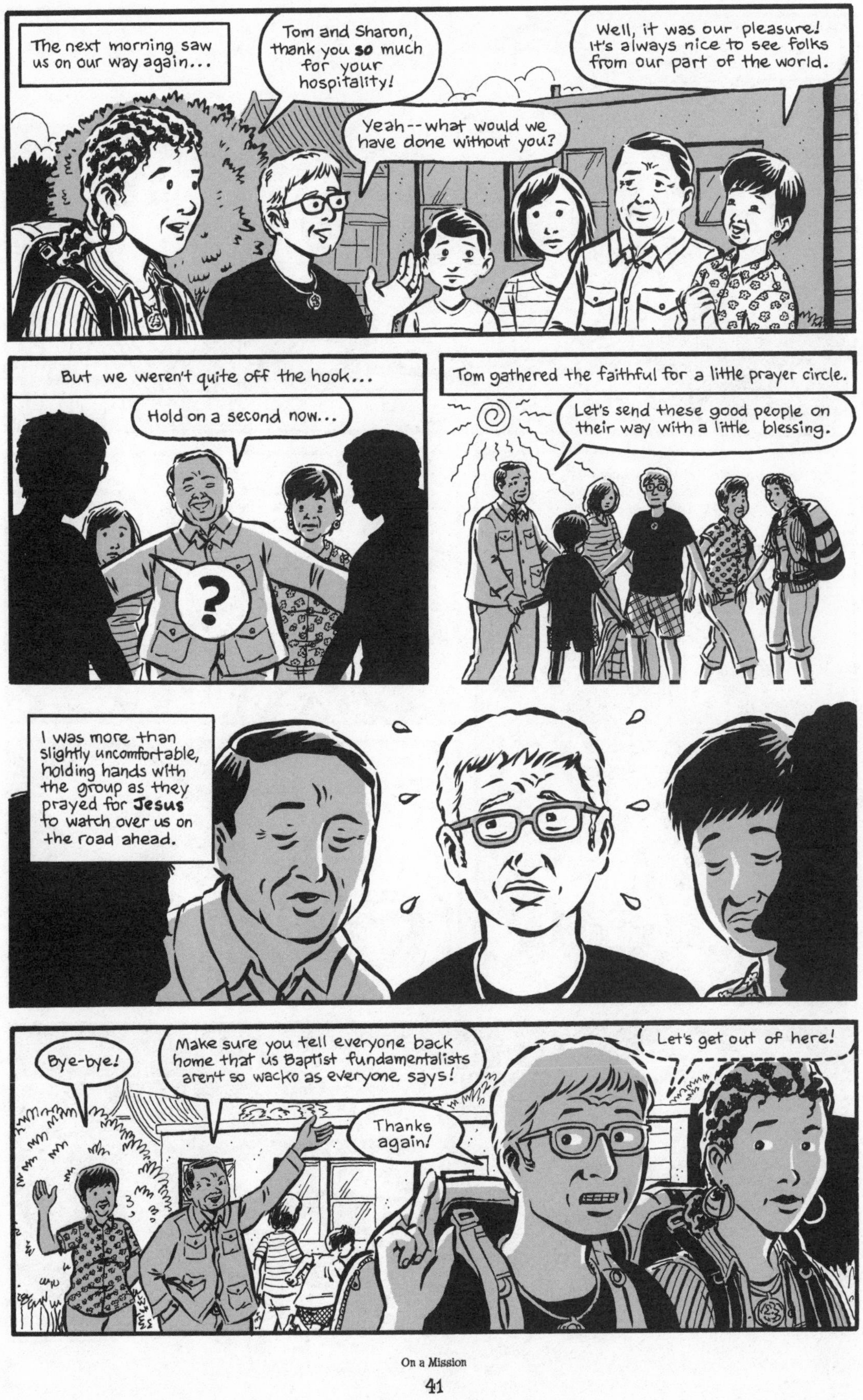
The next morning saw us on our way again...
Tom and Sharon, thank you **so** much for your hospitality!
Yeah--what would we have done without you?
Well, it was our pleasure! It's always nice to see folks from our part of the world.
But we weren't quite off the hook...
Hold on a second now...
?
Tom gathered the faithful for a little prayer circle.
Let's send these good people on their way with a little blessing.
I was more than slightly uncomfortable, holding hands with the group as they prayed for **Jesus** to watch over us on the road ahead.
Bye-bye!
Make sure you tell everyone back home that us Baptist fundamentalists aren't so wacko as everyone says!
Thanks again!
Let's get out of here!

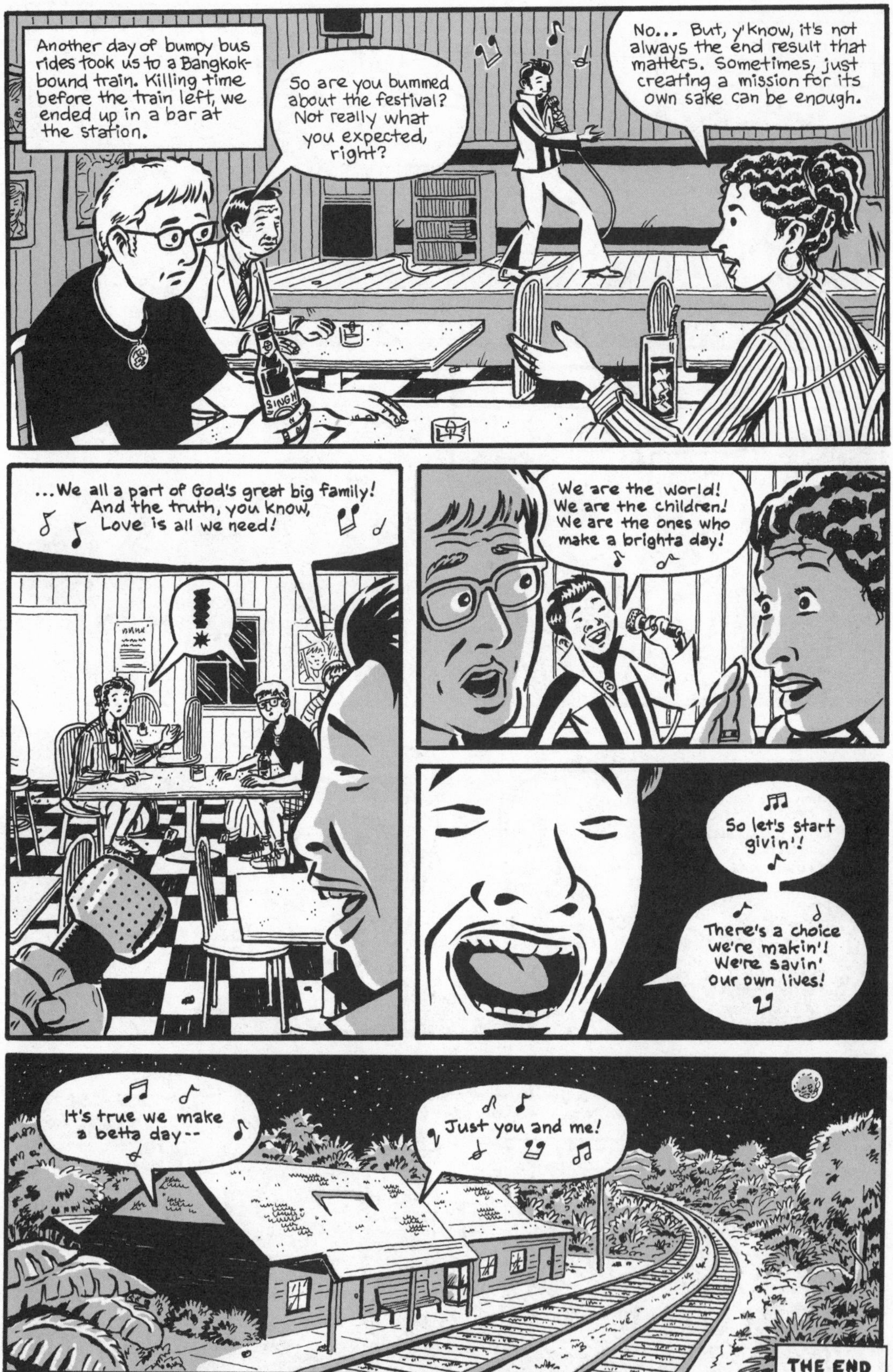
Another day of bumpy bus rides took us to a Bangkok-bound train. Killing time before the train left, we ended up in a bar at the station.
So are you bummed about the festival? Not really what you expected, right?
No... But, y'know, it's not always the end result that matters. Sometimes, just creating a mission for its own sake can be enough.
...We all a part of God's great big family! And the truth, you know, Love is all we need!
We are the world! We are the children! We are the ones who make a brighta day!
So let's start givin'!
There's a choice we're makin'! We're savin' our own lives!
It's true we make a betta day--
Just you and me!
THE END

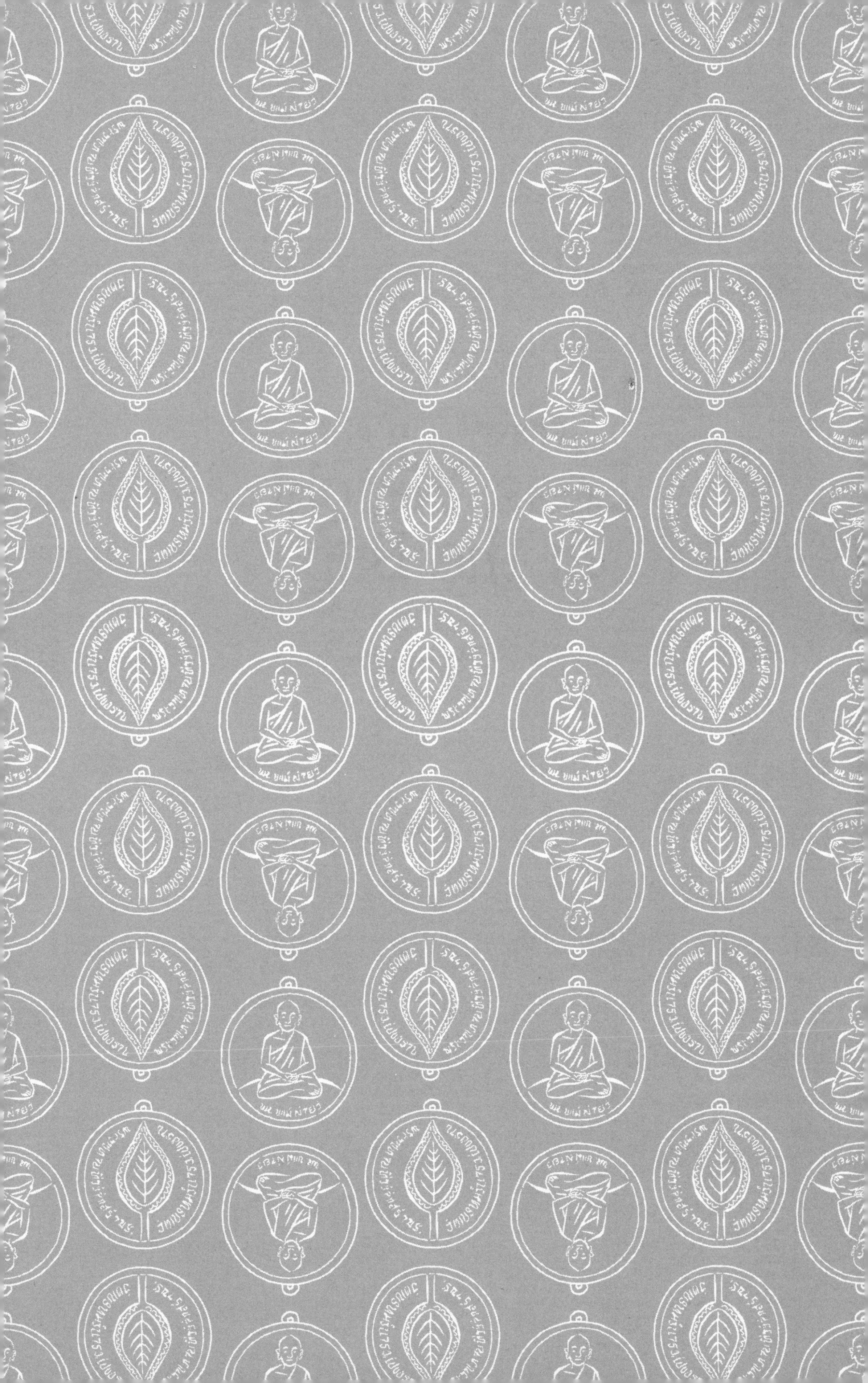

Travel Tip #3:
Less Weight
in the Bag

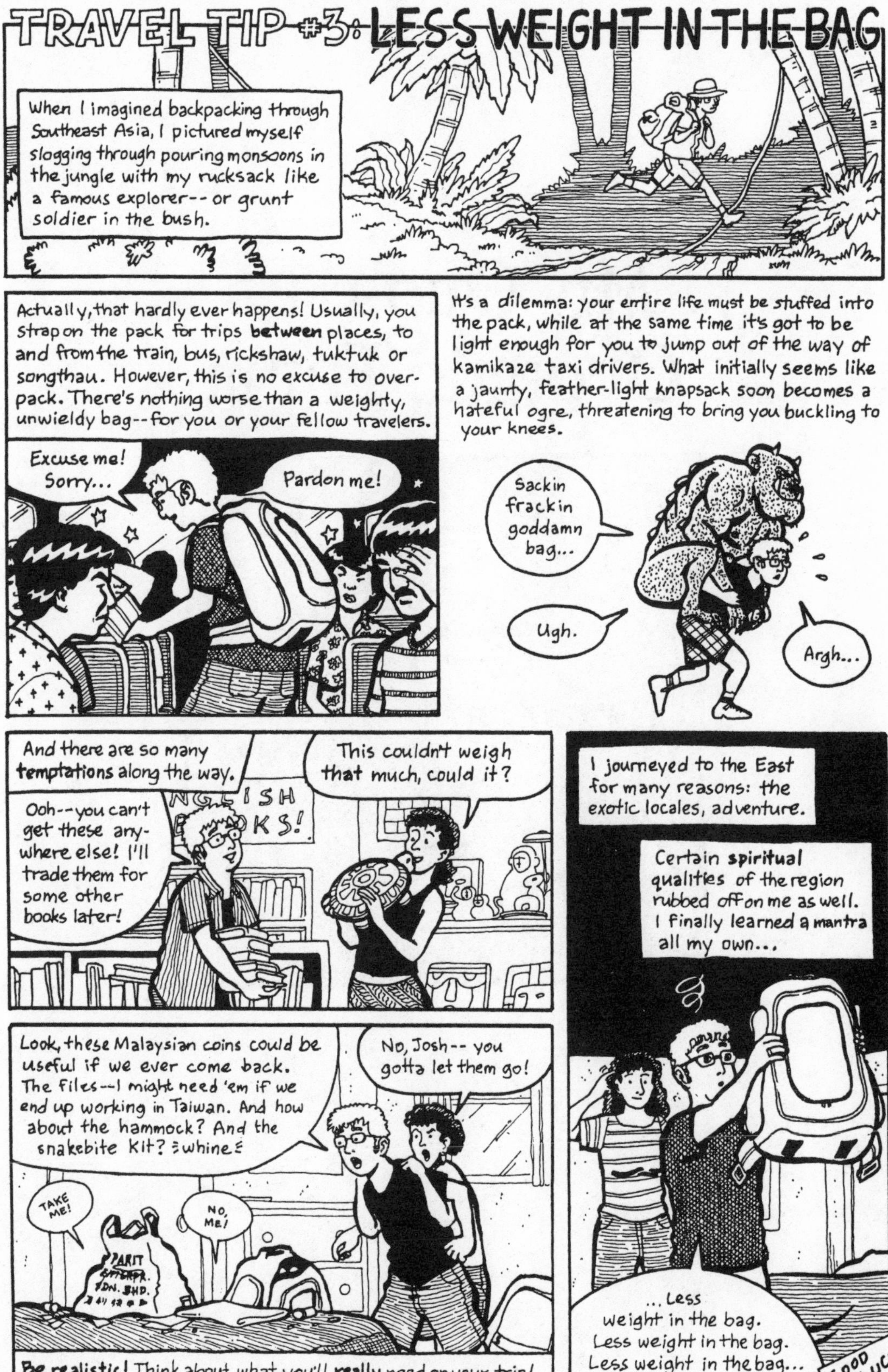
TRAVEL TIP #3: LESS WEIGHT IN THE BAG
When I imagined backpacking through Southeast Asia, I pictured myself slogging through pouring monsoons in the jungle with my rucksack like a famous explorer-- or grunt soldier in the bush.
Actually, that hardly ever happens! Usually, you strap on the pack for trips **between** places, to and from the train, bus, rickshaw, tuktuk or songthau. However, this is no excuse to over-pack. There's nothing worse than a weighty, unwieldy bag--for you or your fellow travelers.
Excuse me! Sorry...
Pardon me!
It's a dilemma: your entire life must be stuffed into the pack, while at the same time it's got to be light enough for you to jump out of the way of kamikaze taxi drivers. What initially seems like a jaunty, feather-light knapsack soon becomes a hateful ogre, threatening to bring you buckling to your knees.
Sackin frackin goddamn bag...
Ugh.
Argh...
And there are so many **temptations** along the way.
This couldn't weigh **that** much, could it?
Ooh--you can't get these anywhere else! I'll trade them for some other books later!
Look, these Malaysian coins could be useful if we ever come back. The files--I might need 'em if we end up working in Taiwan. And how about the hammock? And the snakebite kit? ≡whine≡
No, Josh-- you gotta let them go!
TAKE ME!
NO, ME!
Be realistic! Think about what you'll **really** need on your trip!
I journeyed to the East for many reasons: the exotic locales, adventure.
Certain **spiritual** qualities of the region rubbed off on me as well. I finally learned a **mantra** all my own...
...Less weight in the bag. Less weight in the bag. Less weight in the bag...
GOOD LUCK!

Mr. Ong's Organic Farm

Telok Bahang
George Town
PENANG
MALAYSIA
Strait of Malacca

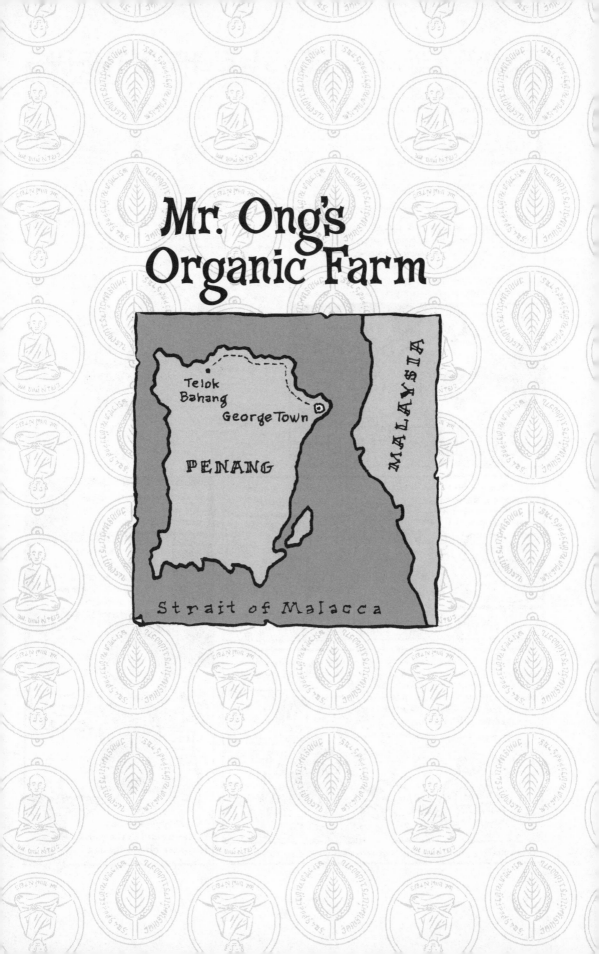

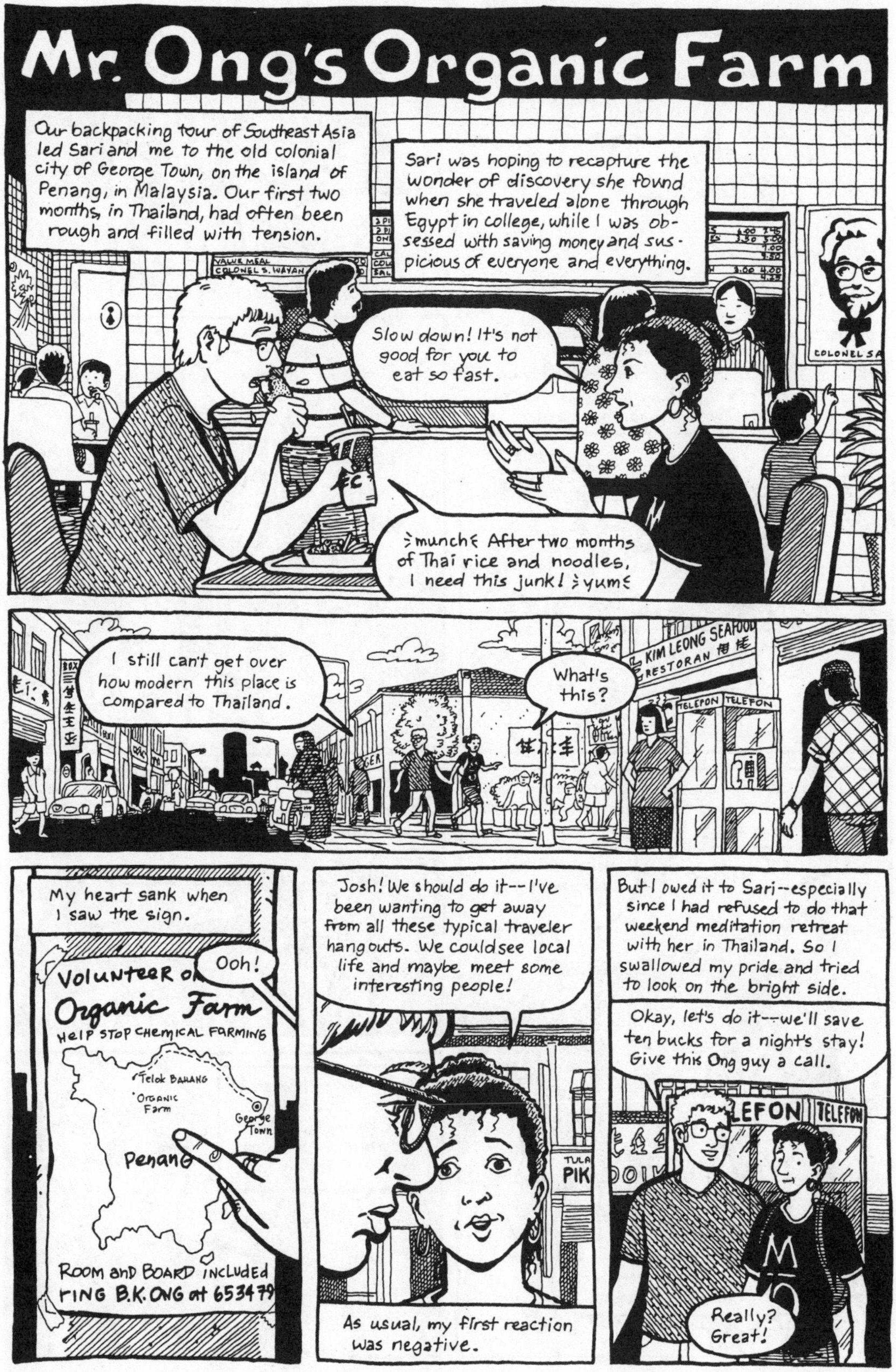
Mr. Ong's Organic Farm
Our backpacking tour of Southeast Asia led Sari and me to the old colonial city of George Town, on the island of Penang, in Malaysia. Our first two months, in Thailand, had often been rough and filled with tension.
Sari was hoping to recapture the wonder of discovery she found when she traveled alone through Egypt in college, while I was obsessed with saving money and suspicious of everyone and everything.
Slow down! It's not good for you to eat so fast.
≥munch≤ After two months of Thai rice and noodles, I need this junk! ≥yum≤
COLONEL SA
I still can't get over how modern this place is compared to Thailand.
What's this?
KIM LEONG SEAFOOD RESTORAN
TELEFON TELEFON
My heart sank when I saw the sign.
Ooh!
Volunteer on Organic Farm
Help stop chemical farming
Telok Bahang
Organic Farm
George Town
Penang
Room and Board included
ring B.K. Ong at 653479
Josh! We should do it--I've been wanting to get away from all these typical traveler hangouts. We could see local life and maybe meet some interesting people!
As usual, my first reaction was negative.
But I owed it to Sari--especially since I had refused to do that weekend meditation retreat with her in Thailand. So I swallowed my pride and tried to look on the bright side.
Okay, let's do it--we'll save ten bucks for a night's stay! Give this Ong guy a call.
Really? Great!

Sari reached Mr. Ong on the first try. He told us to take a bus to a small town on the other side of the island, where he would meet us and take us to the farm.

At Mr. Ong's suggestion, we bought some canned goods at a supermarket in George Town which we brought with us to help with that evening's dinner.

I wondered what the farm would be like, imagining something like the ranches I remembered from my childhood in San Diego. Sometimes my mother and I would venture into farm country to get horse manure to use as fertilizer for her garden.

Here we are...

Mr. Ong appeared. He made a strange sight, with his long ponytail and the dozens of scabbed-over mosquito bites on his arms and legs.

Mr. Ong?

Hello. Heh heh. We take this bus to the farm.

He didn't introduce himself or even ask us our names.

Try this nonya. Good village pastry.

As the bus rattled along the dirt roads toward the farm, I couldn't help but wonder what we were getting into.

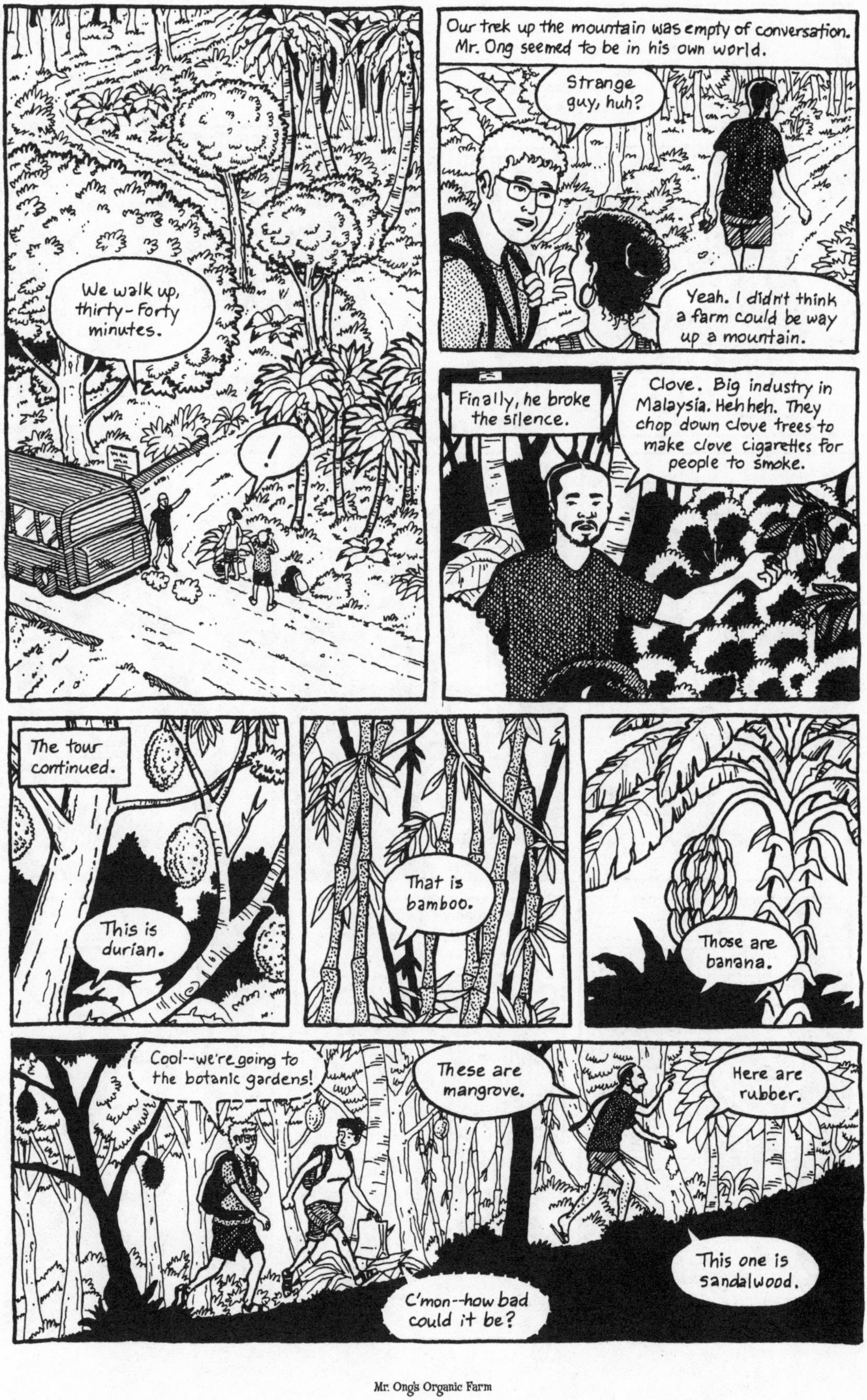
We walk up, thirty-Forty minutes.
!
Our trek up the mountain was empty of conversation. Mr. Ong seemed to be in his own world.
Strange guy, huh?
Yeah. I didn't think a farm could be way up a mountain.
Finally, he broke the silence.
Clove. Big industry in Malaysia. Hehheh. They chop down clove trees to make clove cigarettes for people to smoke.
The tour continued.
This is durian.
That is bamboo.
Those are banana.
Cool--we're going to the botanic gardens!
These are mangrove.
Here are rubber.
This one is sandalwood.
C'mon--how bad could it be?

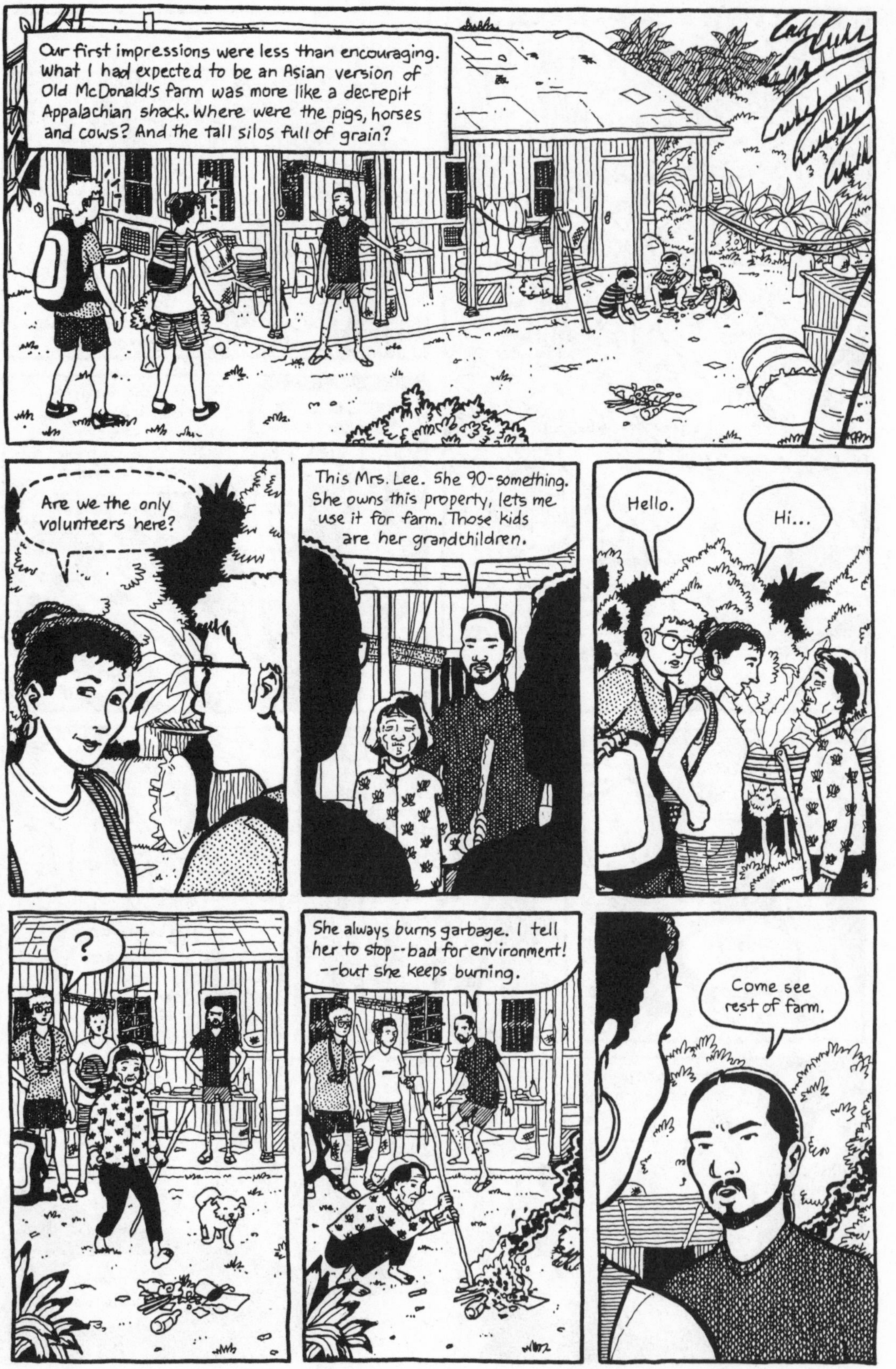
Our first impressions were less than encouraging. What I had expected to be an Asian version of Old McDonald's farm was more like a decrepit Appalachian shack. Where were the pigs, horses and cows? And the tall silos full of grain?
Are we the only volunteers here?
This Mrs. Lee. She 90-something. She owns this property, lets me use it for farm. Those kids are her grandchildren.
Hello.
Hi...
?
She always burns garbage. I tell her to stop--bad for environment! --but she keeps burning.
Come see rest of farm.

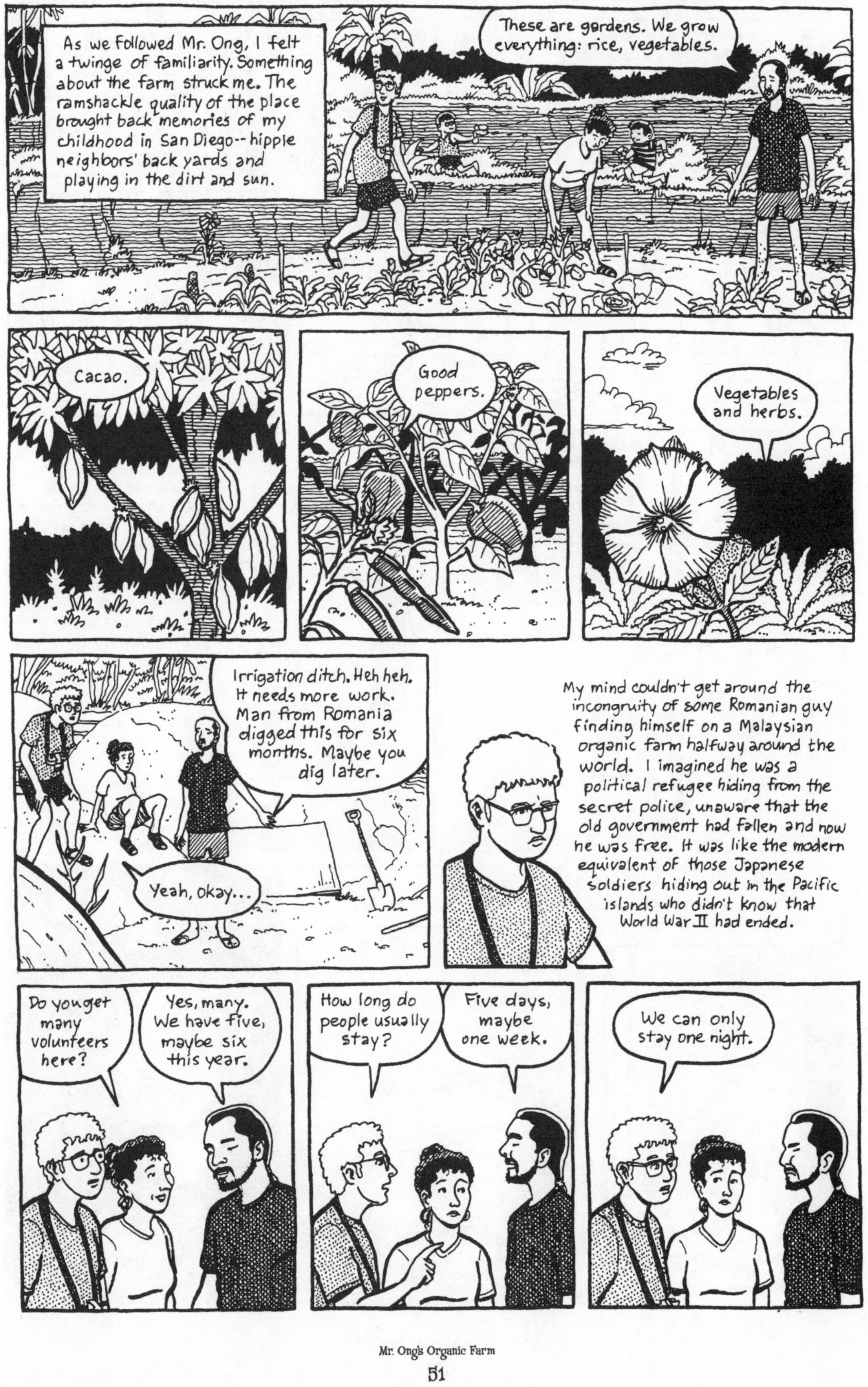
As we followed Mr. Ong, I felt a twinge of familiarity. Something about the farm struck me. The ramshackle quality of the place brought back memories of my childhood in San Diego--hippie neighbors' back yards and playing in the dirt and sun.
These are gardens. We grow everything: rice, vegetables.
Cacao.
Good peppers.
Vegetables and herbs.
Irrigation ditch. Heh heh. It needs more work. Man from Romania digged this for six months. Maybe you dig later.
Yeah, okay...
My mind couldn't get around the incongruity of some Romanian guy finding himself on a Malaysian organic farm halfway around the world. I imagined he was a political refugee hiding from the secret police, unaware that the old government had fallen and now he was free. It was like the modern equivalent of those Japanese soldiers hiding out in the Pacific islands who didn't know that World War II had ended.
Do you get many volunteers here?
Yes, many. We have five, maybe six this year.
How long do people usually stay?
Five days, maybe one week.
We can only stay one night.

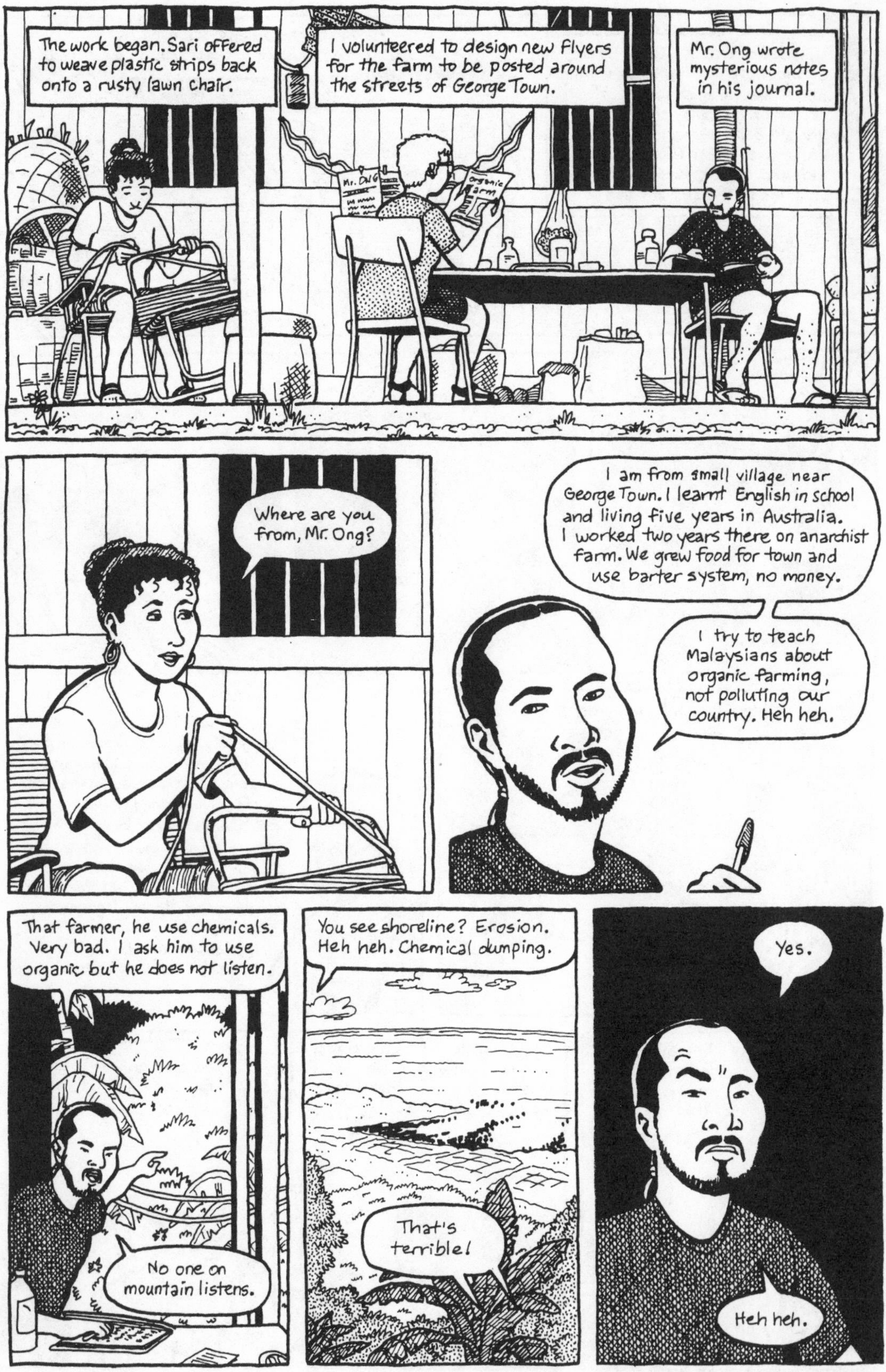
The work began. Sari offered to weave plastic strips back onto a rusty lawn chair.
I volunteered to design new flyers for the farm to be posted around the streets of George Town.
Mr. Ong wrote mysterious notes in his journal.
Mr. ONG
Organic Farm
Where are you from, Mr. Ong?
I am from small village near George Town. I learnt English in school and living five years in Australia. I worked two years there on anarchist farm. We grew food for town and use barter system, no money.
I try to teach Malaysians about organic farming, not polluting our country. Heh heh.
That farmer, he use chemicals. Very bad. I ask him to use organic but he does not listen.
No one on mountain listens.
You see shoreline? Erosion. Heh heh. Chemical dumping.
That's terrible!
Yes.
Heh heh.

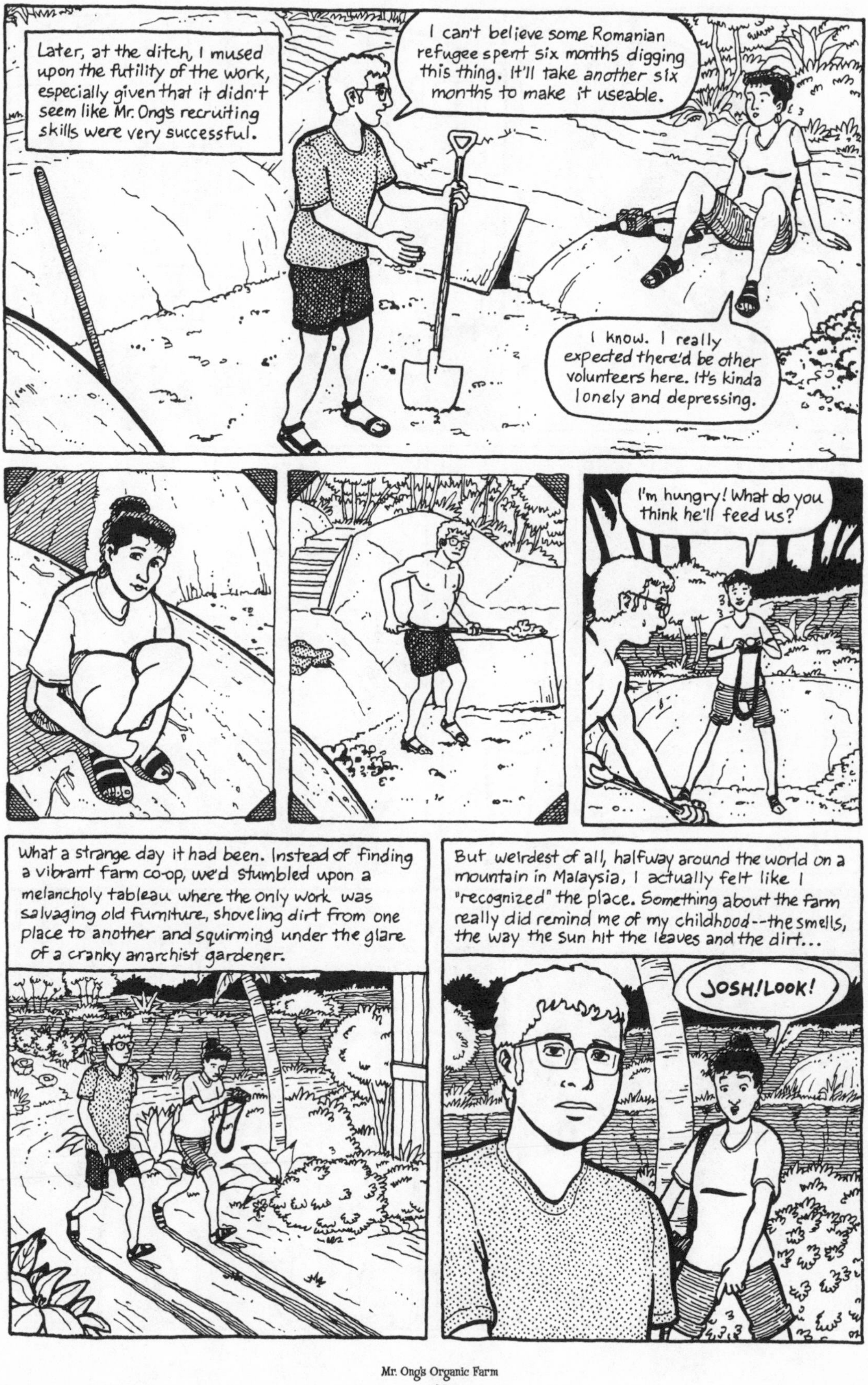
Later, at the ditch, I mused upon the futility of the work, especially given that it didn't seem like Mr. Ong's recruiting skills were very successful.
I can't believe some Romanian refugee spent six months digging this thing. It'll take another six months to make it useable.
I know. I really expected there'd be other volunteers here. It's kinda lonely and depressing.
I'm hungry! What do you think he'll feed us?
What a strange day it had been. Instead of finding a vibrant farm co-op, we'd stumbled upon a melancholy tableau where the only work was salvaging old furniture, shoveling dirt from one place to another and squirming under the glare of a cranky anarchist gardener.
But weirdest of all, halfway around the world on a mountain in Malaysia, I actually felt like I "recognized" the place. Something about the farm really did remind me of my childhood--the smells, the way the sun hit the leaves and the dirt...
JOSH! LOOK!

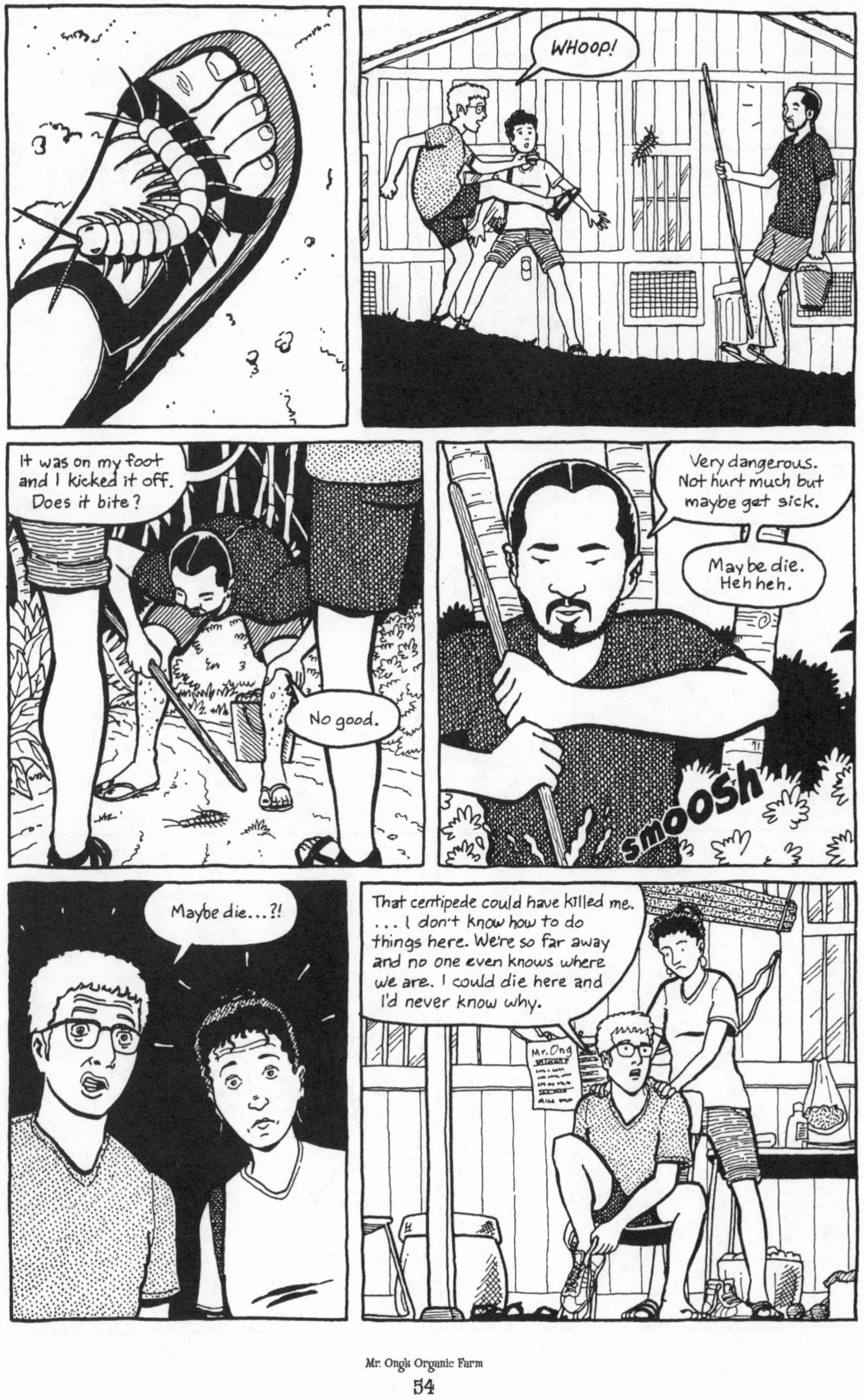
WHOOP!
It was on my foot and I kicked it off. Does it bite?
No good.
Very dangerous. Not hurt much but maybe get sick.
Maybe die. Heh heh.
smoosh
Maybe die...?!
That centipede could have killed me. ... I don't know how to do things here. We're so far away and no one even knows where we are. I could die here and I'd never know why.
Mr. Ong

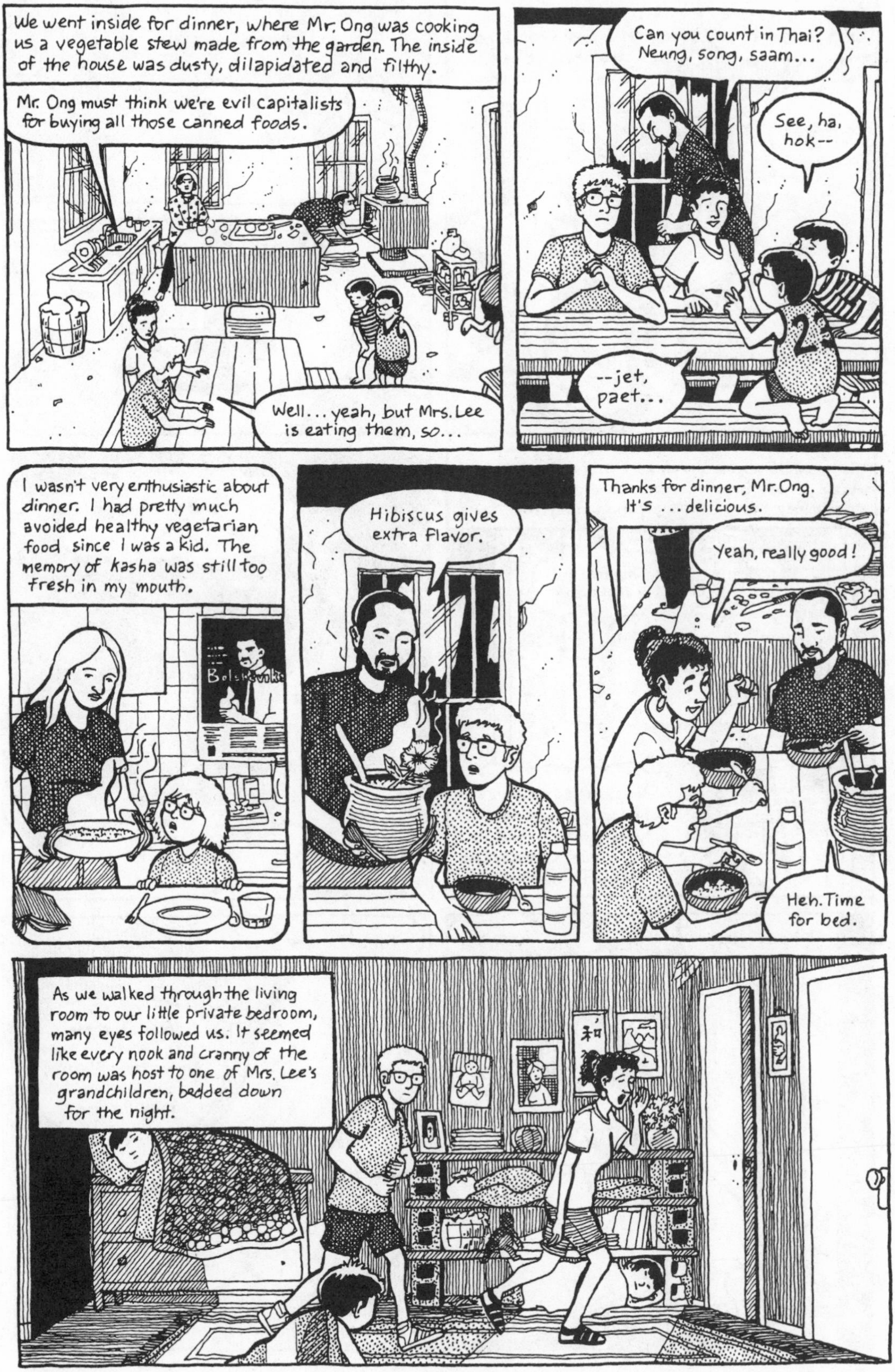
We went inside for dinner, where Mr. Ong was cooking us a vegetable stew made from the garden. The inside of the house was dusty, dilapidated and filthy.
Mr. Ong must think we're evil capitalists for buying all those canned foods.
Well... yeah, but Mrs. Lee is eating them, so...
Can you count in Thai? Neung, song, saam...
See, ha, hok--
--jet, paet...
I wasn't very enthusiastic about dinner. I had pretty much avoided healthy vegetarian food since I was a kid. The memory of kasha was still too fresh in my mouth.
Hibiscus gives extra flavor.
Thanks for dinner, Mr. Ong. It's ...delicious.
Yeah, really good!
Heh. Time for bed.
As we walked through the living room to our little private bedroom, many eyes followed us. It seemed like every nook and cranny of the room was host to one of Mrs. Lee's grandchildren, bedded down for the night.

How'd you manage with dinner?
Oh yeah--you know how much I *love* that kind of cuisine... oh well, you can't beat the price!
A few hours into the night, I was suddenly wide awake.
The moon lit up the porch as I stepped outside. Again, I was brought back to my childhood, to summer camp and sleeping under the stars.
This really is traveling.
Things are so relative. When we go back to the city tomorrow it'll be like going home... Going home to George Town! *Malaysia!*
It was worth it just for this.
epilogue
≷Mmmm≶ How'd you sleep?
Okay, I guess...
What do you mean?
Look at these itchy hives--I don't think that *healthy* food was so good for me.
END

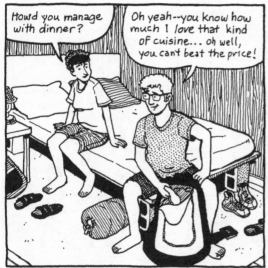

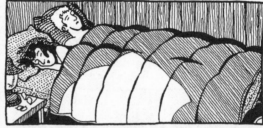

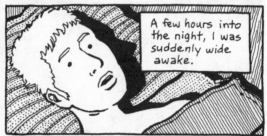

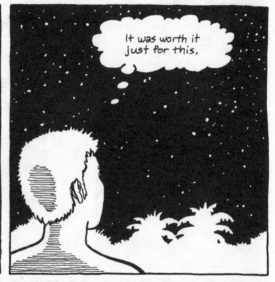

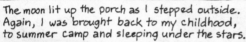

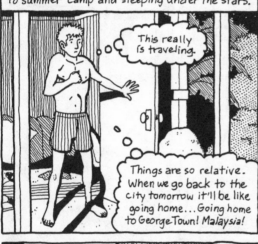

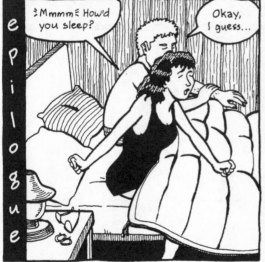

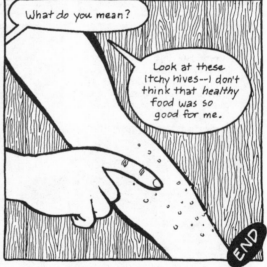

Travel Tip #22:
How to Star in a Singaporean Soap Opera

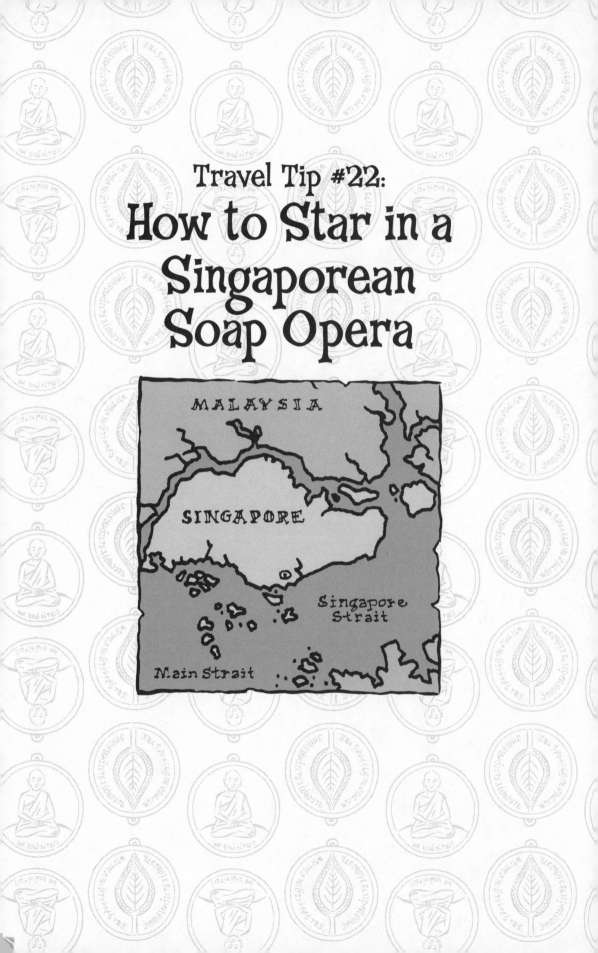

MALAYSIA

SINGAPORE

Singapore Strait

Main Strait

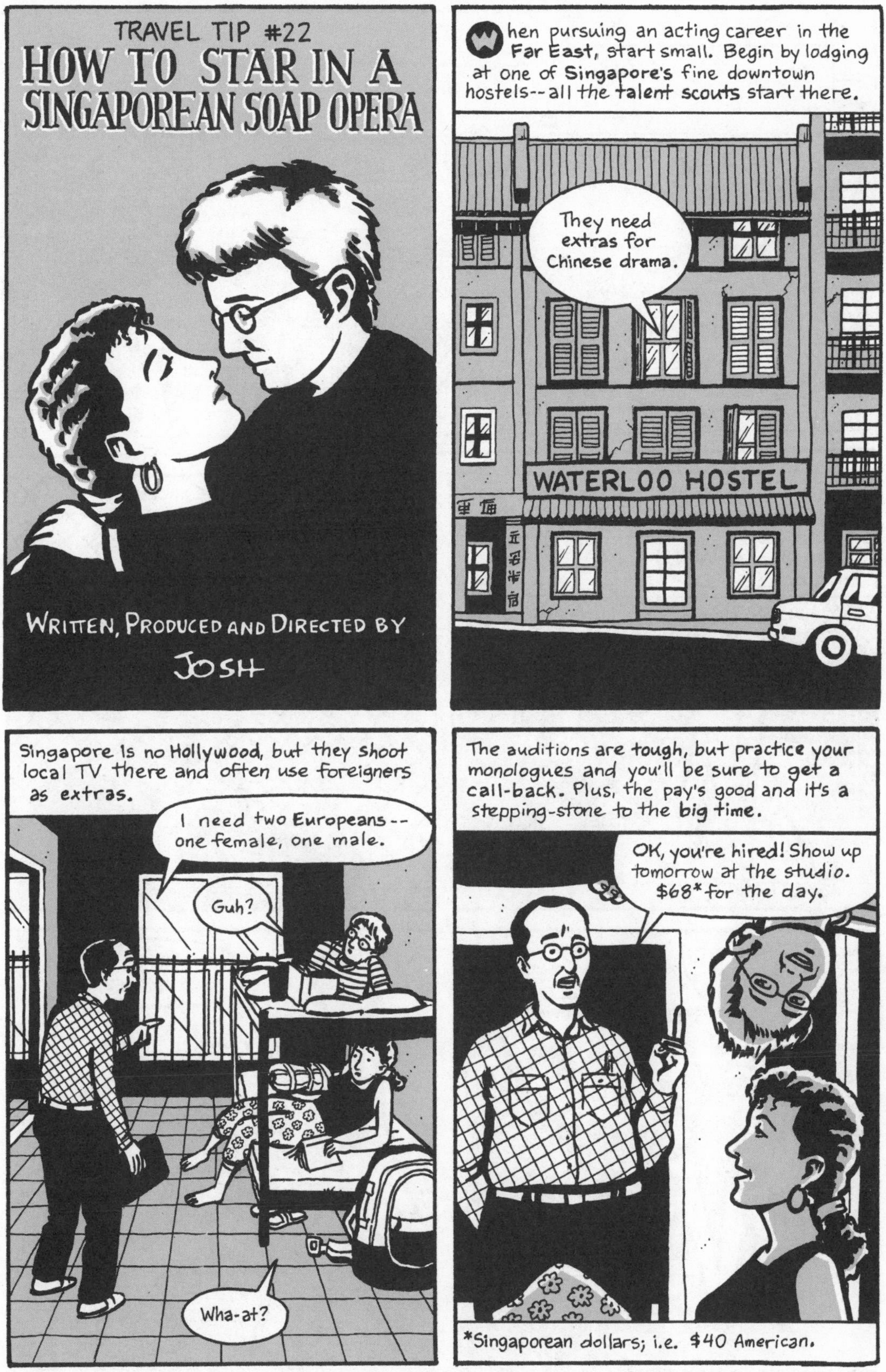
TRAVEL TIP #22
HOW TO STAR IN A SINGAPOREAN SOAP OPERA
WRITTEN, PRODUCED AND DIRECTED BY
JOSH
When pursuing an acting career in the Far East, start small. Begin by lodging at one of Singapore's fine downtown hostels--all the talent scouts start there.
They need extras for Chinese drama.
WATERLOO HOSTEL
Singapore is no Hollywood, but they shoot local TV there and often use foreigners as extras.
I need two Europeans--one female, one male.
Guh?
Wha-at?
The auditions are tough, but practice your monologues and you'll be sure to get a call-back. Plus, the pay's good and it's a stepping-stone to the big time.
OK, you're hired! Show up tomorrow at the studio. $68* for the day.
*Singaporean dollars; i.e. $40 American.

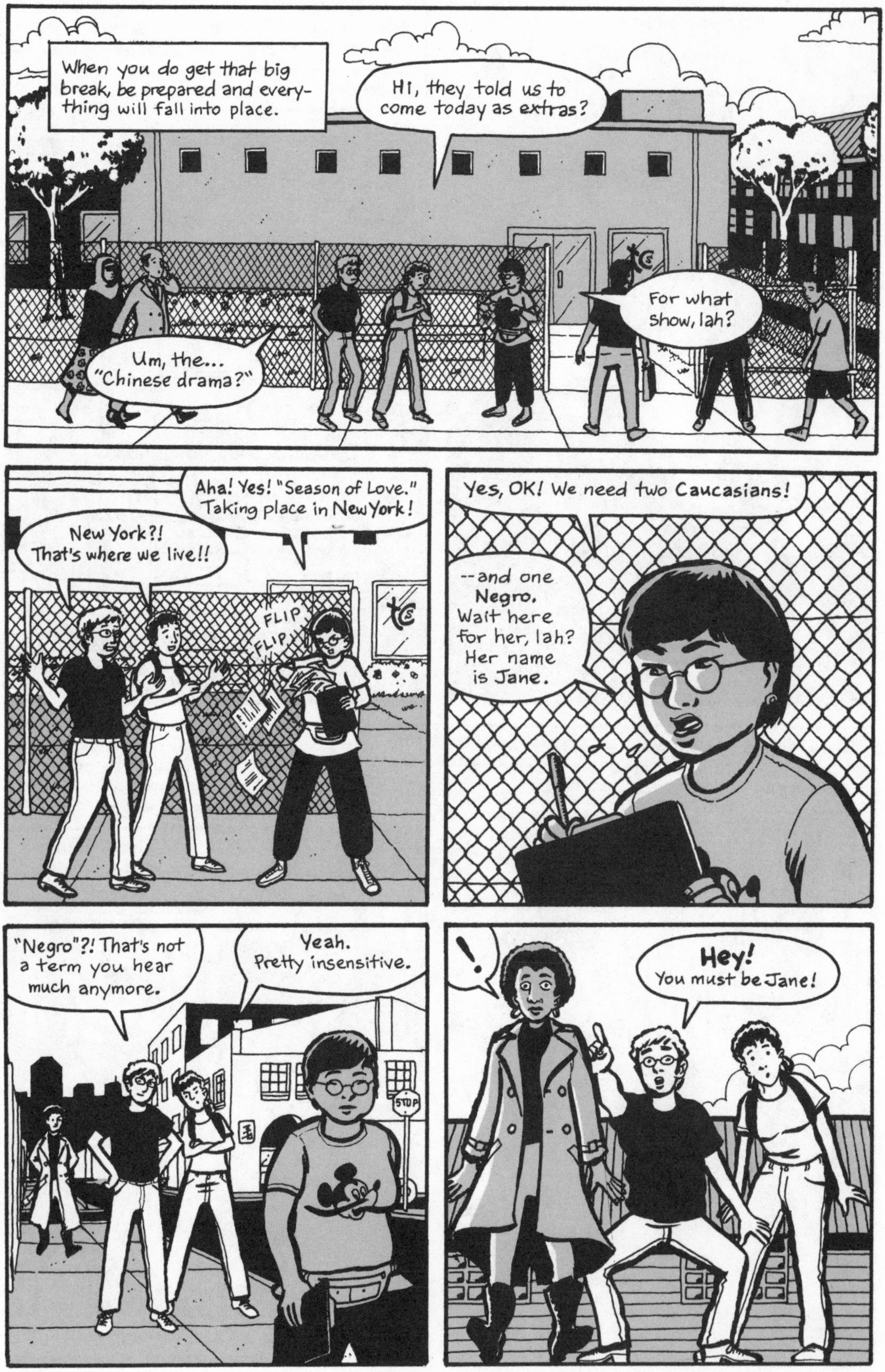
When you do get that big break, be prepared and everything will fall into place.
Hi, they told us to come today as extras?
For what show, lah?
Um, the... "Chinese drama?"
Aha! Yes! "Season of Love." Taking place in New York!
New York?! That's where we live!!
FLIP FLIP
Yes, OK! We need two Caucasians!
--and one Negro. Wait here for her, lah? Her name is Jane.
"Negro"?! That's not a term you hear much anymore.
Yeah. Pretty insensitive.
STOP
!
Hey! You must be Jane!

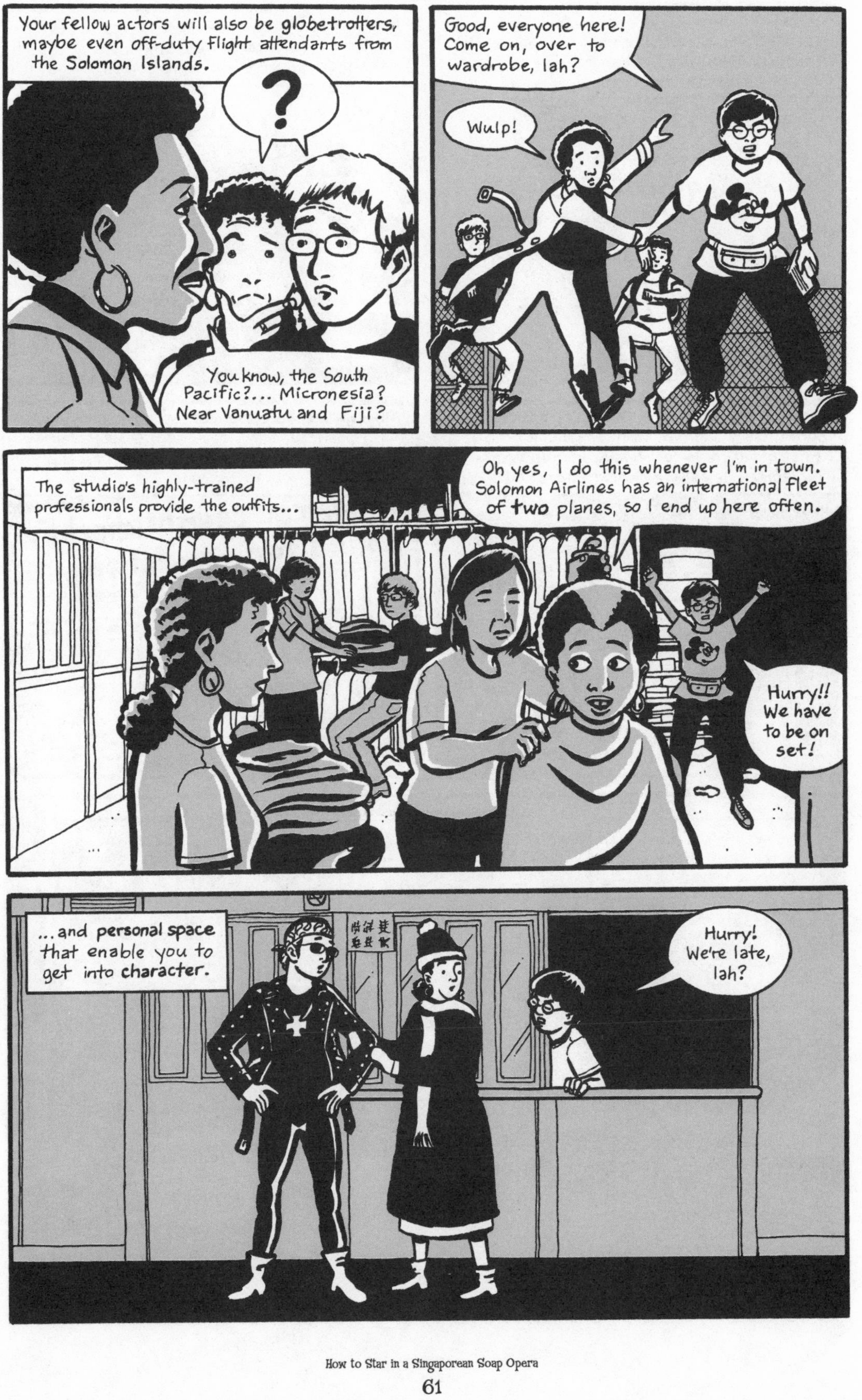
Your fellow actors will also be globetrotters, maybe even off-duty flight attendants from the Solomon Islands.
?
You know, the South Pacific?... Micronesia? Near Vanuatu and Fiji?
Good, everyone here! Come on, over to wardrobe, lah?
Wulp!
The studio's highly-trained professionals provide the outfits...
Oh yes, I do this whenever I'm in town. Solomon Airlines has an international fleet of two planes, so I end up here often.
Hurry!! We have to be on set!
...and personal space that enable you to get into character.
Hurry! We're late, lah?

Singapore's **tumultuous** history has produced a multi-ethnic society composed mainly of Chinese, Malay and Indian peoples, with the odd European thrown in.

Unlike the **rough-and-tumble** cities of other Southeast Asian countries, Singapore prides itself on civility and cleanliness.

Singapore is a wealthy, modern metropolis, but it has a vested interest in celebrating its colorful past--especially if this benefits the sometimes **sluggish** tourist trade.

Hey there, big boy!

YE OLDE ORCHARD ST. SALOON

Ahr! How much, me lassie?

Although Singapore **embraces** Western technology and commerce, there have been some notable clashes between their ordered society and our more "decadent" one.

American teen Michael Fay caned for vandalism

SINGAPORE — Four lashes of a bamboo cane and it was done. After all the months of controversy and spectacle, Singapore prison authorities yesterday carried out the prescribed punishment on American Michael Fay, 17, of Florida.

He had been arrested last summer after engaging in a wild spree through a downtown district.

Despite protests by "human rights" organizations and a personal

...it happened: A Sing...

The result is a portrayal of the West that can border on the **surreal.**

This is supposed to be New York?! "Sesame Street," is more like it.

BANK OF NEW YORK

DICK LEE PASTRY

Yeah... Crossed with "Gunsmoke."

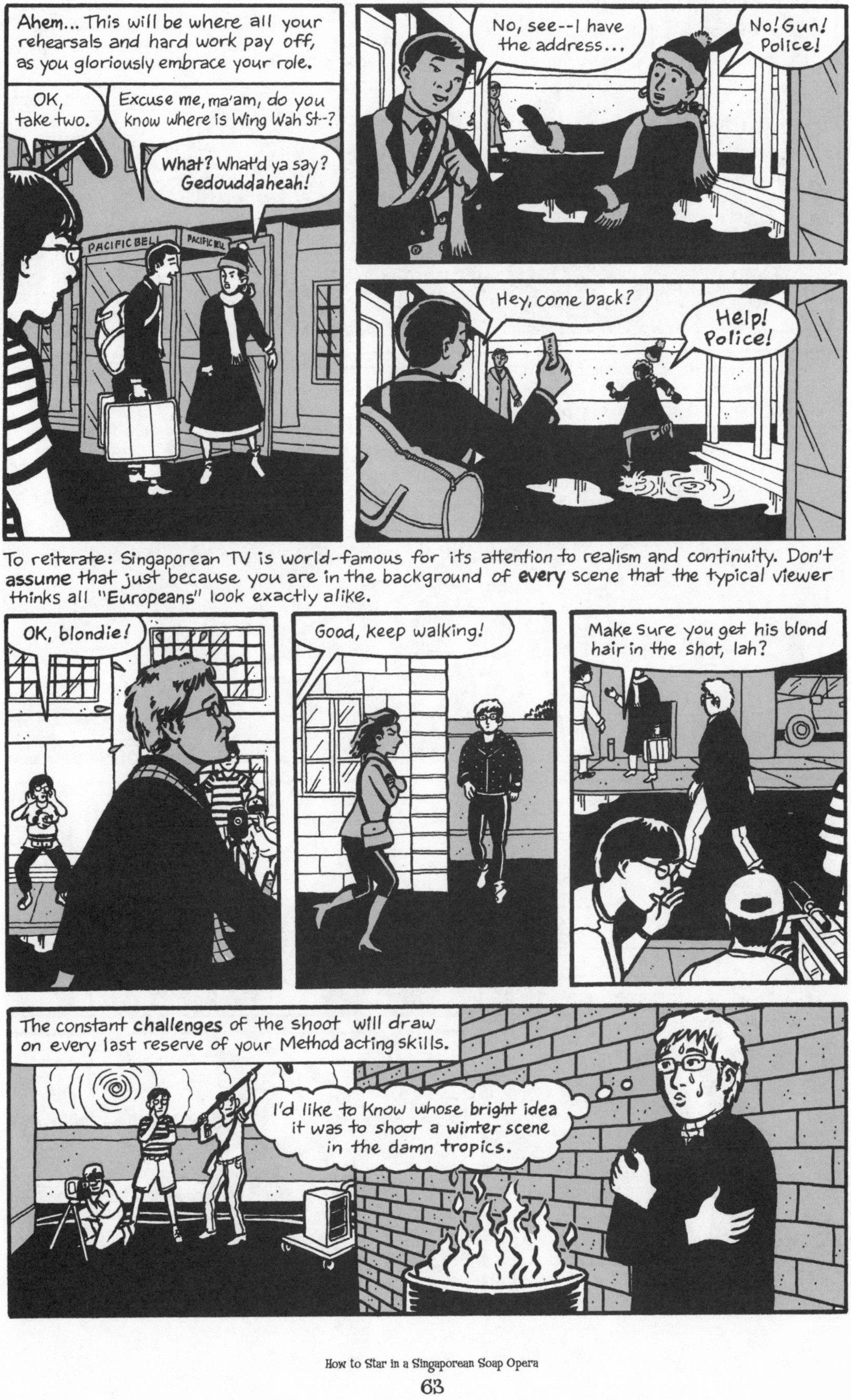
Ahem... This will be where all your rehearsals and hard work pay off, as you gloriously embrace your role.
OK, take two.
Excuse me, ma'am, do you know where is Wing Wah St--?
What? What'd ya say? Gedouddaheah!
PACIFIC BELL
PACIFIC BELL
No, see--I have the address...
No! Gun! Police!
Hey, come back?
Help! Police!
To reiterate: Singaporean TV is world-famous for its attention to realism and continuity. Don't **assume** that just because you are in the background of **every** scene that the typical viewer thinks all "Europeans" look exactly alike.
OK, blondie!
Good, keep walking!
Make sure you get his blond hair in the shot, lah?
The constant **challenges** of the shoot will draw on every last reserve of your Method acting skills.
I'd like to know whose bright idea it was to shoot a winter scene in the damn tropics.

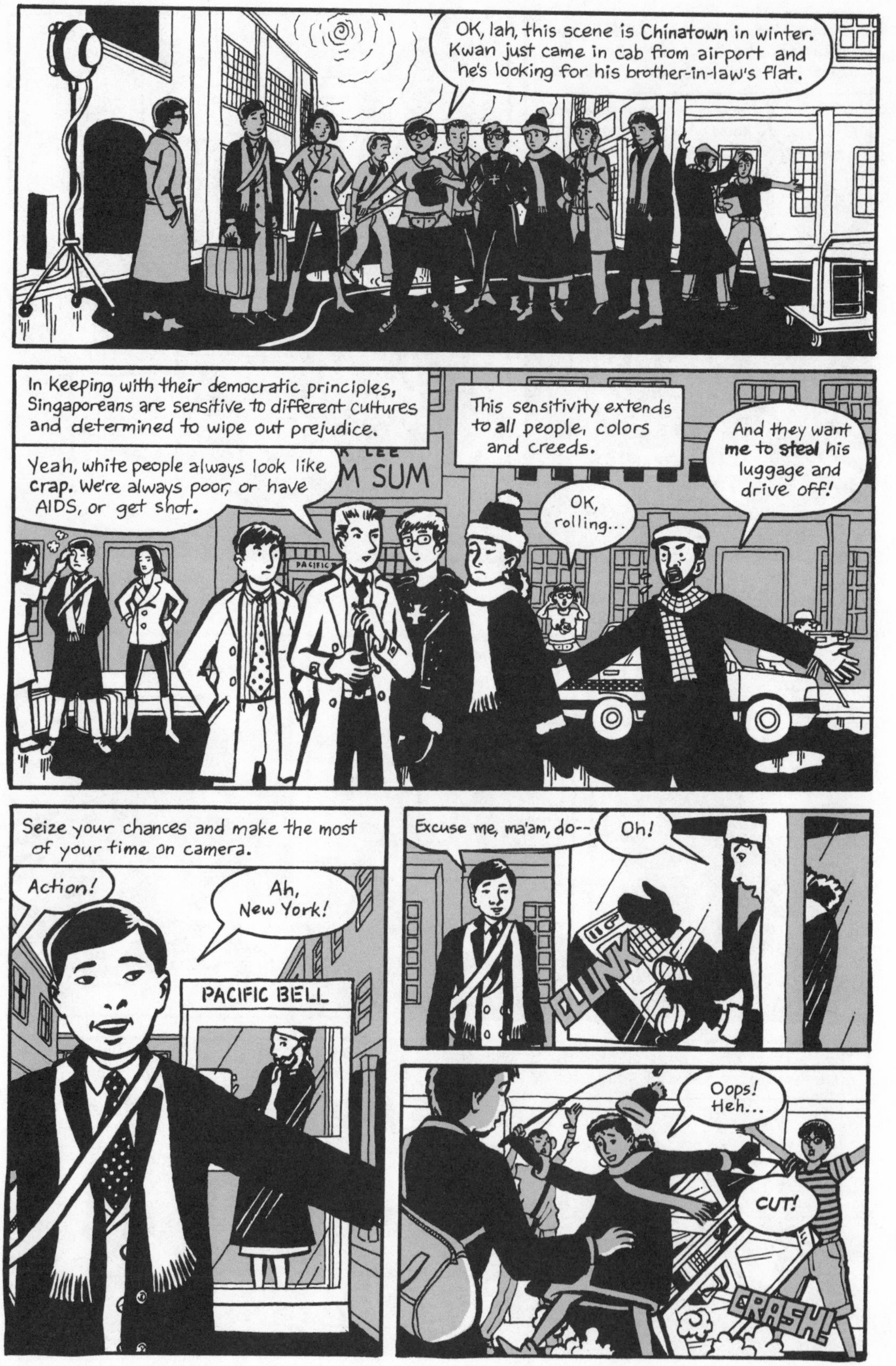
OK, lah, this scene is Chinatown in winter. Kwan just came in cab from airport and he's looking for his brother-in-law's flat.
In keeping with their democratic principles, Singaporeans are sensitive to different cultures and determined to wipe out prejudice.
Yeah, white people always look like crap. We're always poor, or have AIDS, or get shot.
This sensitivity extends to all people, colors and creeds.
OK, rolling...
And they want me to steal his luggage and drive off!
M SUM
Seize your chances and make the most of your time on camera.
Action!
Ah, New York!
PACIFIC BELL
Excuse me, ma'am, do--
Oh!
CLUNK
Oops! Heh...
CUT!
CRASH!

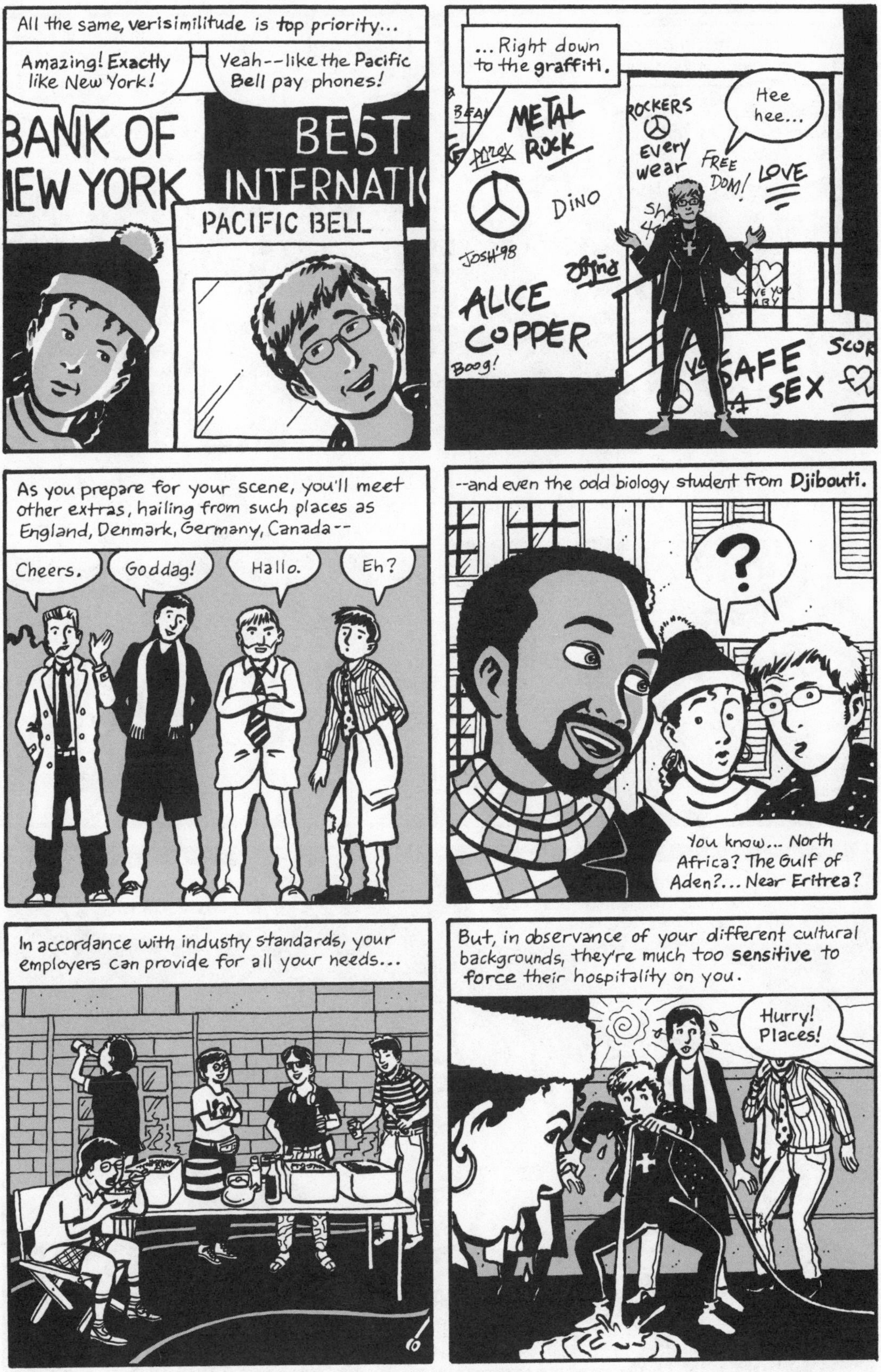

All the same, verisimilitude is top priority...
Amazing! Exactly like New York!
Yeah--like the Pacific Bell pay phones!
BANK OF NEW YORK
BEST INTERNATI
PACIFIC BELL
...Right down to the graffiti.
METAL ROCK
ROCKERS
Every wear
FREE DOM!
LOVE
Hee hee...
DINO
JOSH '98
ALICE COPPER
Boog!
SAFE SEX
LOVE YOU BABY
As you prepare for your scene, you'll meet other extras, hailing from such places as England, Denmark, Germany, Canada--
Cheers.
Goddag!
Hallo.
Eh?
--and even the odd biology student from Djibouti.
?
You know... North Africa? The Gulf of Aden?... Near Eritrea?
In accordance with industry standards, your employers can provide for all your needs...
But, in observance of your different cultural backgrounds, they're much too sensitive to force their hospitality on you.
Hurry! Places!

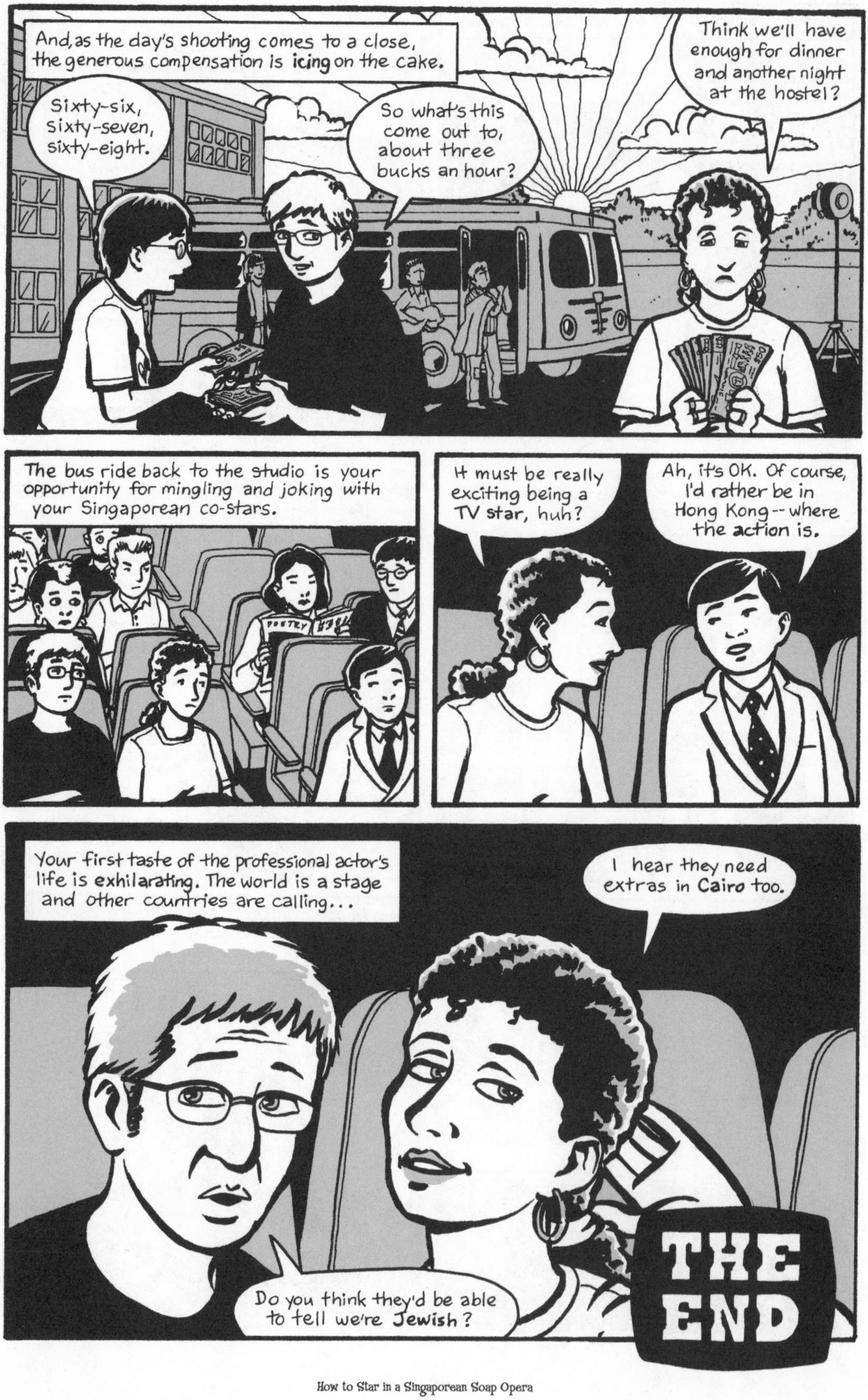
And, as the day's shooting comes to a close, the generous compensation is icing on the cake.
Sixty-six, sixty-seven, sixty-eight.
So what's this come out to, about three bucks an hour?
Think we'll have enough for dinner and another night at the hostel?
The bus ride back to the studio is your opportunity for mingling and joking with your Singaporean co-stars.
POETRY
It must be really exciting being a TV star, huh?
Ah, it's OK. Of course, I'd rather be in Hong Kong -- where the action is.
Your first taste of the professional actor's life is exhilarating. The world is a stage and other countries are calling...
I hear they need extras in Cairo too.
Do you think they'd be able to tell we're Jewish?
THE END

Travel Tip #45:
Gynecology
on the Go

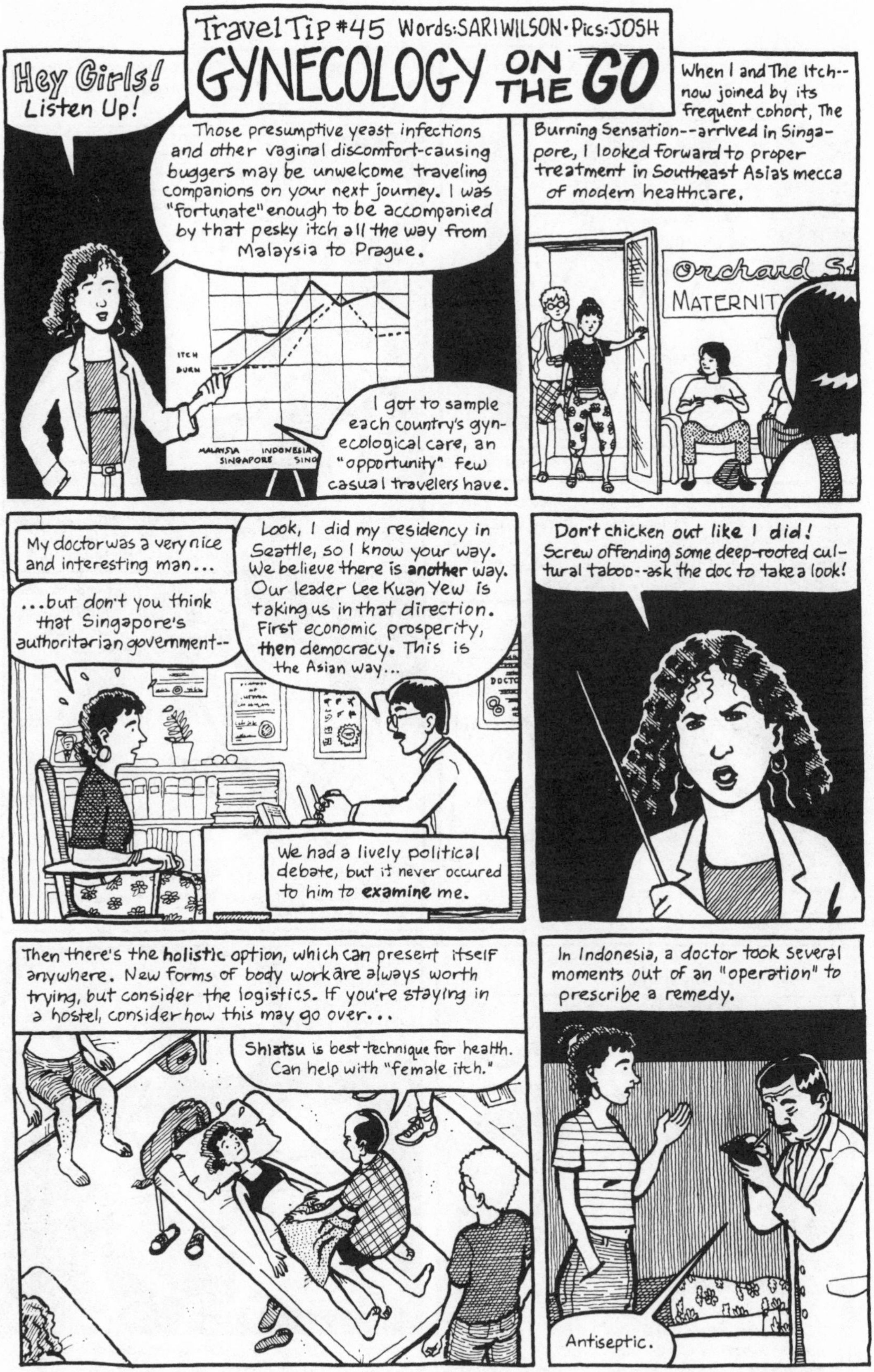
Travel Tip #45 Words: SARI WILSON • Pics: JOSH
GYNECOLOGY ON THE GO
Hey Girls! Listen Up!
Those presumptive yeast infections and other vaginal discomfort-causing buggers may be unwelcome traveling companions on your next journey. I was "fortunate" enough to be accompanied by that pesky itch all the way from Malaysia to Prague.
ITCH
BURN
MALAYSIA
SINGAPORE
INDONESIA
I got to sample each country's gynecological care, an "opportunity" few casual travelers have.
When I and The Itch--now joined by its frequent cohort, The Burning Sensation--arrived in Singapore, I looked forward to proper treatment in Southeast Asia's mecca of modern healthcare.
Orchard
MATERNITY
My doctor was a very nice and interesting man...
...but don't you think that Singapore's authoritarian government--
Look, I did my residency in Seattle, so I know your way. We believe there is another way. Our leader Lee Kuan Yew is taking us in that direction. First economic prosperity, then democracy. This is the Asian way...
We had a lively political debate, but it never occured to him to examine me.
Don't chicken out like I did! Screw offending some deep-rooted cultural taboo--ask the doc to take a look!
Then there's the holistic option, which can present itself anywhere. New forms of body work are always worth trying, but consider the logistics. If you're staying in a hostel, consider how this may go over...
Shiatsu is best technique for health. Can help with "female itch."
In Indonesia, a doctor took several moments out of an "operation" to prescribe a remedy.
Antiseptic.

His solution, which involved soaking in a tubful of mysterious water-dissolved crystals, was colorful but ineffective.
My rear end was stained purple for several weeks.
The soothing landscape of Bali, where nature abounds, recalled to me that time-worn natural remedy-- yogurt and a spoon.
Mmmmm! Good, eh?
The home-made yogurt was tasty but didn't do the job.
Yeah... Great.
A month later, in Prague, I got to experience the joys of communist-era medicine. After wading through the requisite red tape, the doctor actually examined me and took a culture. The god of medical science had finally intervened.
But gods don't always speak fluent English.
Good?
Uh... ne velmi dobré. Er. No...
I demanded to see an English-speaking doc. So they sent me to Dr. Chlebiček, who spoke it fluently. However, in Czech his name means "little bread."
Yeast reduction is important for your diet.
Here--try zis cream.
Pay attention to names! A guy named Doctor Little Bread just shouldn't be in the business of yeast reduction...
Finally, I resorted to trying the incipient art of Czech acupuncture.
Still no luck, although it did clear up my Czech cuisine-induced chronic indigestion.
In the end, I didn't get the thing resolved until I got back to the States.
Next time I'll take some prior precautions. Remember: twelve pounds of well-packed prevention is worth a world of exotic cures!
ACIDOPHILUS
YOGURT
MASSENGIL
SUPPOSITORIES
DOUCHES
DOUCHES
ROSEMARY
MONO-STAT 7
VINEGAR
Write in with your own "gynecology on the go" tips. Good travels and GOOD LUCK!

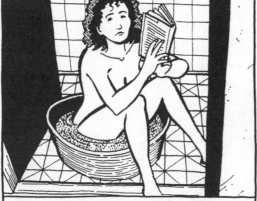

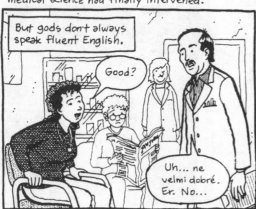

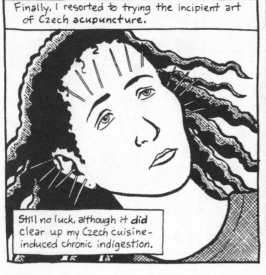

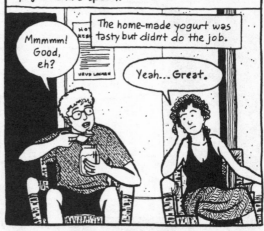

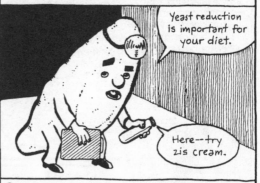

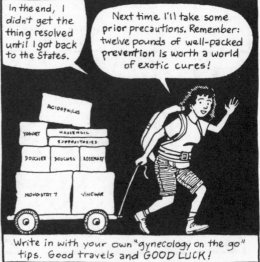

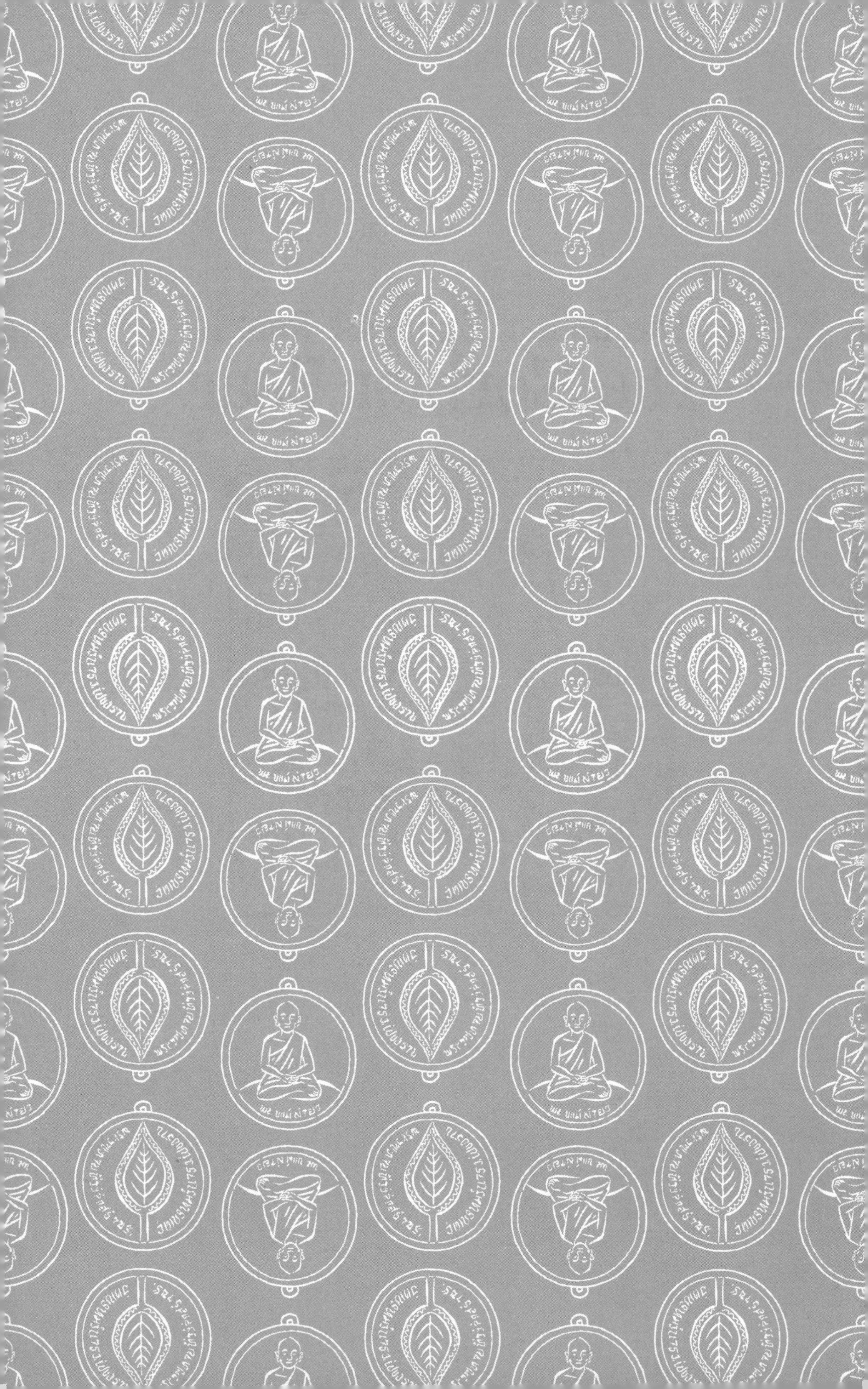

The Balkan Express, Part I:
The Serbian Bear

HUNGARY
ROMANIA
Belgrade
SERBIA
BULGARIA
Black Sea
Sofia
Istanbul
ALBANIA
MACEDONIA
TURKEY
Aegean
GREECE

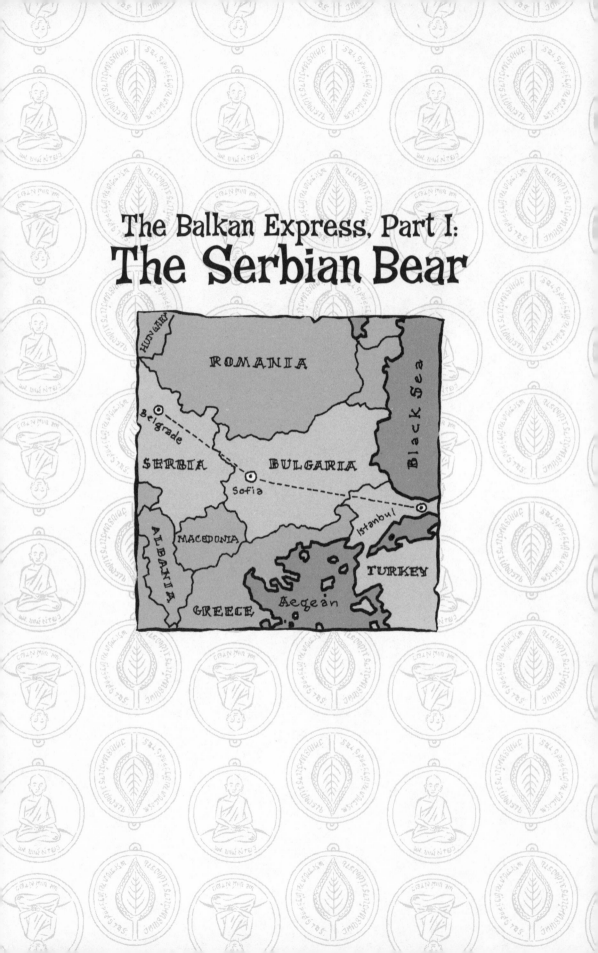

JOSH and SARI in "THE BALKAN EXPRESS, PART ONE"

THE SERBIAN BEAR

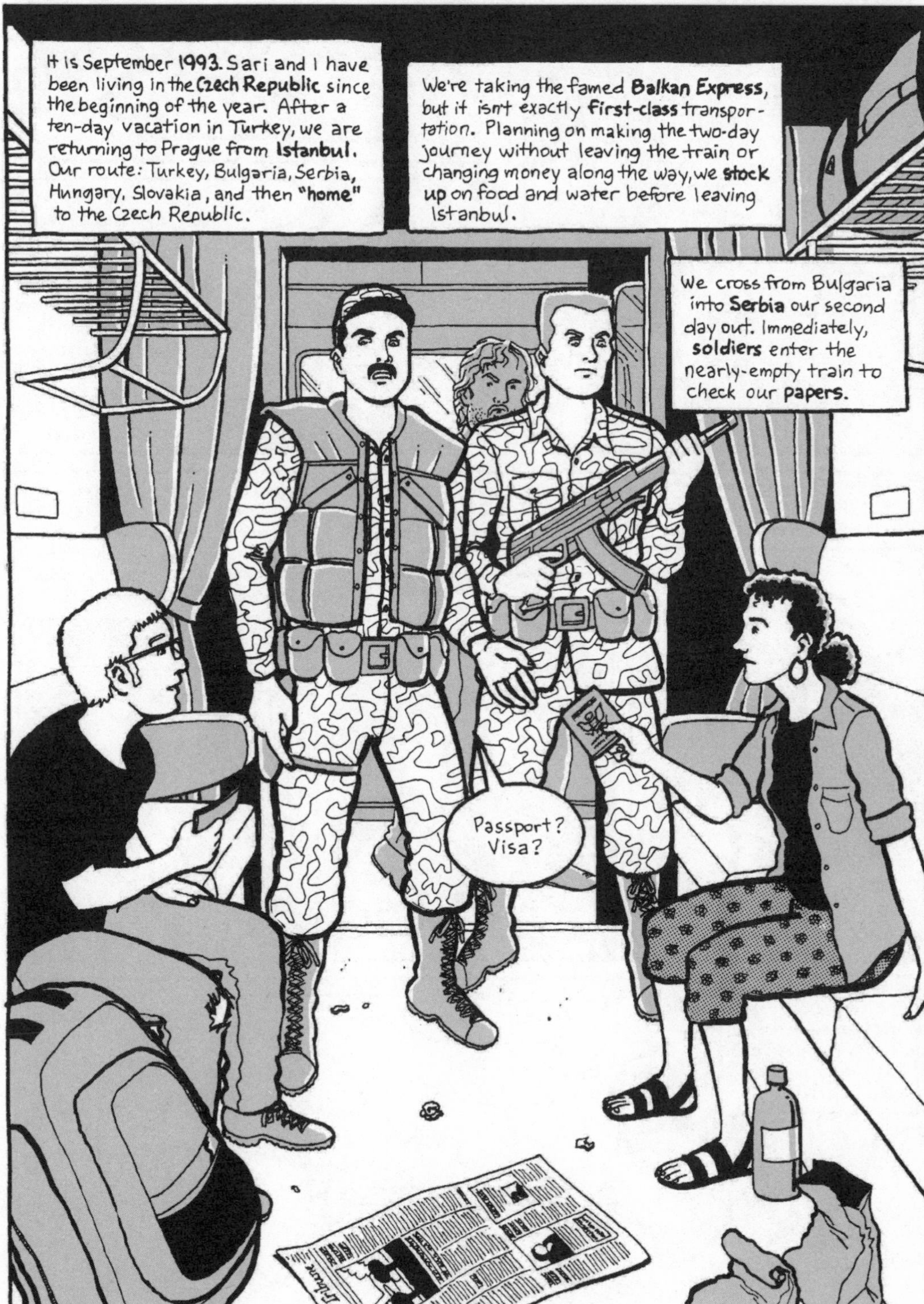
It is September 1993. Sari and I have been living in the Czech Republic since the beginning of the year. After a ten-day vacation in Turkey, we are returning to Prague from Istanbul. Our route: Turkey, Bulgaria, Serbia, Hungary, Slovakia, and then "home" to the Czech Republic.
We're taking the famed Balkan Express, but it isn't exactly first-class transportation. Planning on making the two-day journey without leaving the train or changing money along the way, we stock up on food and water before leaving Istanbul.
We cross from Bulgaria into Serbia our second day out. Immediately, soldiers enter the nearly-empty train to check our papers.
Passport? Visa?

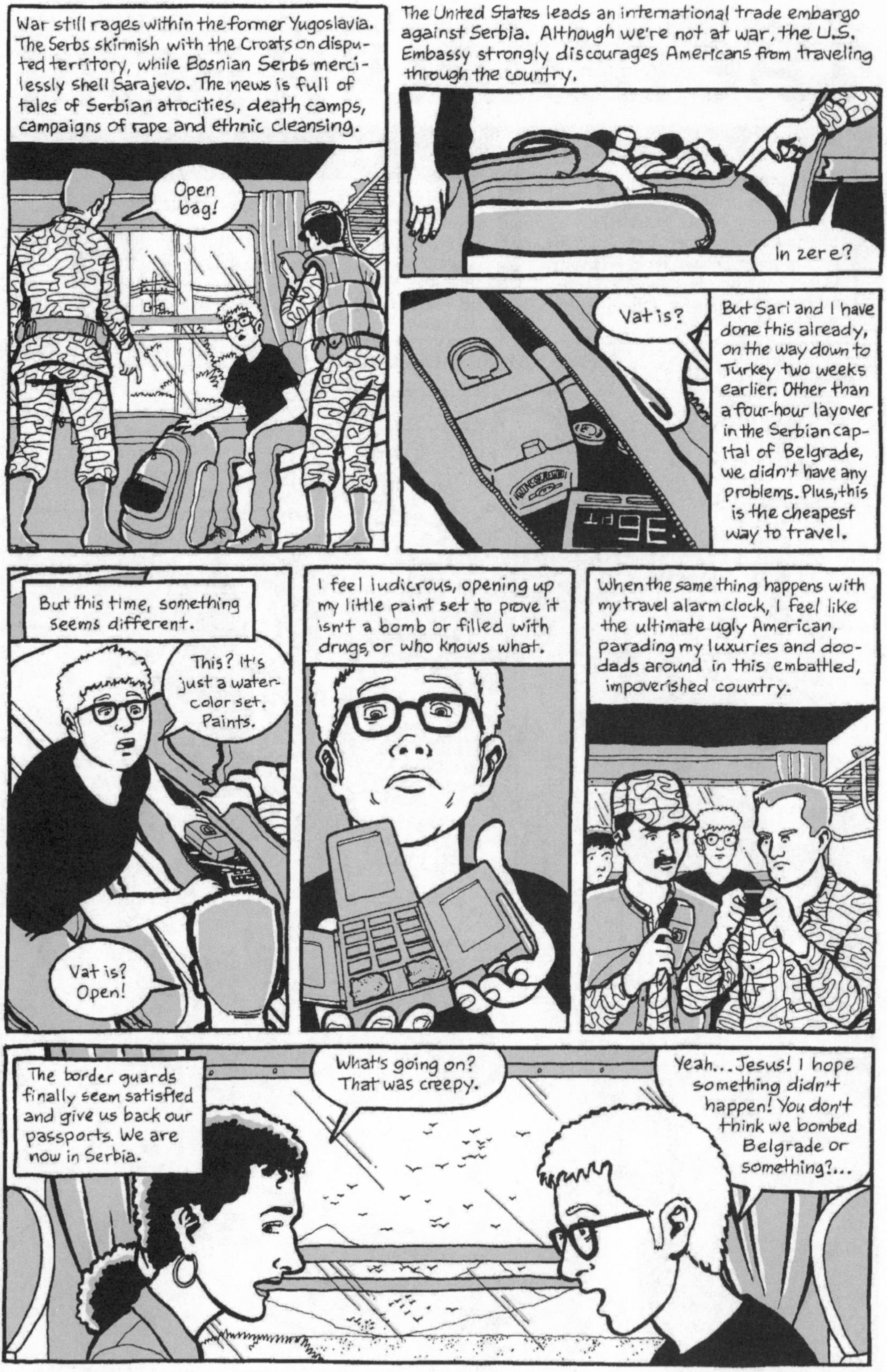
War still rages within the former Yugoslavia. The Serbs skirmish with the Croats on disputed territory, while Bosnian Serbs mercilessly shell Sarajevo. The news is full of tales of Serbian atrocities, death camps, campaigns of rape and ethnic cleansing.
Open bag!
The United States leads an international trade embargo against Serbia. Although we're not at war, the U.S. Embassy strongly discourages Americans from traveling through the country.
In zere?
Vat is?
But Sari and I have done this already, on the way down to Turkey two weeks earlier. Other than a four-hour layover in the Serbian capital of Belgrade, we didn't have any problems. Plus, this is the cheapest way to travel.
But this time, something seems different.
This? It's just a water-color set. Paints.
Vat is? Open!
I feel ludicrous, opening up my little paint set to prove it isn't a bomb or filled with drugs, or who knows what.
When the same thing happens with my travel alarm clock, I feel like the ultimate ugly American, parading my luxuries and doodads around in this embattled, impoverished country.
The border guards finally seem satisfied and give us back our passports. We are now in Serbia.
What's going on? That was creepy.
Yeah... Jesus! I hope something didn't happen! You don't think we bombed Belgrade or something?...

Soon after the border crossing, we come to a small village.

Now what's going on?

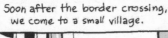

...A celebration...?

Looks like the whole town is here.

Our train car includes three Serbs coming back from Turkey, loaded down with huge, overstuffed bags filled with all sorts of things you can't find in cash-poor Serbia.

Vojnik.
Vojnik.
Soldat.

Man. Those boys are going off to join the army, to go to war-- maybe in Croatia, maybe Bosnia.

Did you see how they didn't let them touch the ground when they put 'em on the train?

The Serbian Bear

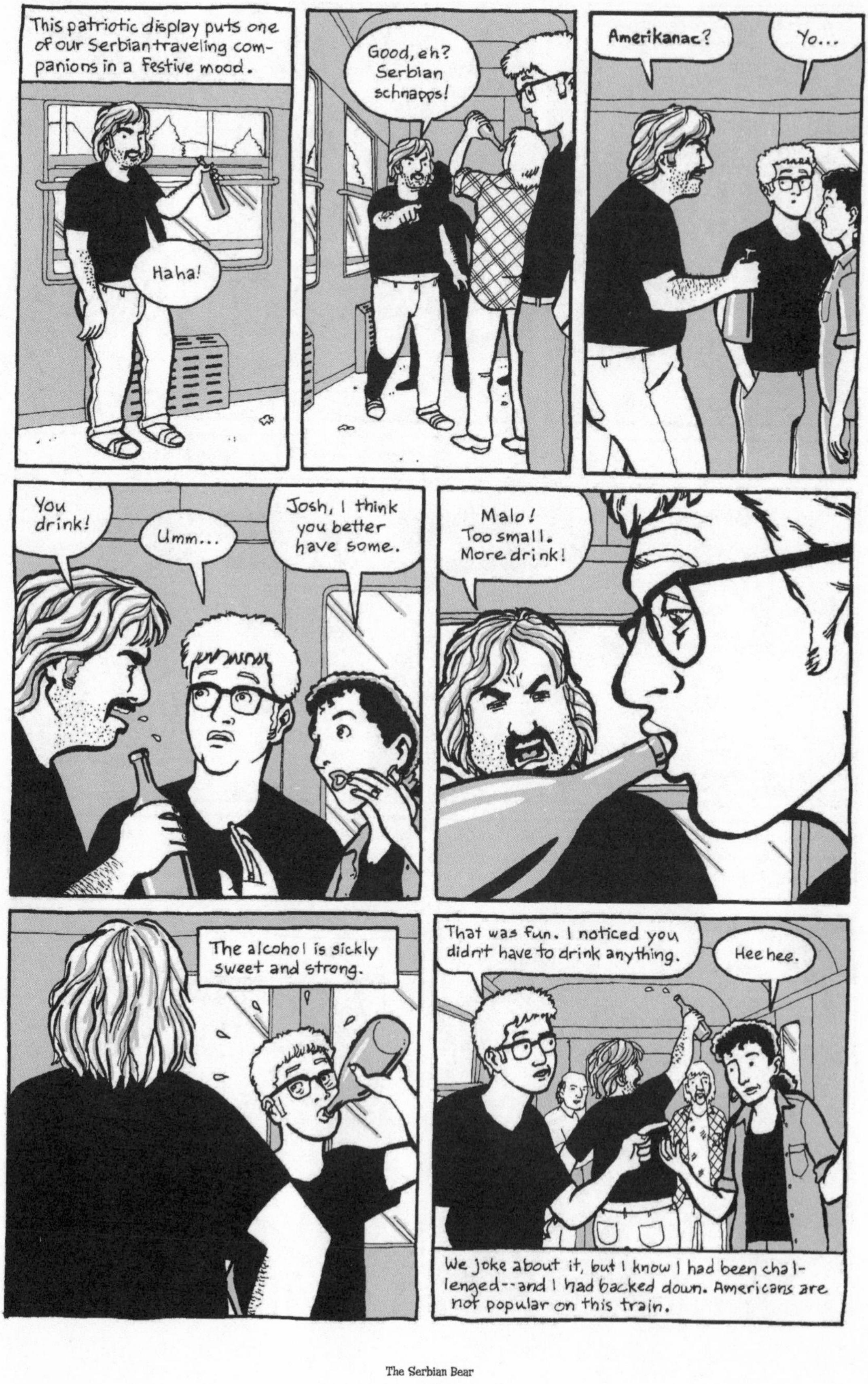
This patriotic display puts one of our Serbian traveling companions in a festive mood.
Haha!
Good, eh? Serbian schnapps!
Amerikanac?
Yo...
You drink!
Umm...
Josh, I think you better have some.
Malo! Too small. More drink!
The alcohol is sickly sweet and strong.
That was fun. I noticed you didn't have to drink anything.
Hee hee.
We joke about it, but I know I had been challenged--and I had backed down. Americans are not popular on this train.

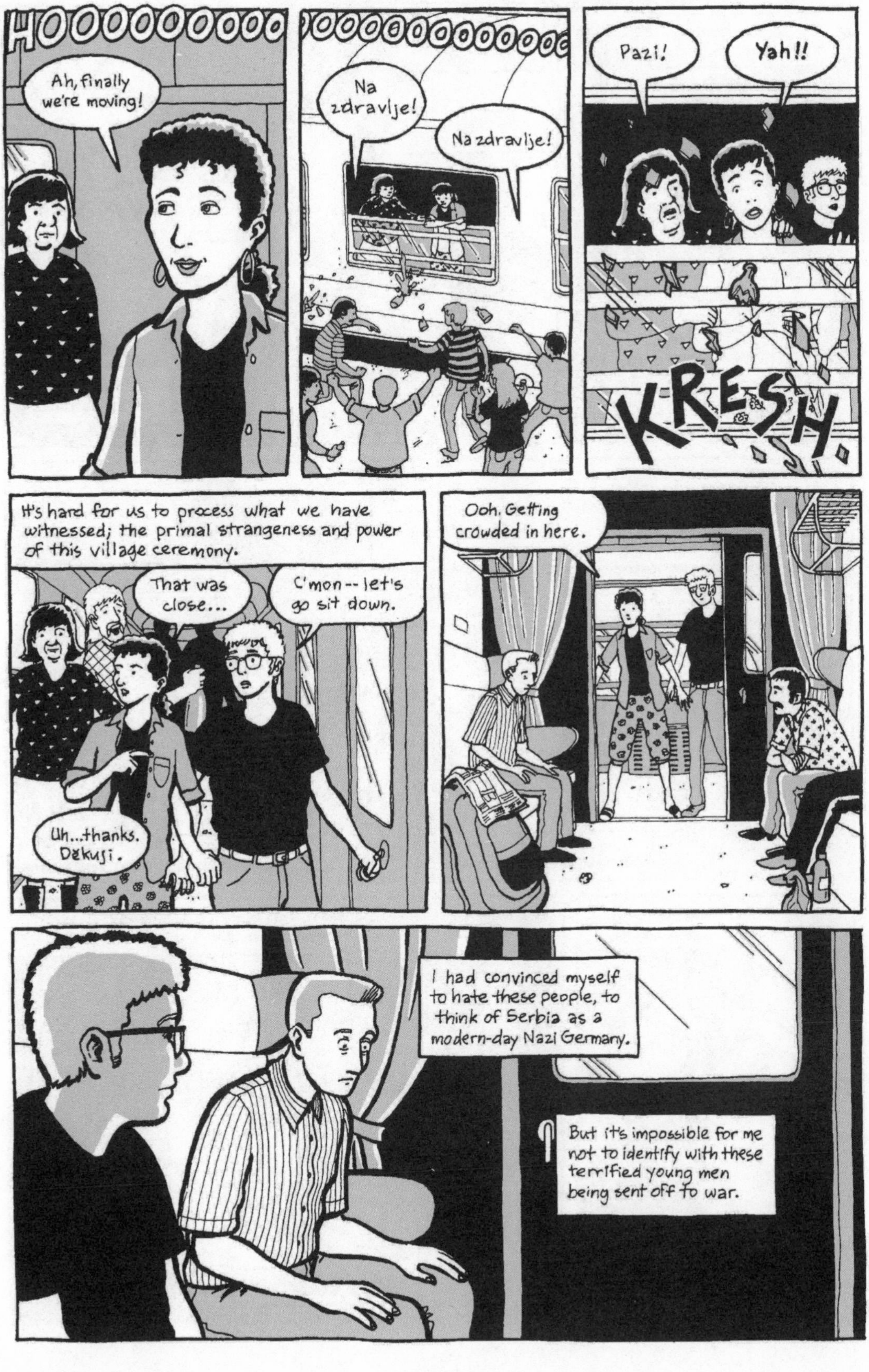
HOOOOOOOOOOOOOOOOOOOOOOOOOOO
Ah, finally we're moving!
Na zdravlje!
Na zdravlje!
Pazi!
Yah!!
KRESH.
It's hard for us to process what we have witnessed; the primal strangeness and power of this village ceremony.
That was close...
C'mon -- let's go sit down.
Uh...thanks. Děkuji.
Ooh. Getting crowded in here.
I had convinced myself to hate these people, to think of Serbia as a modern-day Nazi Germany.
But it's impossible for me not to identify with these terrified young men being sent off to war.

The **Serbian Bear** is on the prowl again.

Amerikanac? Aha!

And I am still his **prey**.

I'm starting to get **buzzed**.

As the **journey** continues, we pass through more villages sending their young men off to join the Serbian army. The closer we get to Belgrade, the more **nationalistic** and **patriotic** the crowds become.

And the Bear keeps coming back. And back. **And back.**

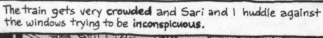

The train gets very **crowded** and Sari and I huddle against the windows trying to be **inconspicuous.**

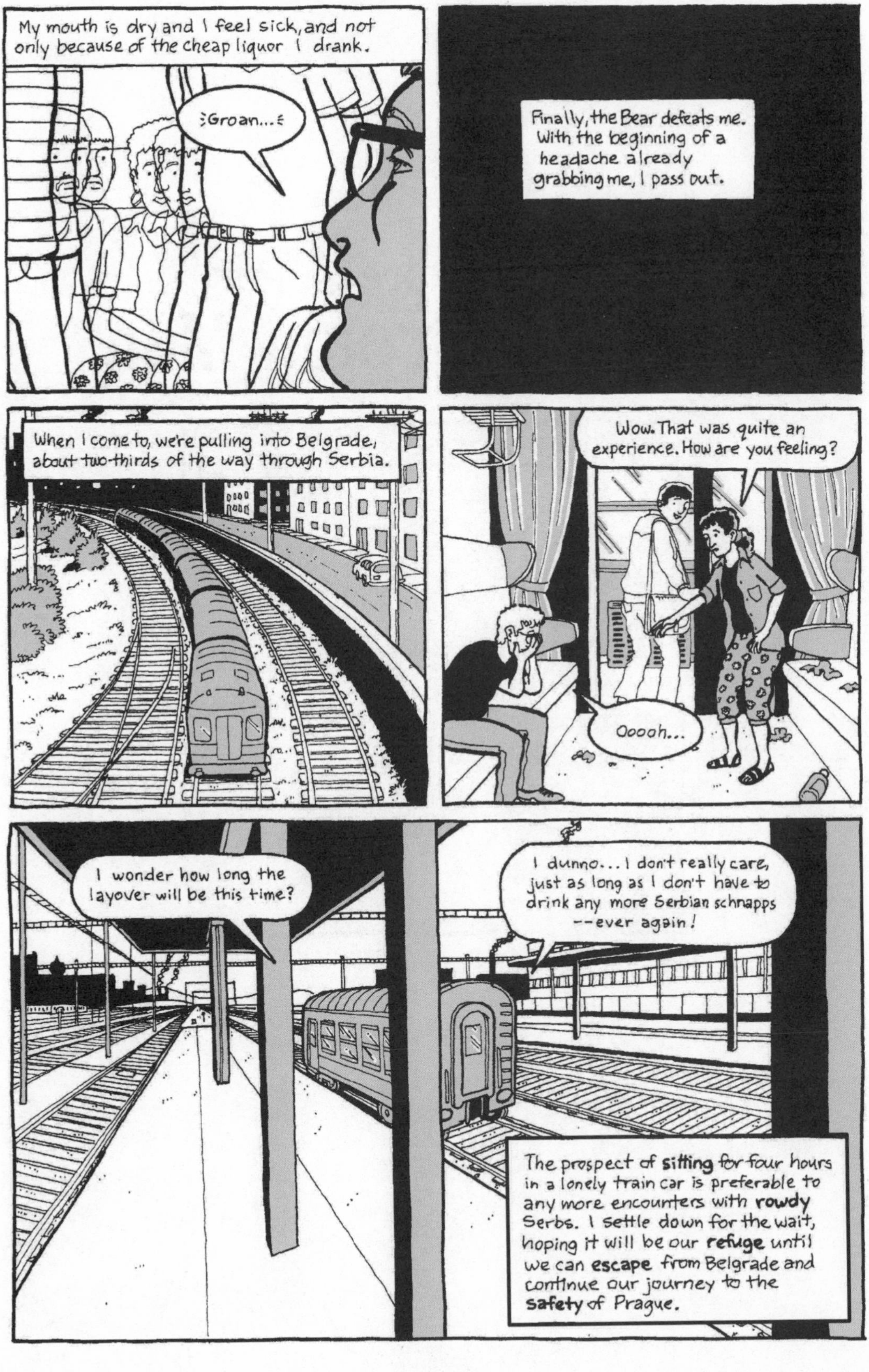

My mouth is dry and I feel sick, and not only because of the cheap liquor I drank.
Groan...
Finally, the Bear defeats me. With the beginning of a headache already grabbing me, I pass out.
When I come to, we're pulling into Belgrade, about two-thirds of the way through Serbia.
Wow. That was quite an experience. How are you feeling?
Ooooh...
I wonder how long the layover will be this time?
I dunno... I don't really care, just as long as I don't have to drink any more Serbian schnapps --ever again!
The prospect of **sitting** for four hours in a lonely train car is preferable to any more encounters with **rowdy** Serbs. I settle down for the wait, hoping it will be our **refuge** until we can **escape** from Belgrade and continue our journey to the **safety** of Prague.

The Balkan Express, Part II:
The Ice Cream Man

HUNGARY
ROMANIA
CROATIA
Belgrade
BOSNIA-
HERZE-
GOVINA
SERBIA

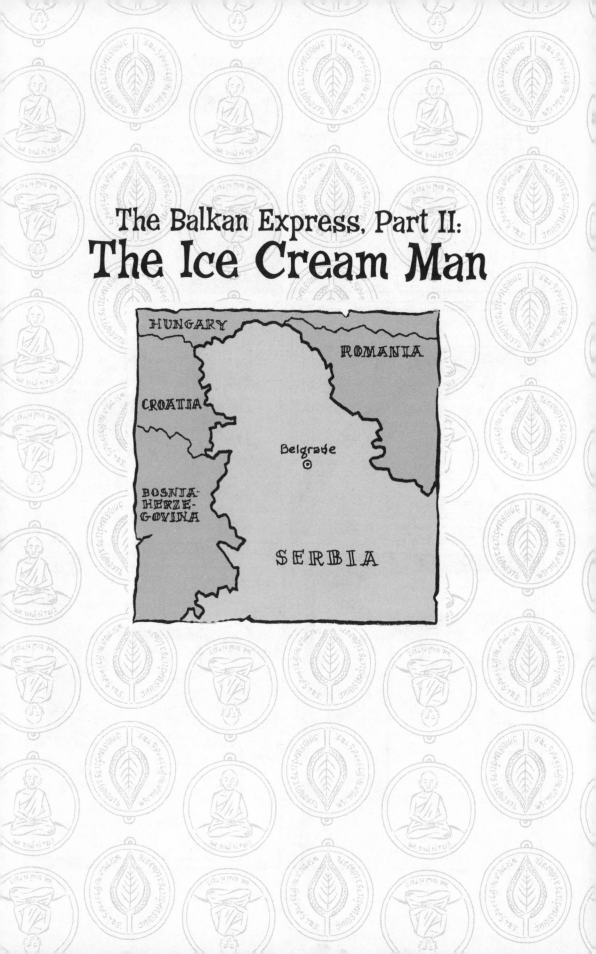

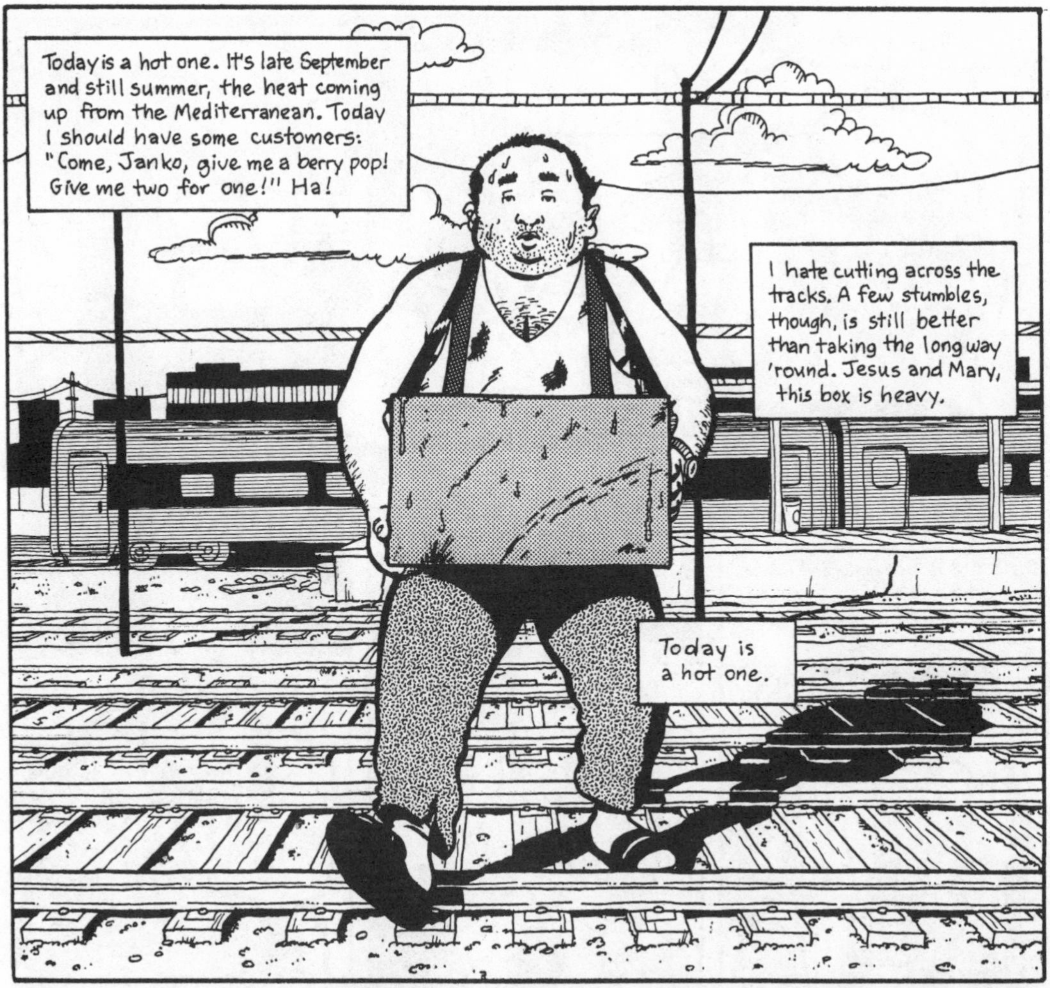
Today is a hot one. It's late September and still summer, the heat coming up from the Mediterranean. Today I should have some customers: "Come, Janko, give me a berry pop! Give me two for one!" Ha!
I hate cutting across the tracks. A few stumbles, though, is still better than taking the long way 'round. Jesus and Mary, this box is heavy.
Today is a hot one.

TH3 BALKAN EXPR3SS PART II The Ice Cream Man

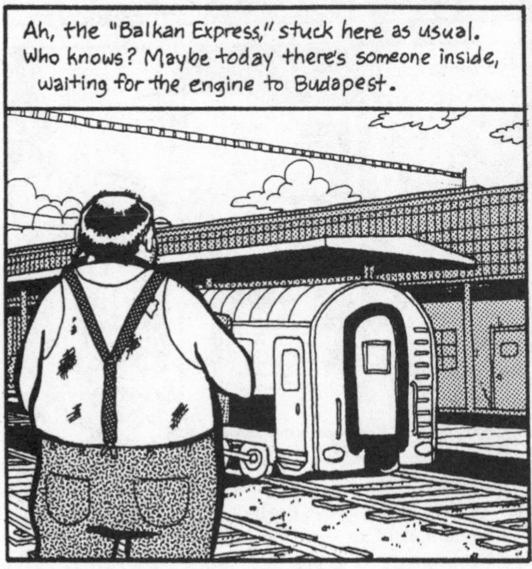
Ah, the "Balkan Express," stuck here as usual. Who knows? Maybe today there's someone inside, waiting for the engine to Budapest.

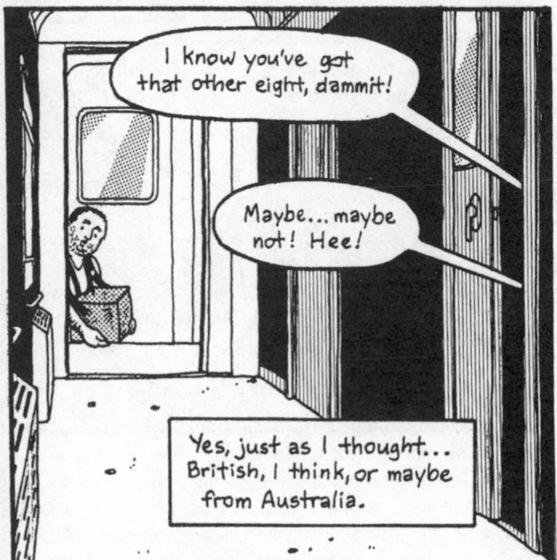
I know you've got that other eight, dammit!
Maybe... maybe not! Hee!
Yes, just as I thought... British, I think, or maybe from Australia.

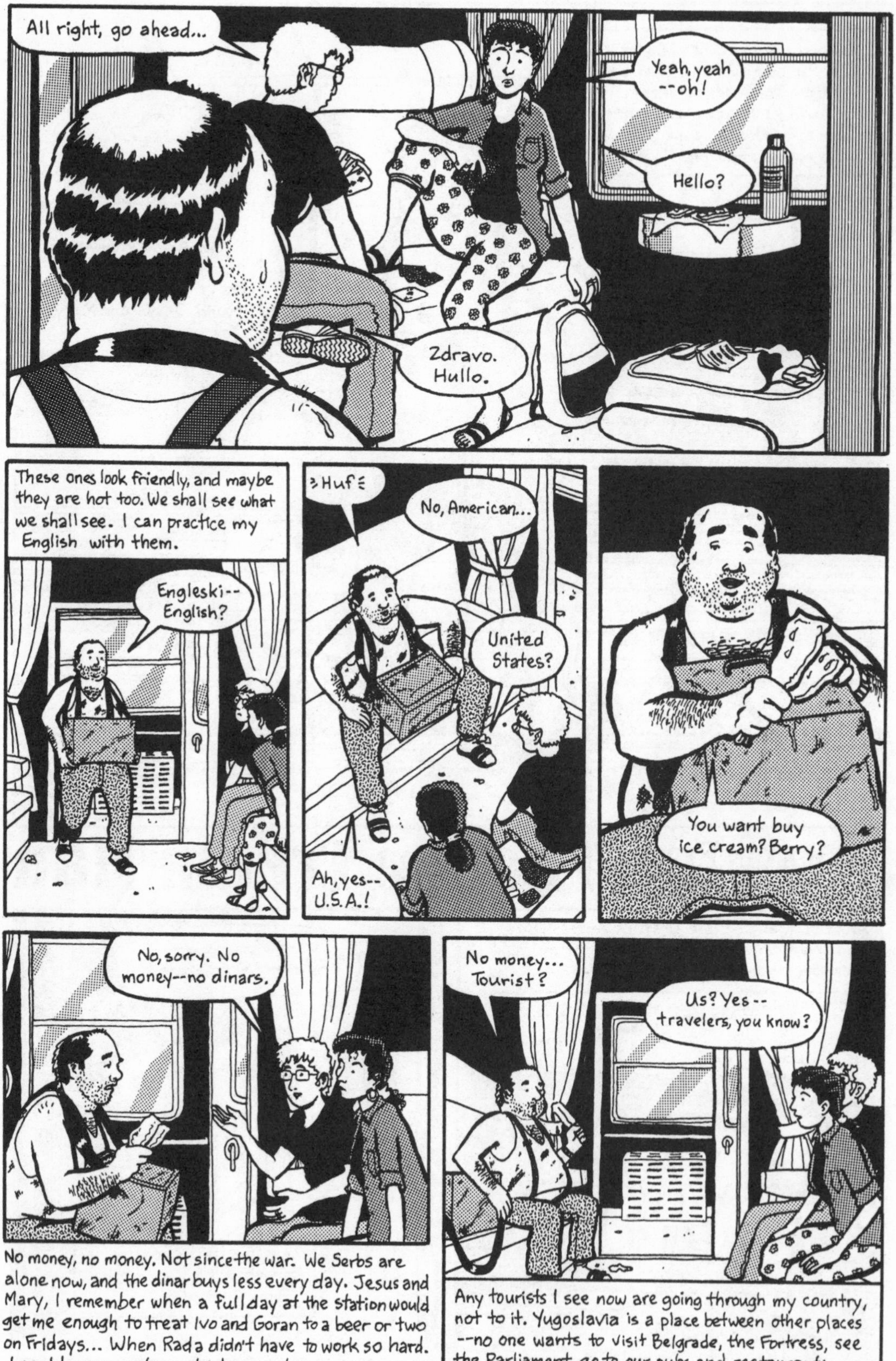
All right, go ahead...
Yeah, yeah --oh!
Hello?
Zdravo. Hullo.
These ones look friendly, and maybe they are hot too. We shall see what we shall see. I can practice my English with them.
Engleski-- English?
Huf
No, American...
United States?
Ah, yes-- U.S.A.!
You want buy ice cream? Berry?
No, sorry. No money--no dinars.
No money, no money. Not since the war. We Serbs are alone now, and the dinar buys less every day. Jesus and Mary, I remember when a full day at the station would get me enough to treat Ivo and Goran to a beer or two on Fridays... When Rada didn't have to work so hard. I could wear a clean shirt every day.
No money... Tourist?
Us? Yes-- travelers, you know?
Any tourists I see now are going through my country, not to it. Yugoslavia is a place between other places --no one wants to visit Belgrade, the Fortress, see the Parliament, go to our pubs and restaurants...

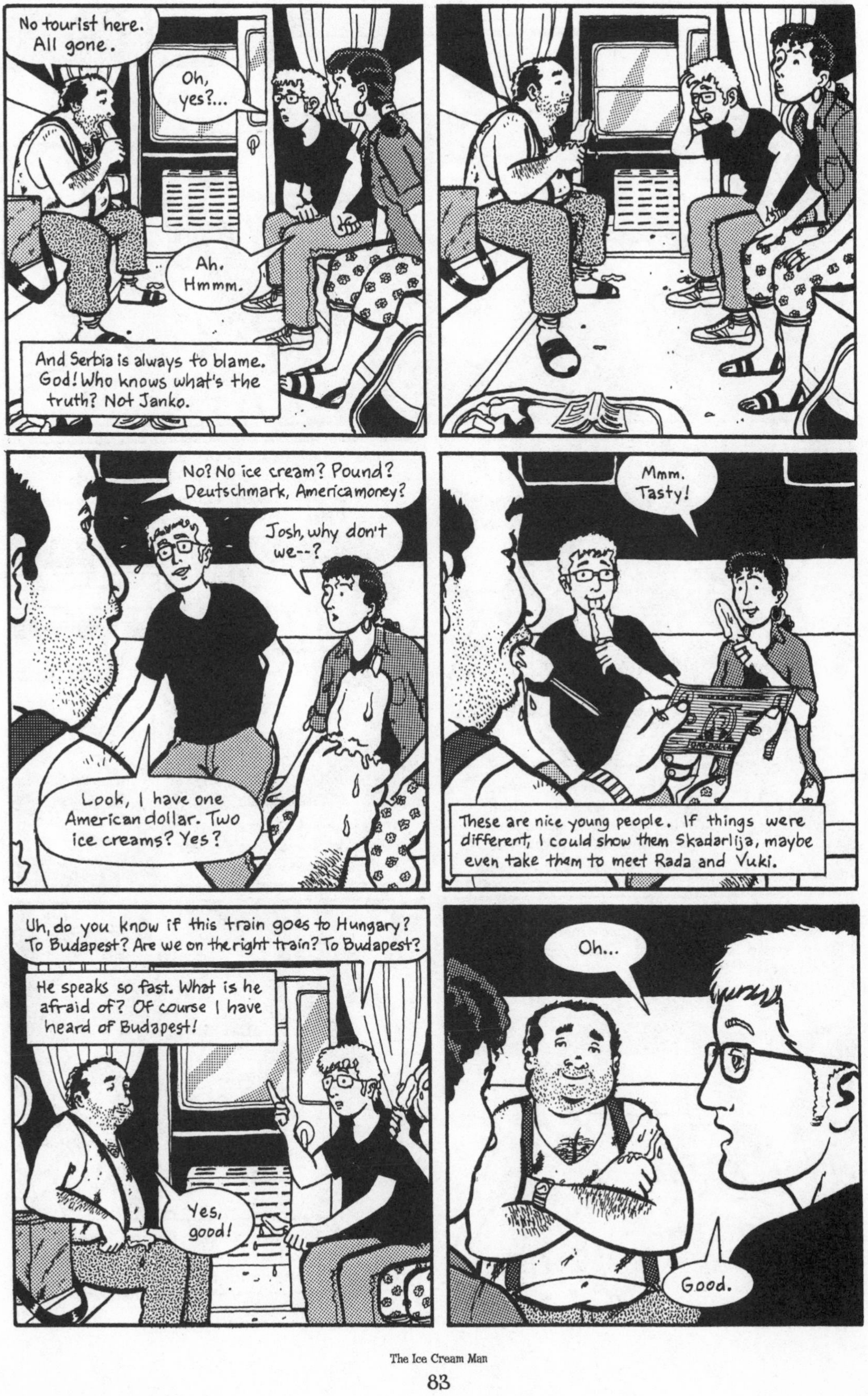
No tourist here. All gone.
Oh, yes?...
Ah. Hmmm.
And Serbia is always to blame. God! Who knows what's the truth? Not Janko.
No? No ice cream? Pound? Deutschmark, Americamoney?
Josh, why don't we--?
Look, I have one American dollar. Two ice creams? Yes?
Mmm. Tasty!
These are nice young people. If things were different, I could show them Skadarlija, maybe even take them to meet Rada and Vuki.
Uh, do you know if this train goes to Hungary? To Budapest? Are we on the right train? To Budapest?
He speaks so fast. What is he afraid of? Of course I have heard of Budapest!
Yes, good!
Oh...
Good.

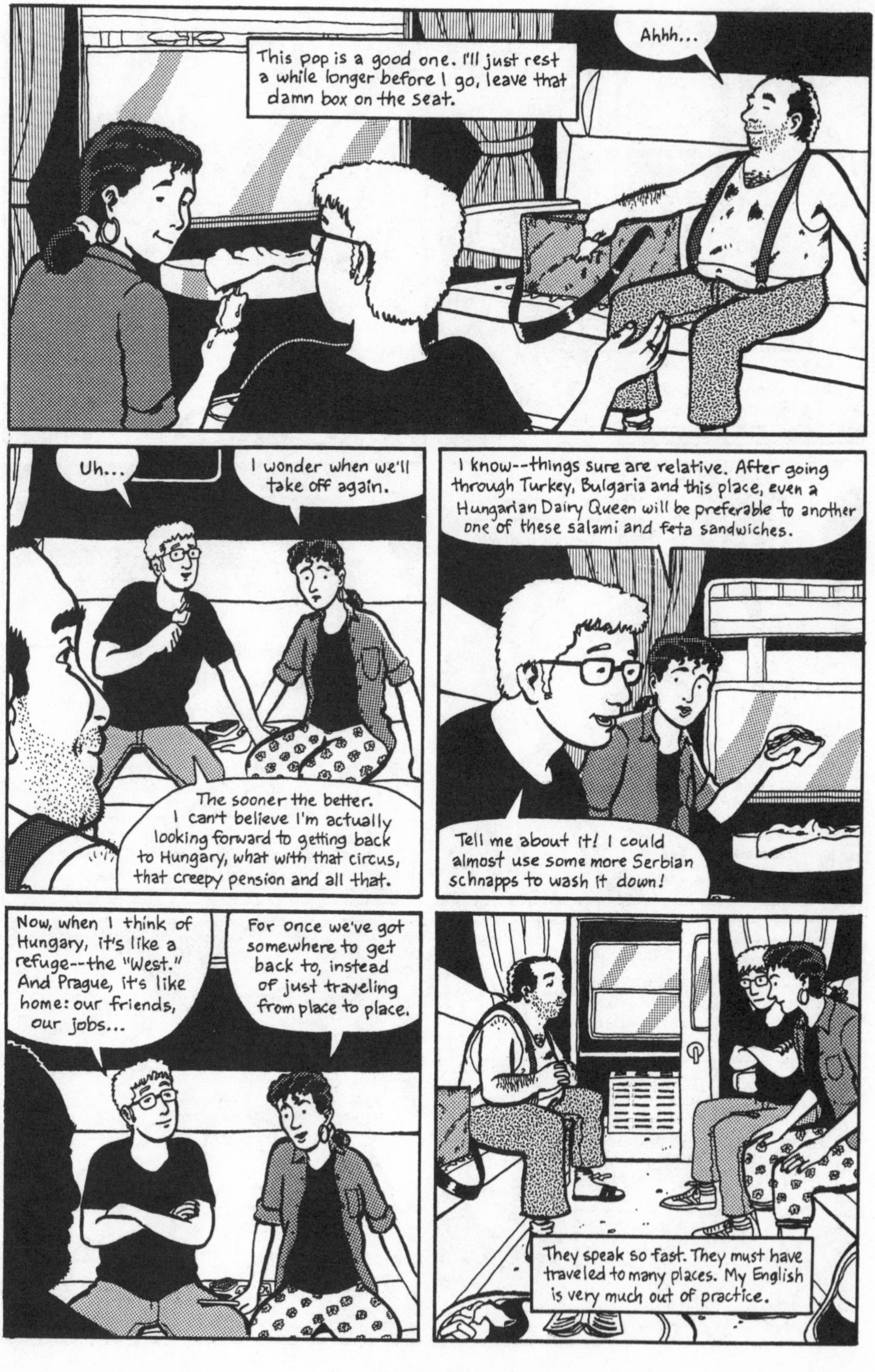
This pop is a good one. I'll just rest a while longer before I go, leave that damn box on the seat.
Ahhh...
Uh...
I wonder when we'll take off again.
The sooner the better. I can't believe I'm actually looking forward to getting back to Hungary, what with that circus, that creepy pension and all that.
I know--things sure are relative. After going through Turkey, Bulgaria and this place, even a Hungarian Dairy Queen will be preferable to another one of these salami and feta sandwiches.
Tell me about it! I could almost use some more Serbian schnapps to wash it down!
Now, when I think of Hungary, it's like a refuge--the "West." And Prague, it's like home: our friends, our jobs...
For once we've got somewhere to get back to, instead of just traveling from place to place.
They speak so fast. They must have traveled to many places. My English is very much out of practice.

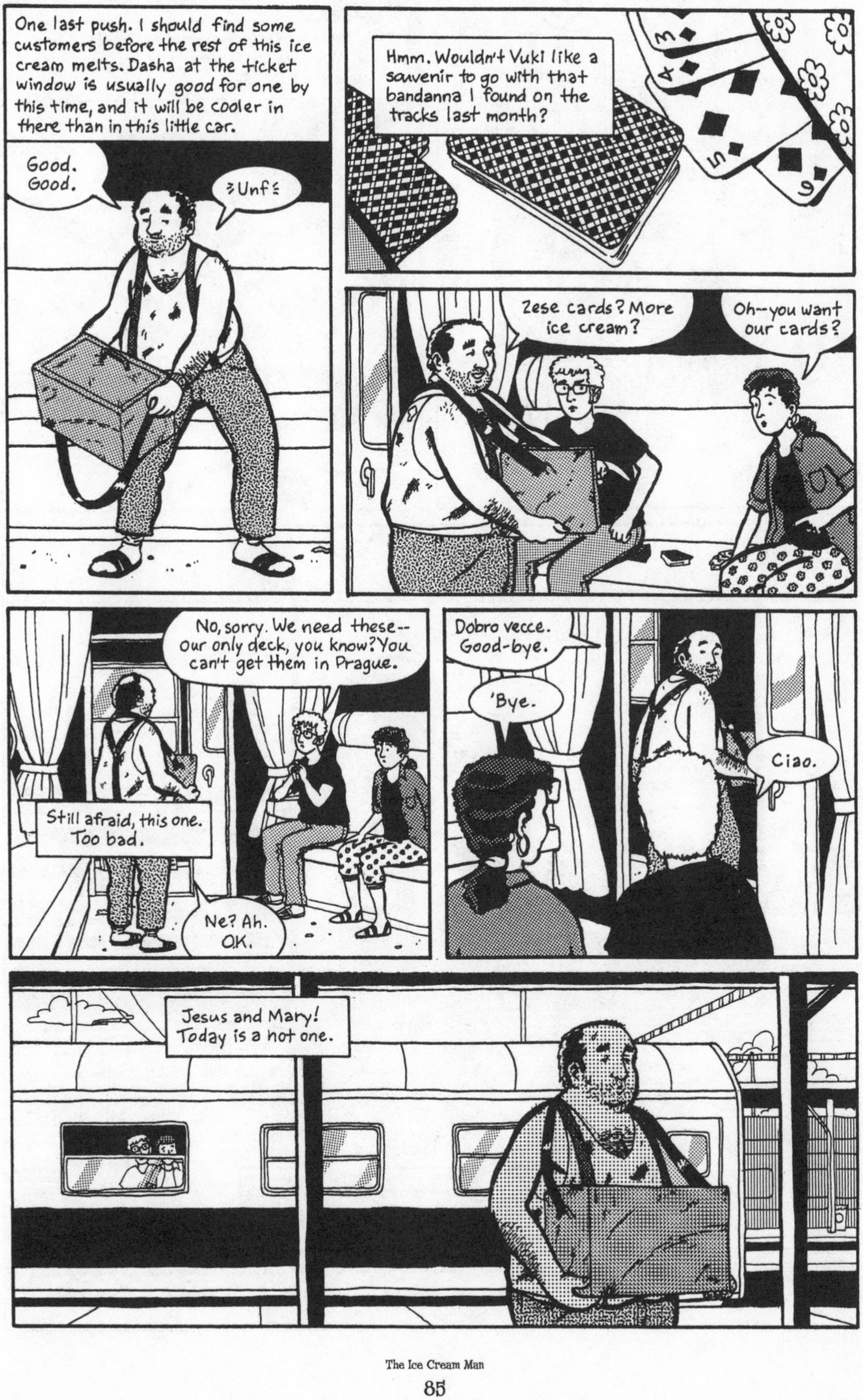
One last push. I should find some customers before the rest of this ice cream melts. Dasha at the ticket window is usually good for one by this time, and it will be cooler in there than in this little car.
Good. Good.
Unf
Hmm. Wouldn't Vuki like a souvenir to go with that bandanna I found on the tracks last month?
Zese cards? More ice cream?
Oh--you want our cards?
No, sorry. We need these--our only deck, you know? You can't get them in Prague.
Still afraid, this one. Too bad.
Ne? Ah. OK.
Dobro vecce. Good-bye.
'Bye.
Ciao.
Jesus and Mary! Today is a hot one.

The "Express" is on the move again. Ha! Only a two-hour wait this time. Off you go, young Americans.

Who knows what the Balkan Express will bring me tomorrow?

We shall see what we shall see.

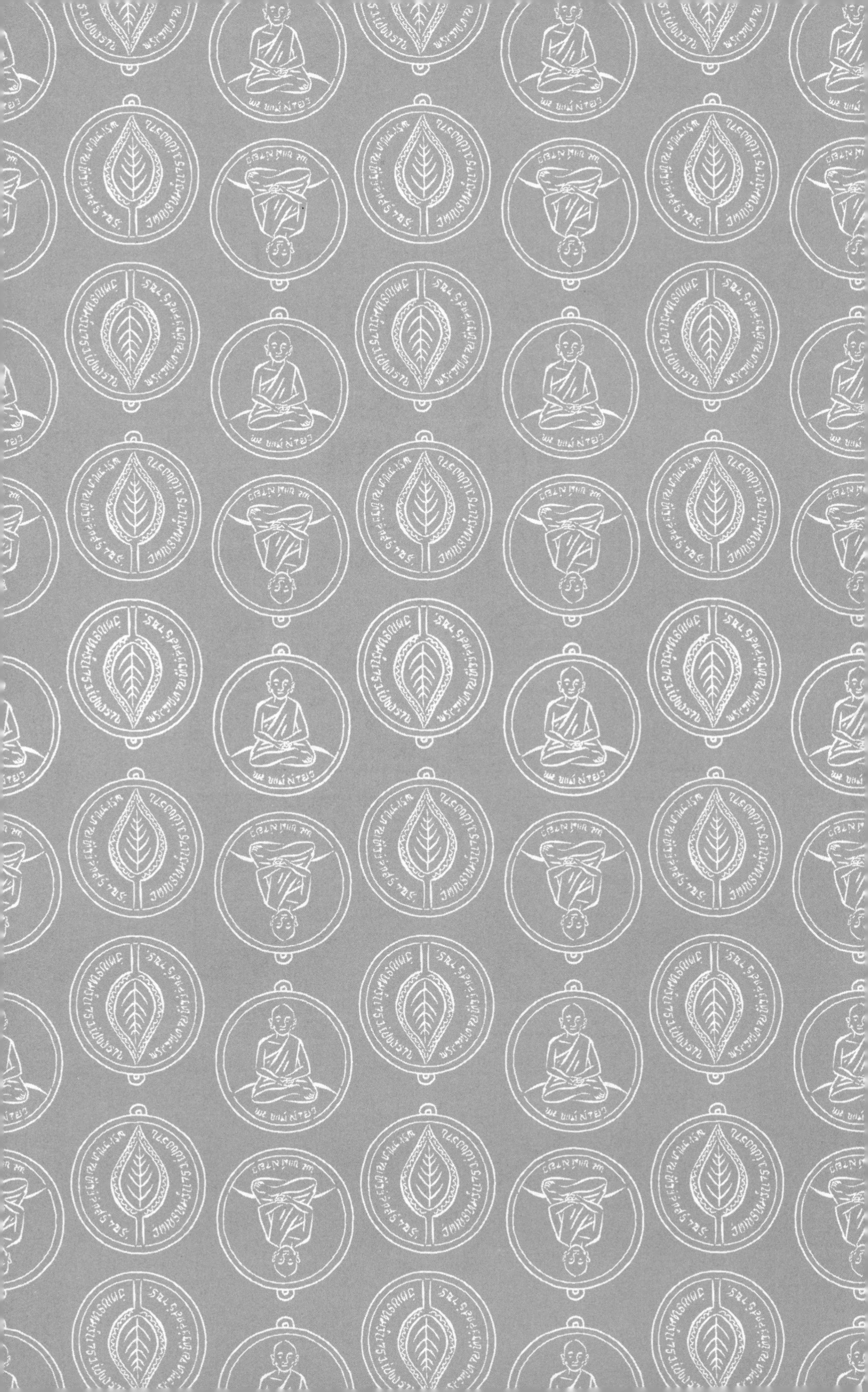

Tribal Rituals, Part II: Cremations, Cubicles, and Cant

Bali Sea
BALI
Indonesian Ocean
GERMANY
POLAND
Prague
CZECH REPUBLIC
SLOVAKIA
AUSTRIA
Lake Erie
CHICAGO
QUEENS
BROOKLYN

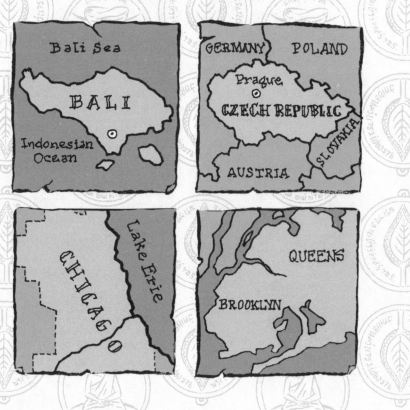

Tribal Rituals, Part II
CREMATIONS, CUBICLES & CANT

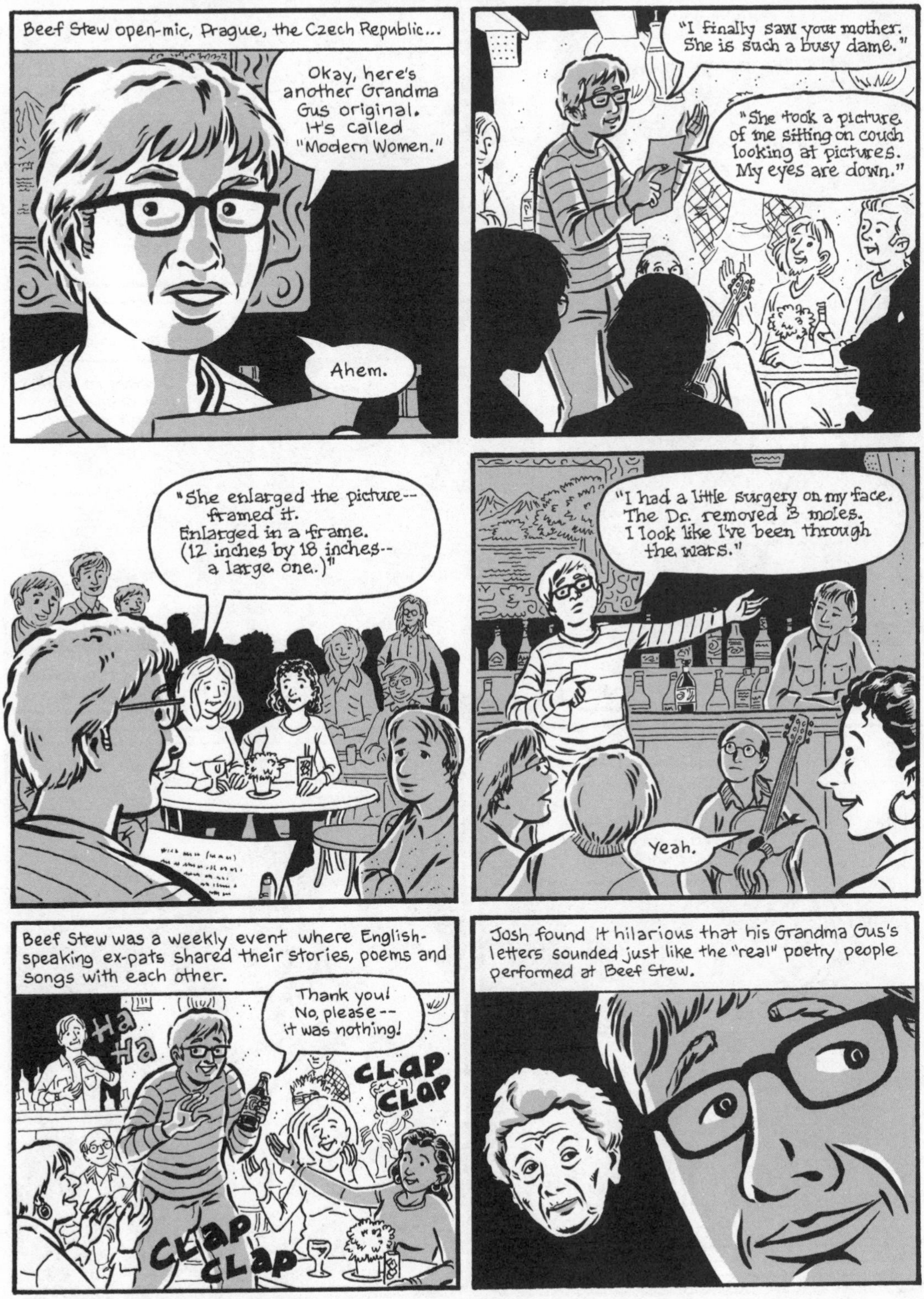

Beef Stew open-mic, Prague, the Czech Republic...
Okay, here's another Grandma Gus original. It's called "Modern Women."
Ahem.
"I finally saw your mother. She is such a busy dame."
"She took a picture of me sitting on couch looking at pictures. My eyes are down."
"She enlarged the picture-- framed it. Enlarged in a frame. (12 inches by 18 inches-- a large one.)"
"I had a little surgery on my face. The Dr. removed 3 moles. I look like I've been through the wars."
Yeah.
Beef Stew was a weekly event where English-speaking ex-pats shared their stories, poems and songs with each other.
Thank you! No, please -- it was nothing!
Ha Ha
CLAP CLAP
CLAP CLAP
Josh found it hilarious that his Grandma Gus's letters sounded just like the "real" poetry people performed at Beef Stew.

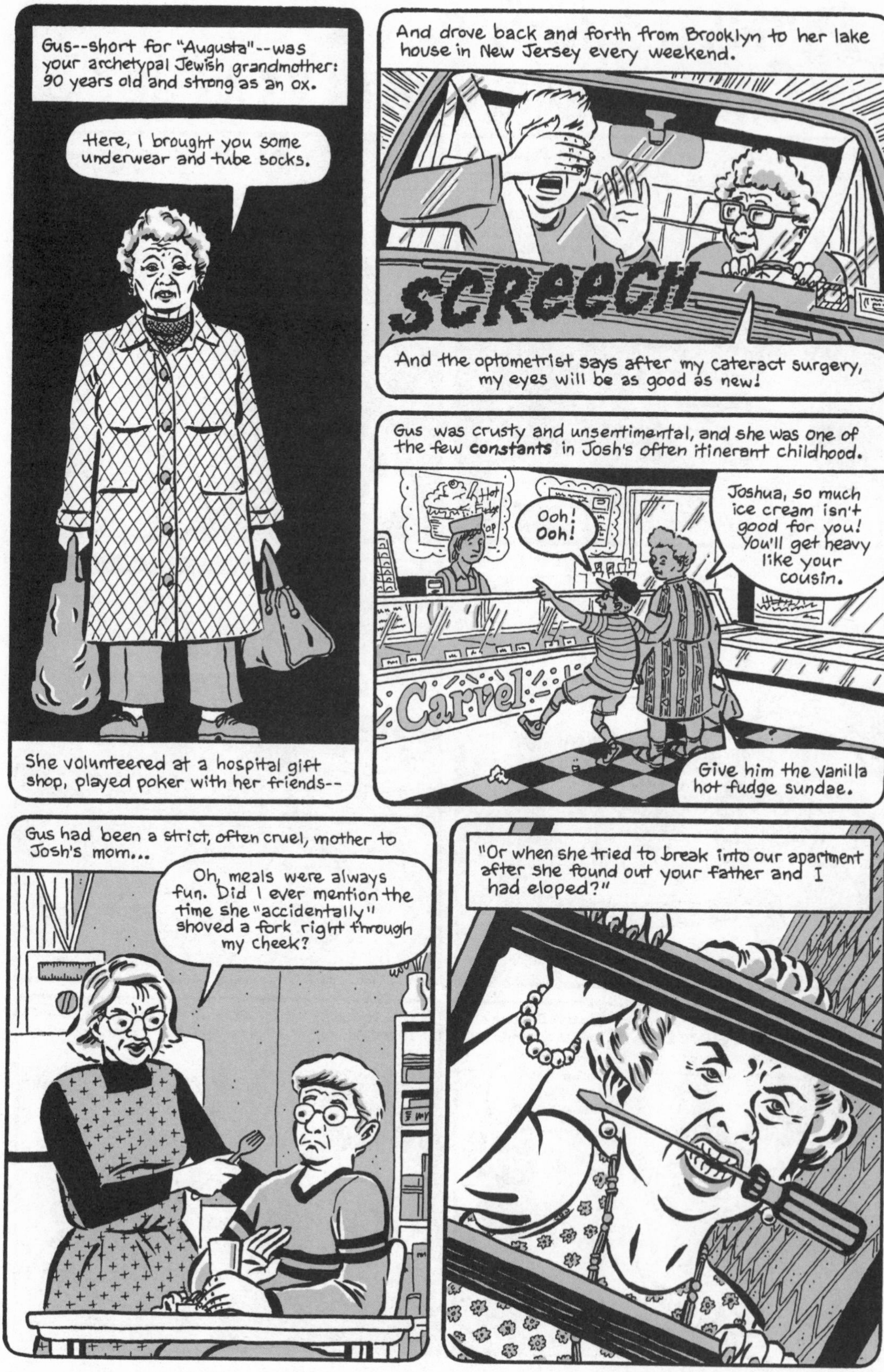
Gus--short for "Augusta"--was your archetypal Jewish grandmother: 90 years old and strong as an ox.
Here, I brought you some underwear and tube socks.
She volunteered at a hospital gift shop, played poker with her friends--
And drove back and forth from Brooklyn to her lake house in New Jersey every weekend.
SCREECH
And the optometrist says after my cateract surgery, my eyes will be as good as new!
Gus was crusty and unsentimental, and she was one of the few **constants** in Josh's often itinerant childhood.
Ooh! Ooh!
Joshua, so much ice cream isn't good for you! You'll get heavy like your cousin.
Carvel
Give him the vanilla hot fudge sundae.
Gus had been a strict, often cruel, mother to Josh's mom...
Oh, meals were always fun. Did I ever mention the time she "accidentally" shoved a fork right through my cheek?
"Or when she tried to break into our apartment after she found out your father and I had eloped?"

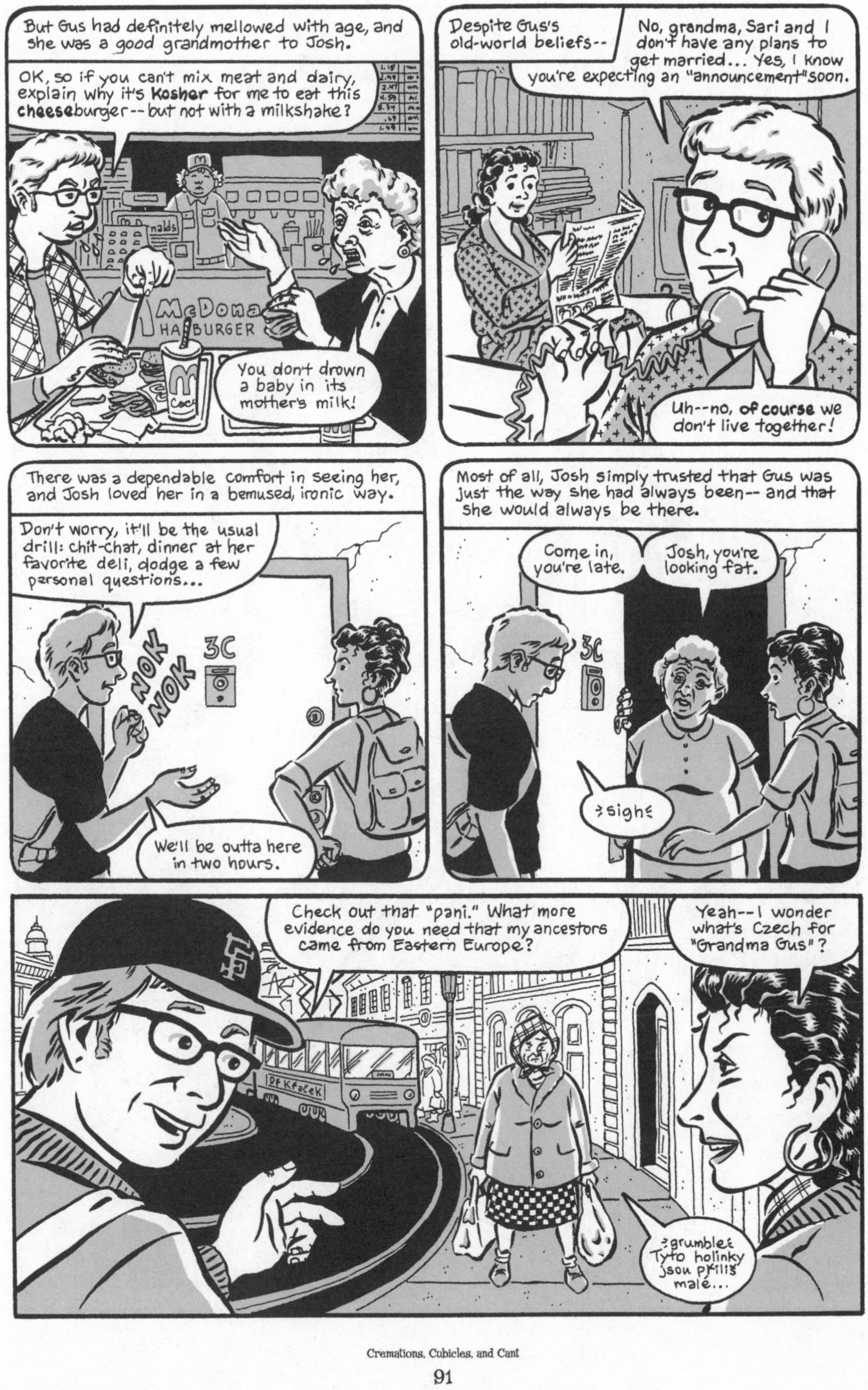

But Gus had definitely mellowed with age, and she was a good grandmother to Josh.
OK, so if you can't mix meat and dairy, explain why it's **Kosher** for me to eat this **cheese**burger -- but not with a milkshake?
You don't drown a baby in its mother's milk!
McDona
HA BURGER
Despite Gus's old-world beliefs--
No, grandma, Sari and I don't have any plans to get married... Yes, I know you're expecting an "announcement" soon.
Uh--no, **of course** we don't live together!
There was a dependable comfort in seeing her, and Josh loved her in a bemused, ironic way.
Don't worry, it'll be the usual drill: chit-chat, dinner at her favorite deli, dodge a few personal questions...
NOK NOK
3C
We'll be outta here in two hours.
Most of all, Josh simply trusted that Gus was just the way she had always been-- and that she would always be there.
Come in, you're late.
Josh, you're looking fat.
3C
sigh
Check out that "pani." What more evidence do you need that my ancestors came from Eastern Europe?
Yeah--I wonder what's Czech for "Grandma Gus"?
grumble
Tyto holinky jsou příliš malé...

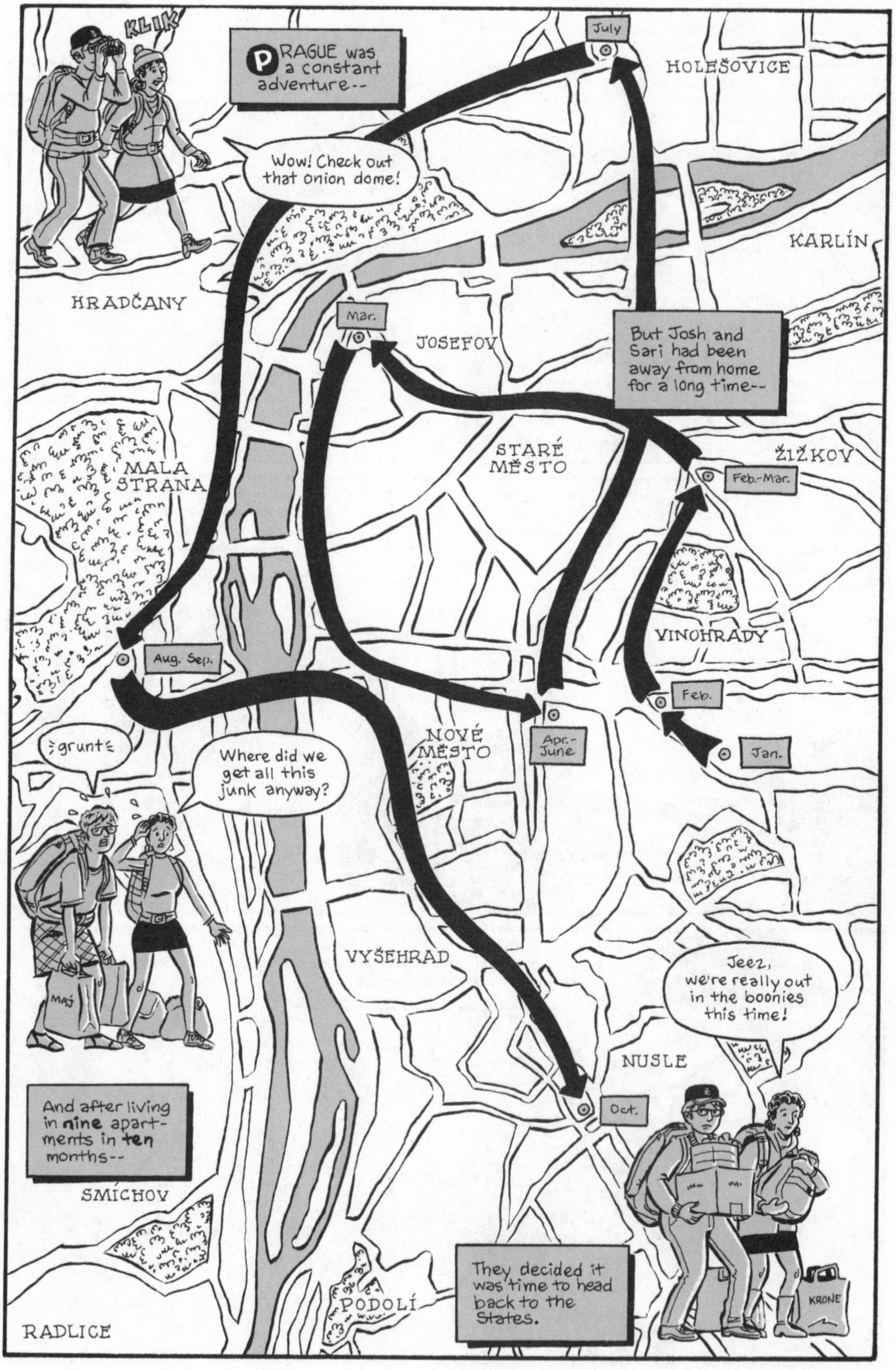
KLIK
PRAGUE was a constant adventure--
Wow! Check out that onion dome!
July
HOLEŠOVICE
KARLÍN
HRADČANY
Mar.
JOSEFOV
But Josh and Sari had been away from home for a long time--
STARÉ MĚSTO
ŽIŽKOV
Feb.-Mar.
MALA STRANA
VINOHRADY
Aug. Sep.
Feb.
NOVÉ MĚSTO
Apr.-June
Jan.
grunt
Where did we get all this junk anyway?
MAJ
VYŠEHRAD
Jeez, we're really out in the boonies this time!
NUSLE
And after living in **nine** apartments in **ten** months--
Oct.
SMÍCHOV
They decided it was time to head back to the States.
PODOLÍ
KRONE
RADLICE

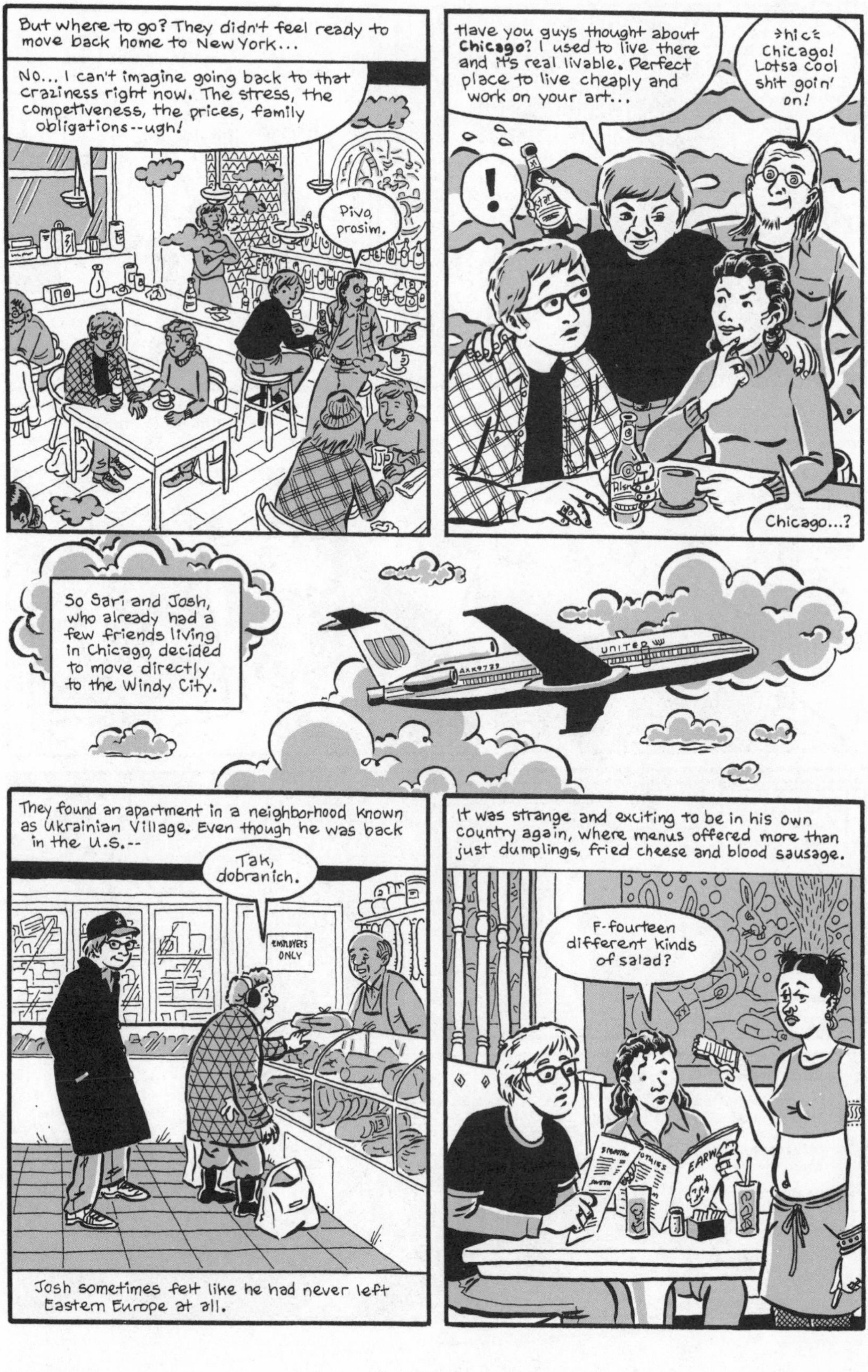

But where to go? They didn't feel ready to move back home to New York...
No... I can't imagine going back to that craziness right now. The stress, the competiveness, the prices, family obligations--ugh!
Pivo, prosim.
Have you guys thought about Chicago? I used to live there and it's real livable. Perfect place to live cheaply and work on your art...
hic Chicago! Lotsa cool shit goin' on!
!
Chicago...?
So Sari and Josh, who already had a few friends living in Chicago, decided to move directly to the Windy City.
UNITED
They found an apartment in a neighborhood known as Ukrainian Village. Even though he was back in the U.S.--
Tak, dobranich.
EMPLOYEES ONLY
Josh sometimes felt like he had never left Eastern Europe at all.
It was strange and exciting to be in his own country again, where menus offered more than just dumplings, fried cheese and blood sausage.
F-fourteen different kinds of salad?

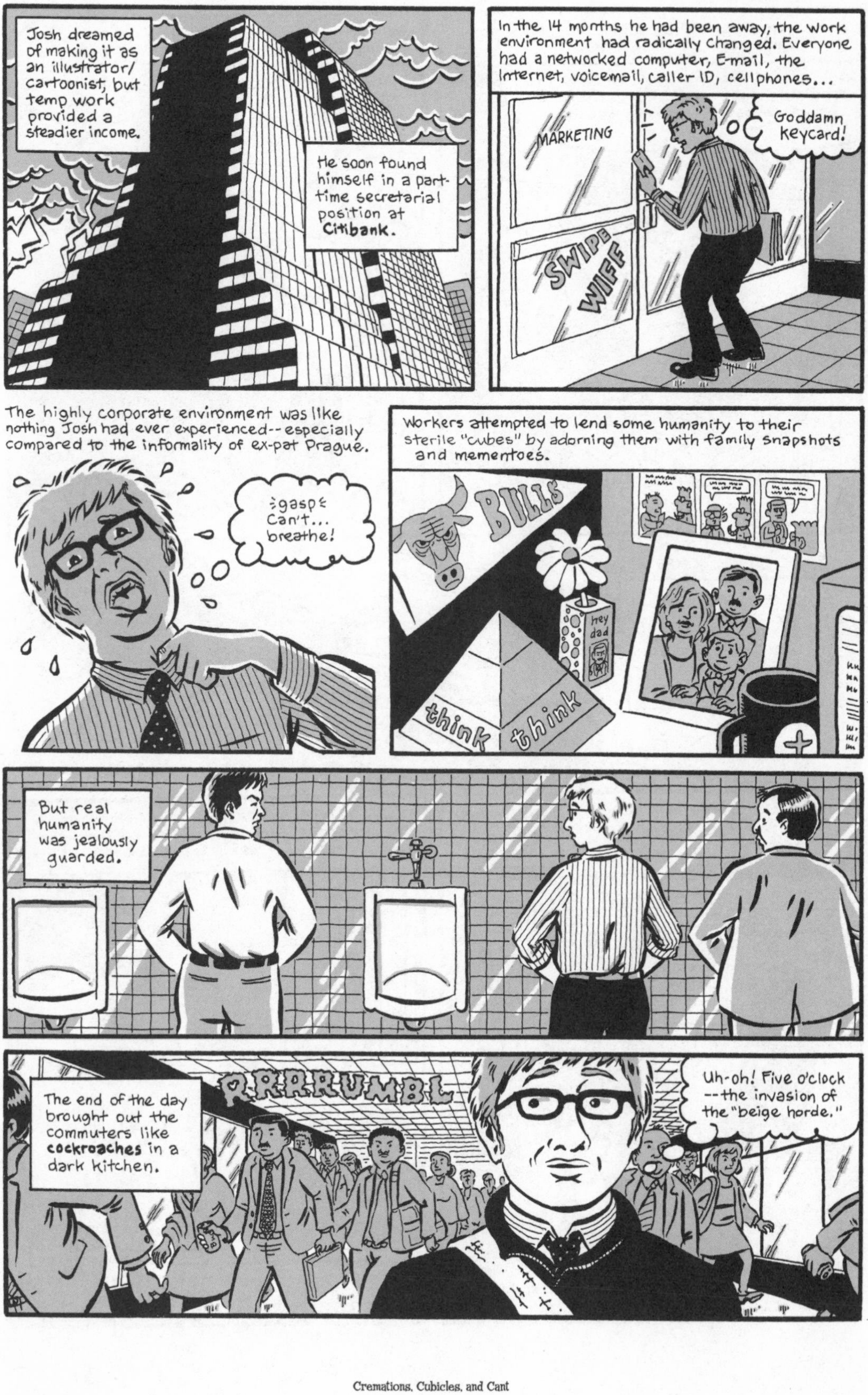
Josh dreamed of making it as an illustrator/ cartoonist, but temp work provided a steadier income.
He soon found himself in a part-time secretarial position at Citibank.
In the 14 months he had been away, the work environment had radically changed. Everyone had a networked computer, E-mail, the Internet, voicemail, caller ID, cellphones...
MARKETING
SWIPE
WIFF
Goddamn keycard!
The highly corporate environment was like nothing Josh had ever experienced--especially compared to the informality of ex-pat Prague.
gasp Can't... breathe!
Workers attempted to lend some humanity to their sterile "cubes" by adorning them with family snapshots and mementoes.
BULLS
hey dad
think
think
But real humanity was jealously guarded.
The end of the day brought out the commuters like cockroaches in a dark kitchen.
RRRRUMBL
Uh-oh! Five o'clock --the invasion of the "beige horde."

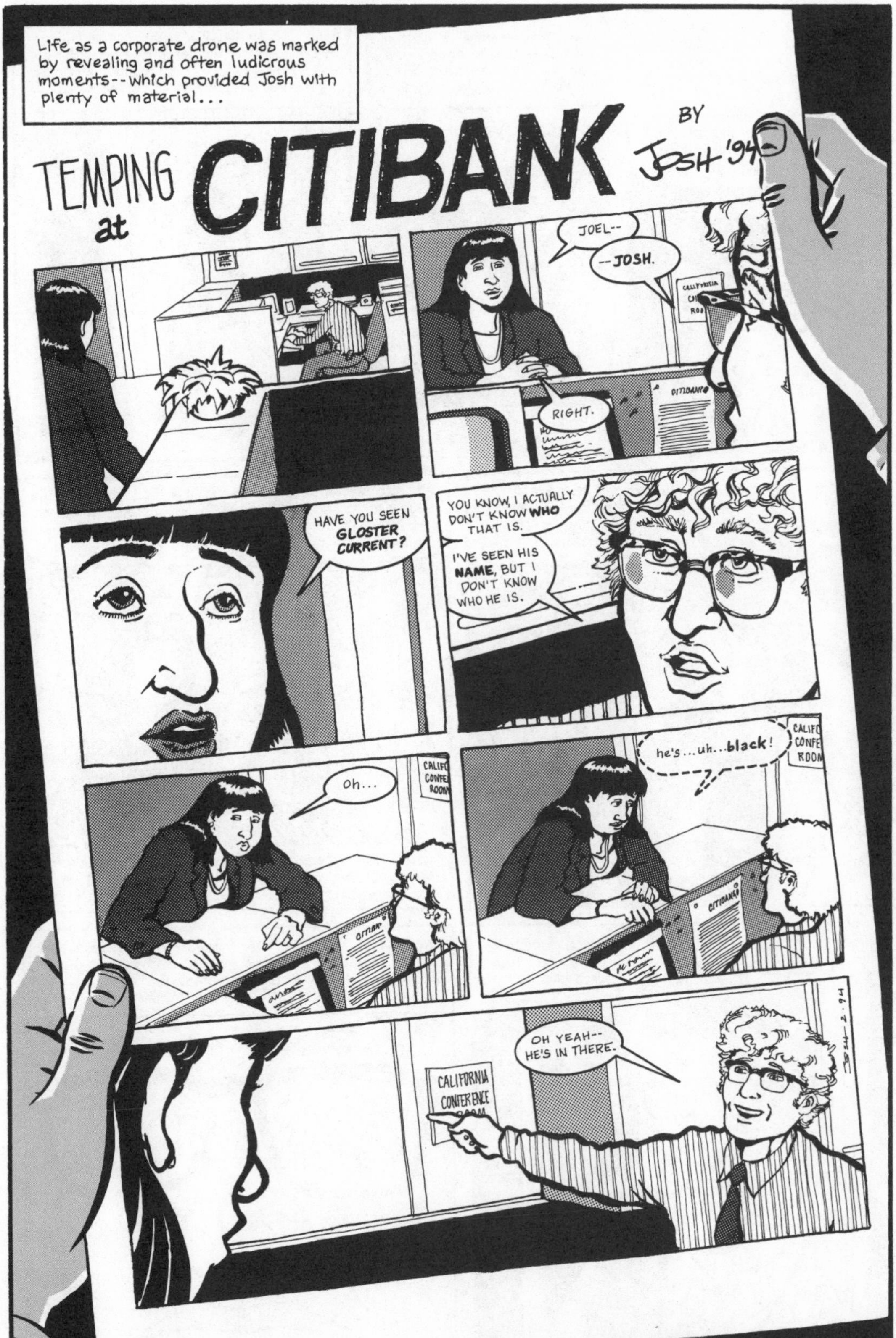

Life as a corporate drone was marked by revealing and often ludicrous moments--which provided Josh with plenty of material...
TEMPING at CITIBANK
BY JOSH '94
JOEL--
--JOSH.
RIGHT.
HAVE YOU SEEN GLOSTER CURRENT?
YOU KNOW, I ACTUALLY DON'T KNOW WHO THAT IS.
I'VE SEEN HIS NAME, BUT I DON'T KNOW WHO HE IS.
Oh...
he's...uh...black!
OH YEAH-- HE'S IN THERE.
CALIFORNIA CONFERENCE ROOM

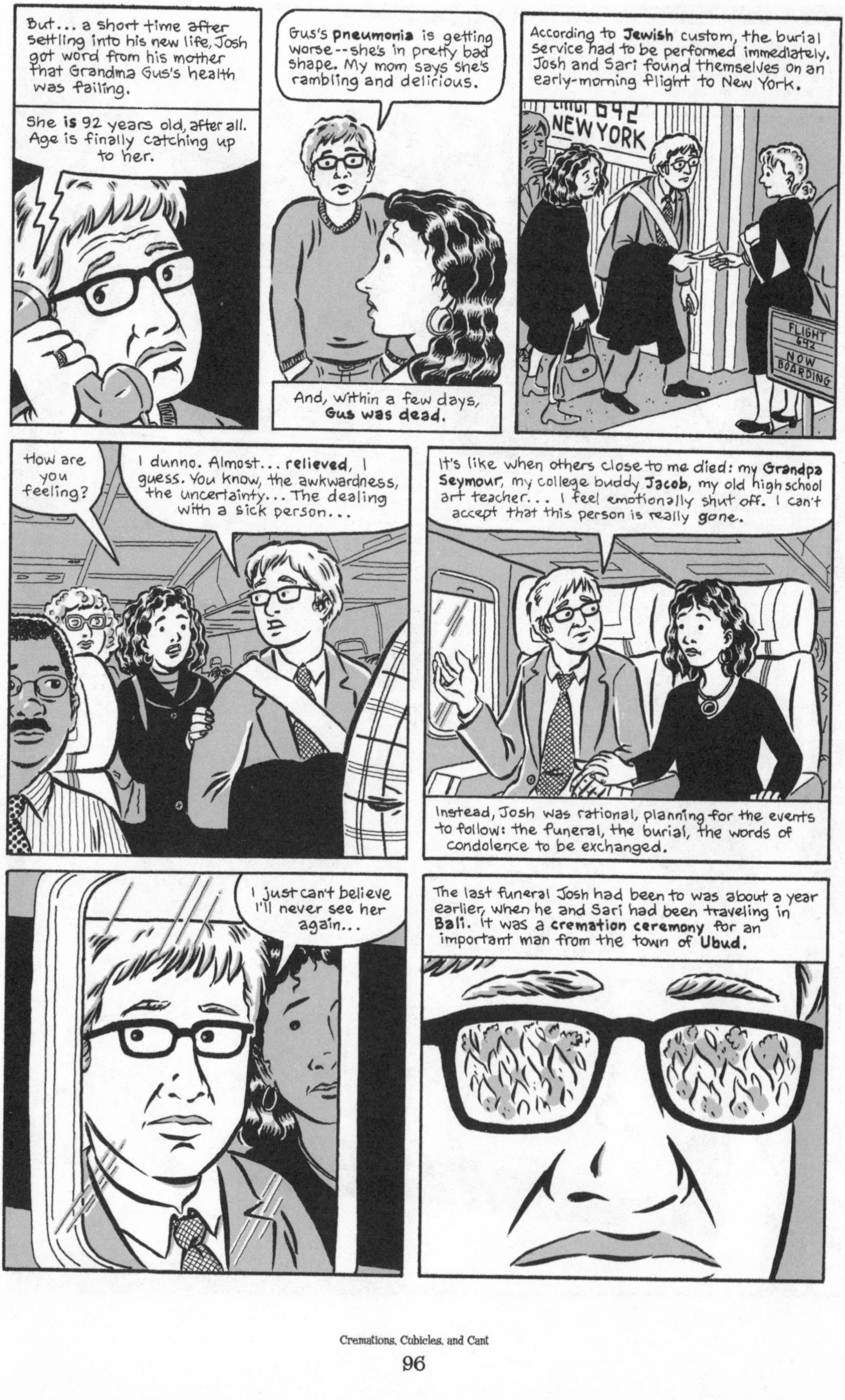
But... a short time after settling into his new life, Josh got word from his mother that Grandma Gus's health was failing.
She is 92 years old, after all. Age is finally catching up to her.
Gus's pneumonia is getting worse--she's in pretty bad shape. My mom says she's rambling and delirious.
And, within a few days, Gus was dead.
According to Jewish custom, the burial service had to be performed immediately. Josh and Sari found themselves on an early-morning flight to New York.
NEW YORK
FLIGHT 642 NOW BOARDING
How are you feeling?
I dunno. Almost... relieved, I guess. You know, the awkwardness, the uncertainty... The dealing with a sick person...
It's like when others close to me died: my Grandpa Seymour, my college buddy Jacob, my old high school art teacher... I feel emotionally shut off. I can't accept that this person is really gone.
Instead, Josh was rational, planning for the events to follow: the funeral, the burial, the words of condolence to be exchanged.
I just can't believe I'll never see her again...
The last funeral Josh had been to was about a year earlier, when he and Sari had been traveling in Bali. It was a cremation ceremony for an important man from the town of Ubud.

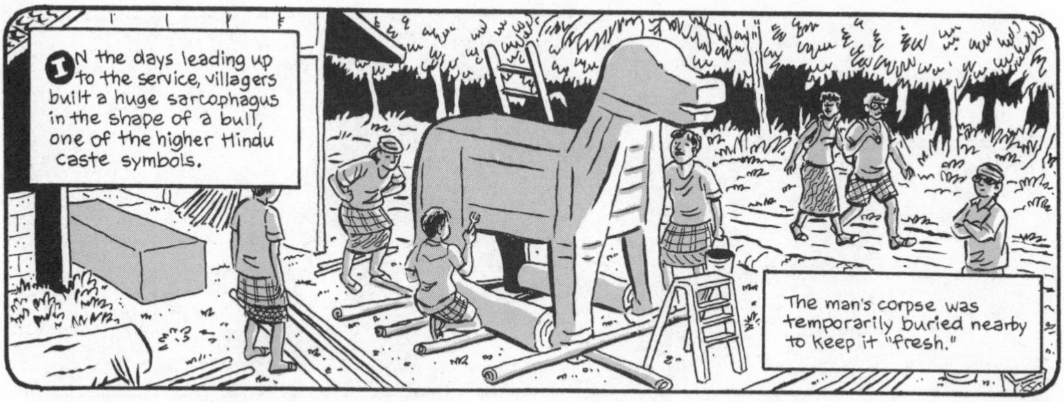
IN the days leading up to the service, villagers built a huge sarcophagus in the shape of a bull, one of the higher Hindu caste symbols.
The man's corpse was temporarily buried nearby to keep it "fresh."

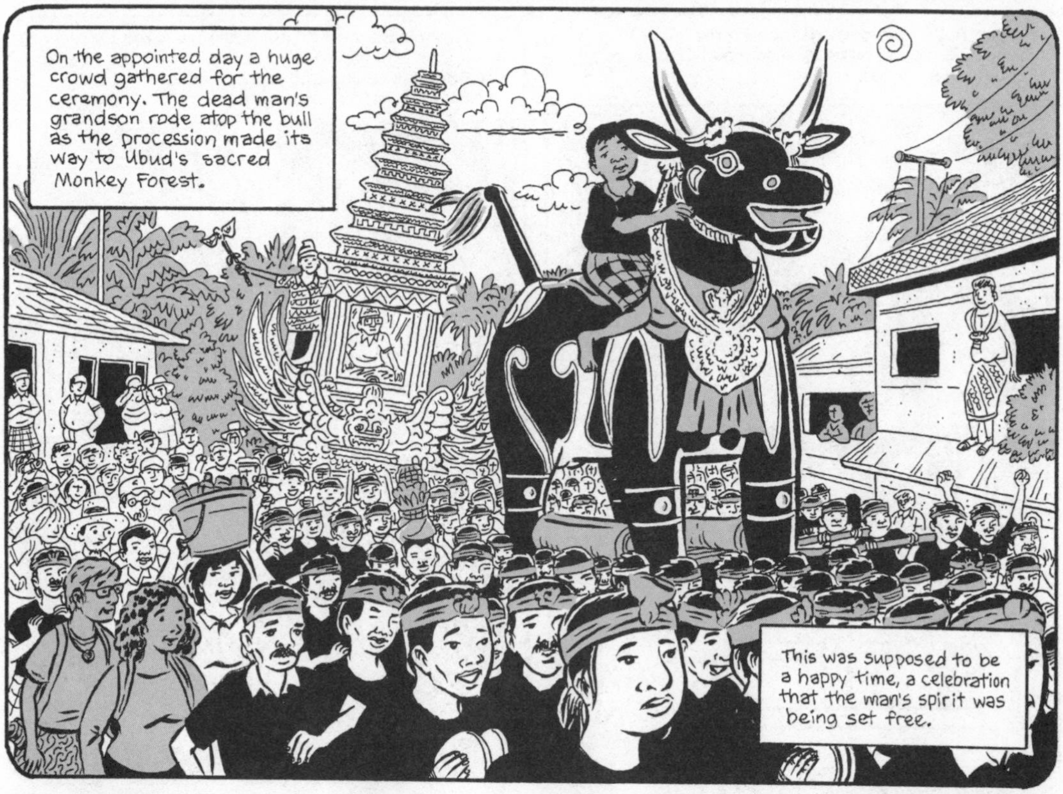
On the appointed day a huge crowd gathered for the ceremony. The dead man's grandson rode atop the bull as the procession made its way to Ubud's sacred Monkey Forest.
This was supposed to be a happy time, a celebration that the man's spirit was being set free.

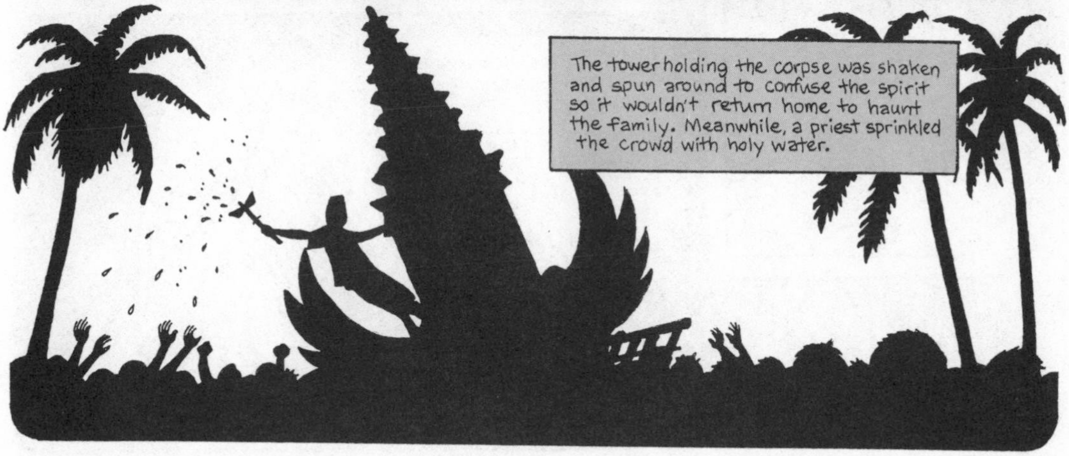
The tower holding the corpse was shaken and spun around to confuse the spirit so it wouldn't return home to haunt the family. Meanwhile, a priest sprinkled the crowd with holy water.

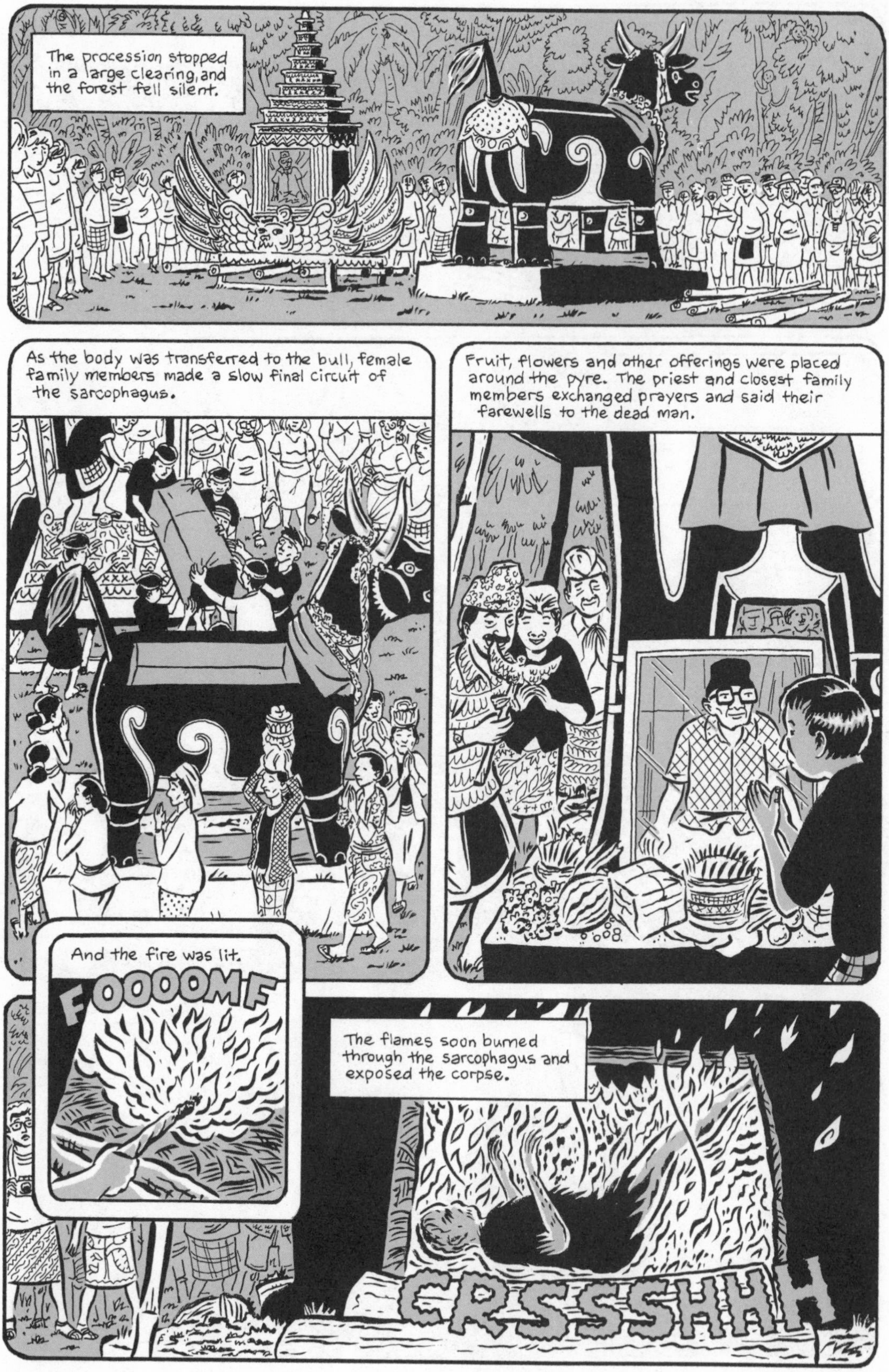
The procession stopped in a large clearing, and the forest fell silent.
As the body was transferred to the bull, female family members made a slow final circuit of the sarcophagus.
Fruit, flowers and other offerings were placed around the pyre. The priest and closest family members exchanged prayers and said their farewells to the dead man.
And the fire was lit.
FOOOOMF
The flames soon burned through the sarcophagus and exposed the corpse.
CRSSSHHH

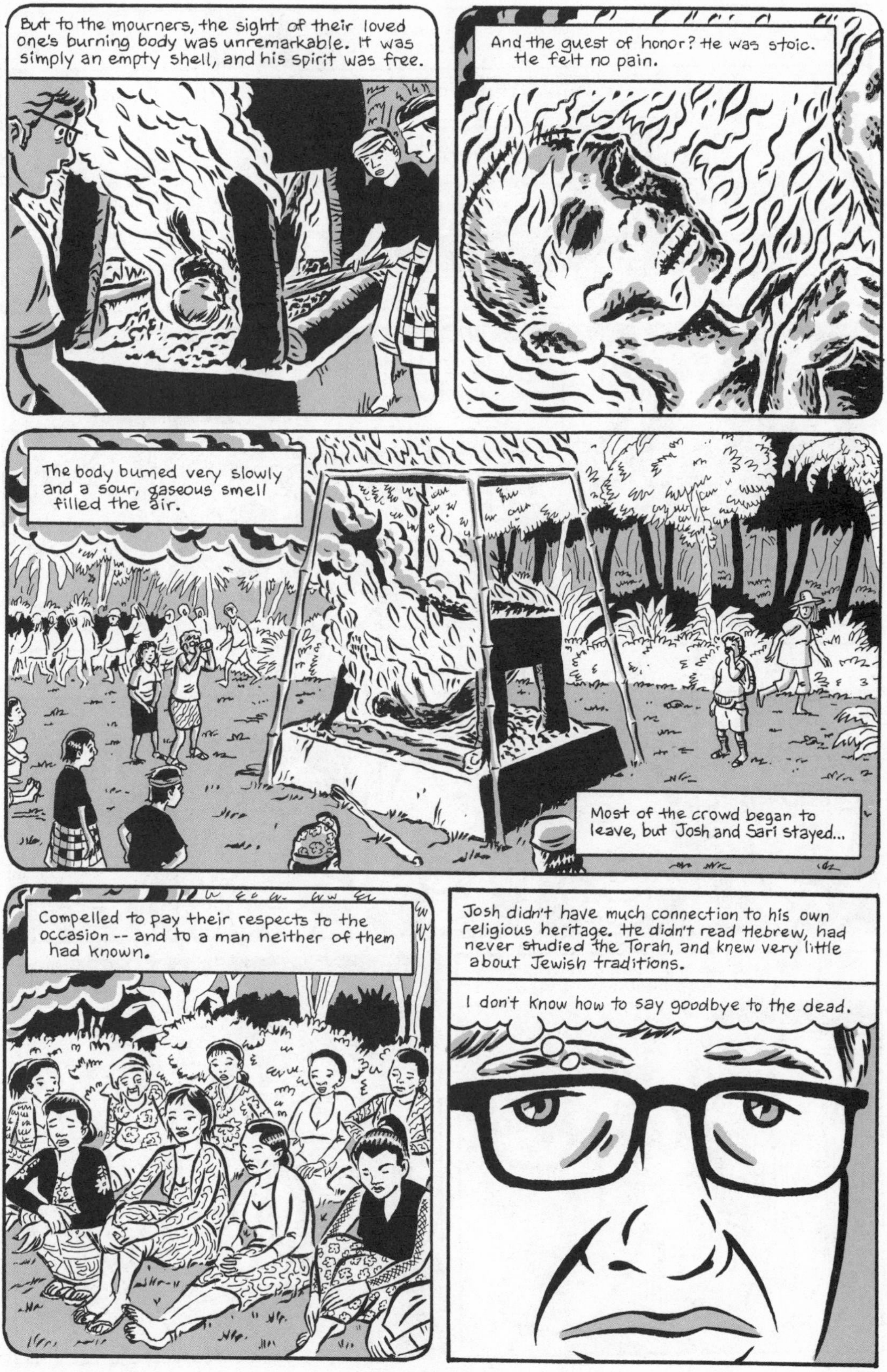
But to the mourners, the sight of their loved one's burning body was unremarkable. It was simply an empty shell, and his spirit was free.
And the guest of honor? He was stoic. He felt no pain.
The body burned very slowly and a sour, gaseous smell filled the air.
Most of the crowd began to leave, but Josh and Sari stayed...
Compelled to pay their respects to the occasion -- and to a man neither of them had known.
Josh didn't have much connection to his own religious heritage. He didn't read Hebrew, had never studied the Torah, and knew very little about Jewish traditions.
I don't know how to say goodbye to the dead.

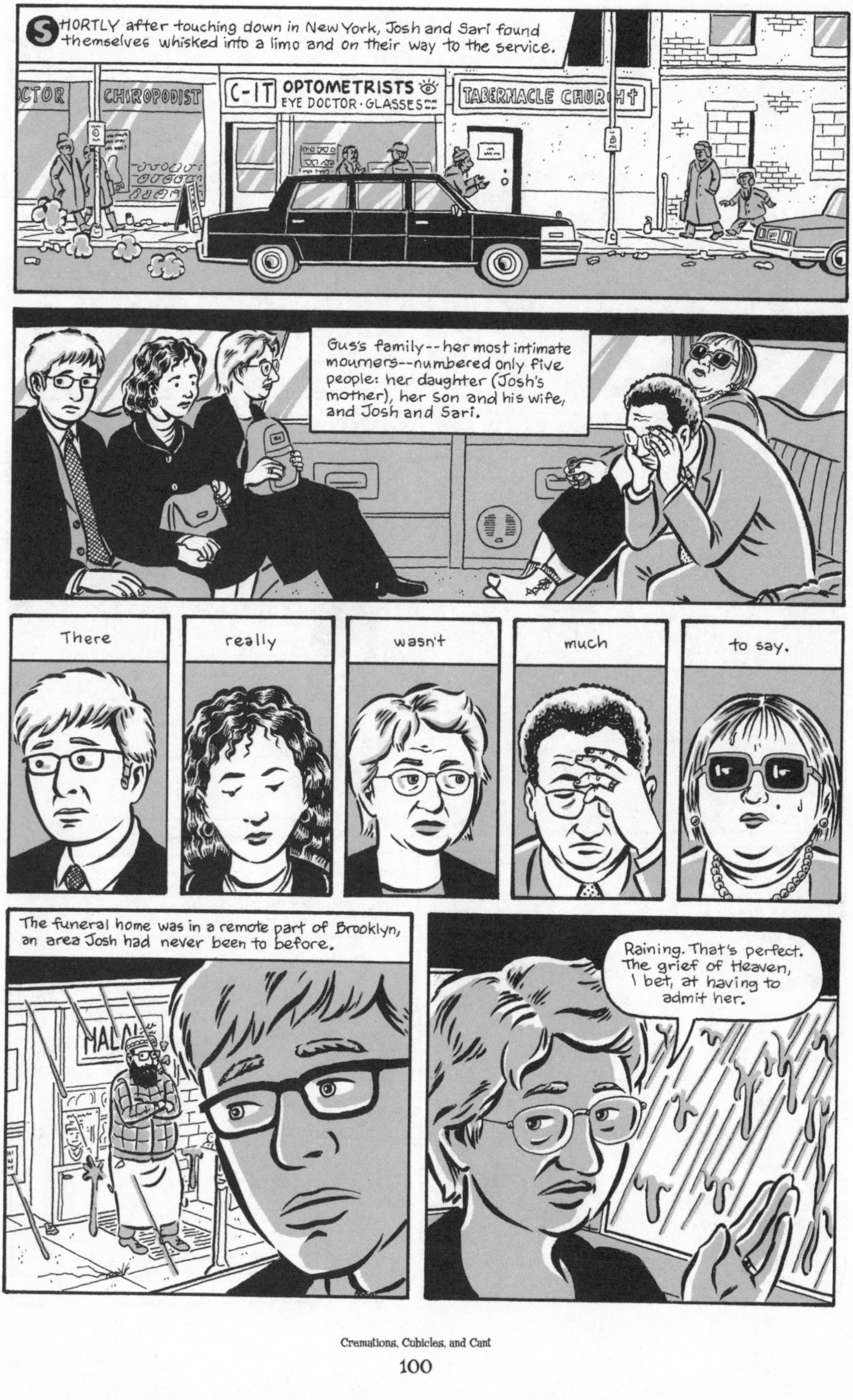
SHORTLY after touching down in New York, Josh and Sari found themselves whisked into a limo and on their way to the service.
CHIROPODIST
C-IT
OPTOMETRISTS
EYE DOCTOR · GLASSES
Gus's family--her most intimate mourners--numbered only five people: her daughter (Josh's mother), her son and his wife, and Josh and Sari.
There
really
wasn't
much
to say.
The funeral home was in a remote part of Brooklyn, an area Josh had never been to before.
Raining. That's perfect. The grief of Heaven, I bet, at having to admit her.

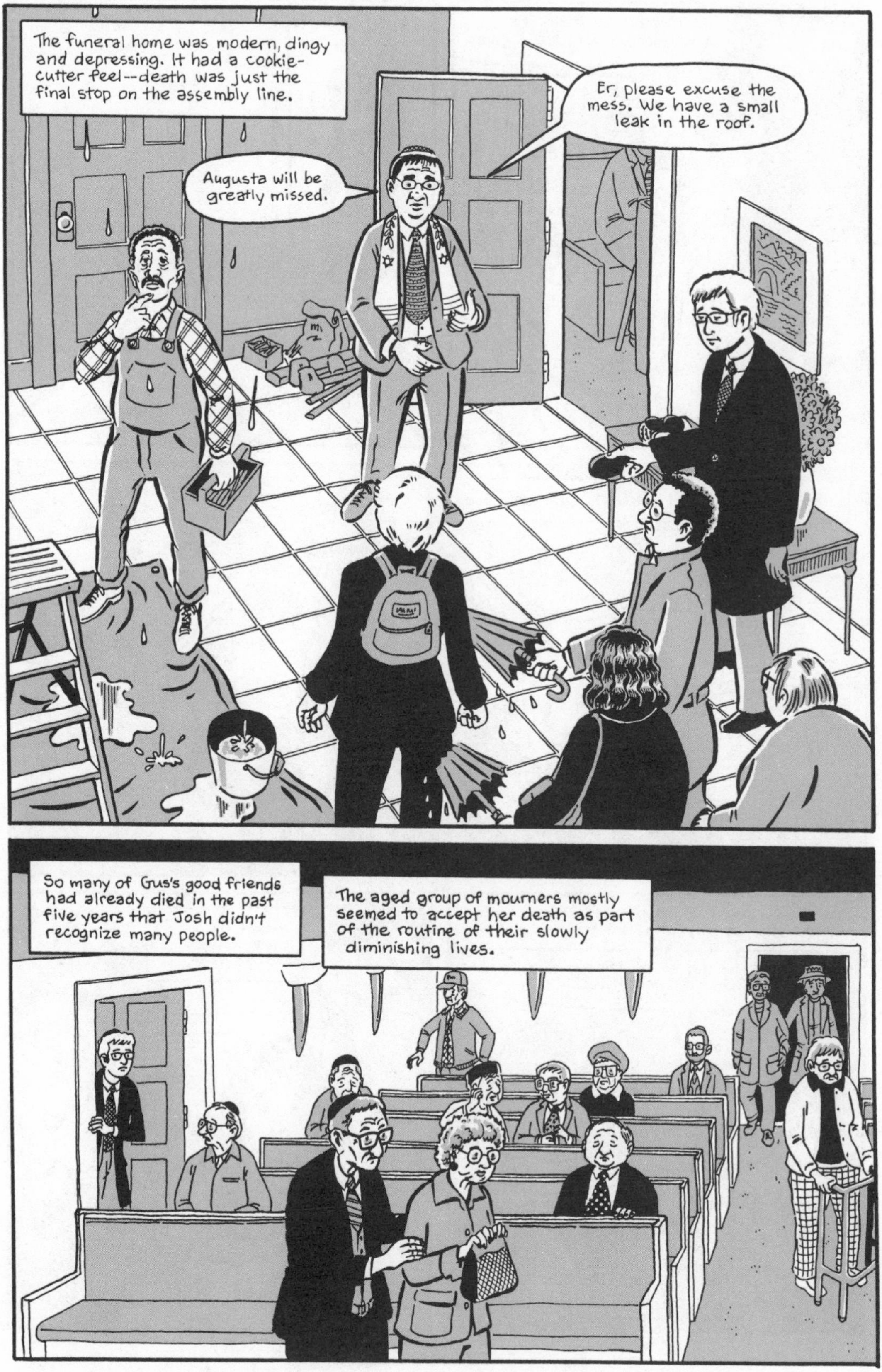
The funeral home was modern, dingy and depressing. It had a cookie-cutter feel--death was just the final stop on the assembly line.
Augusta will be greatly missed.
Er, please excuse the mess. We have a small leak in the roof.
So many of Gus's good friends had already died in the past five years that Josh didn't recognize many people.
The aged group of mourners mostly seemed to accept her death as part of the routine of their slowly diminishing lives.

Mostly.

I drove her to the gift shop every week for fifteen years.

Titleist

The whole affair had a slightly **automatic** quality of grief.

Here are the ribbons for the kriah.

The **kriah**--the ritual rending of the garments-- was as alien as anything Josh had seen on Bali--

Here's the lamentation-of-the-women part. Just rip it a little...

--but its meaning seemed lost to time.

Baruch atah Adonai Eloheinu melekh ha'alom **dayan** ha'emet.

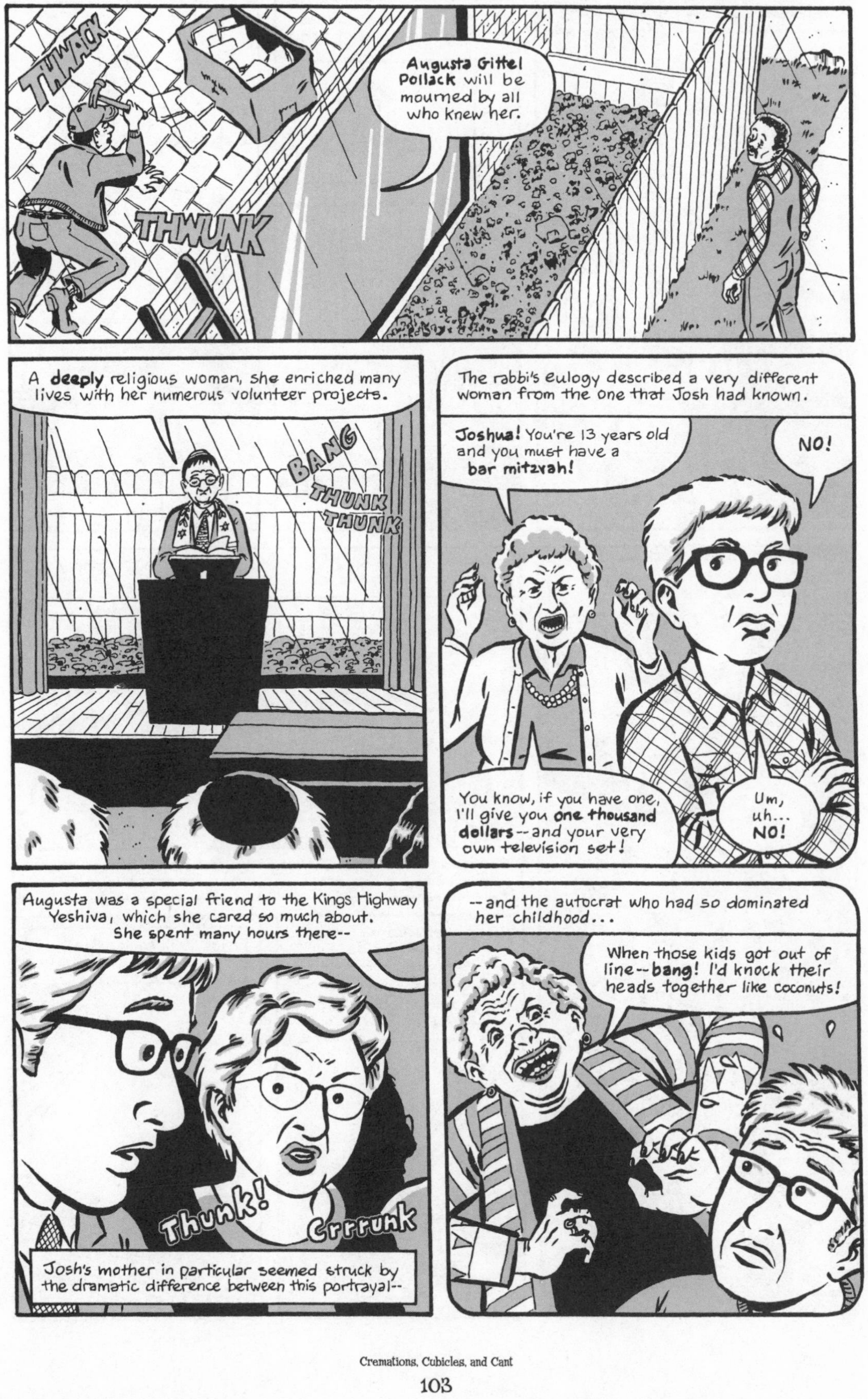
THWACK
Augusta Gittel Pollack will be mourned by all who knew her.
THWUNK
A deeply religious woman, she enriched many lives with her numerous volunteer projects.
BANG
THUNK
THUNK
The rabbi's eulogy described a very different woman from the one that Josh had known.
Joshua! You're 13 years old and you must have a bar mitzvah!
NO!
You know, if you have one, I'll give you one thousand dollars--and your very own television set!
Um, uh... NO!
Augusta was a special friend to the Kings Highway Yeshiva, which she cared so much about. She spent many hours there--
Thunk!
Crrrunk
Josh's mother in particular seemed struck by the dramatic difference between this portrayal--
--and the autocrat who had so dominated her childhood...
When those kids got out of line--bang! I'd knock their heads together like coconuts!

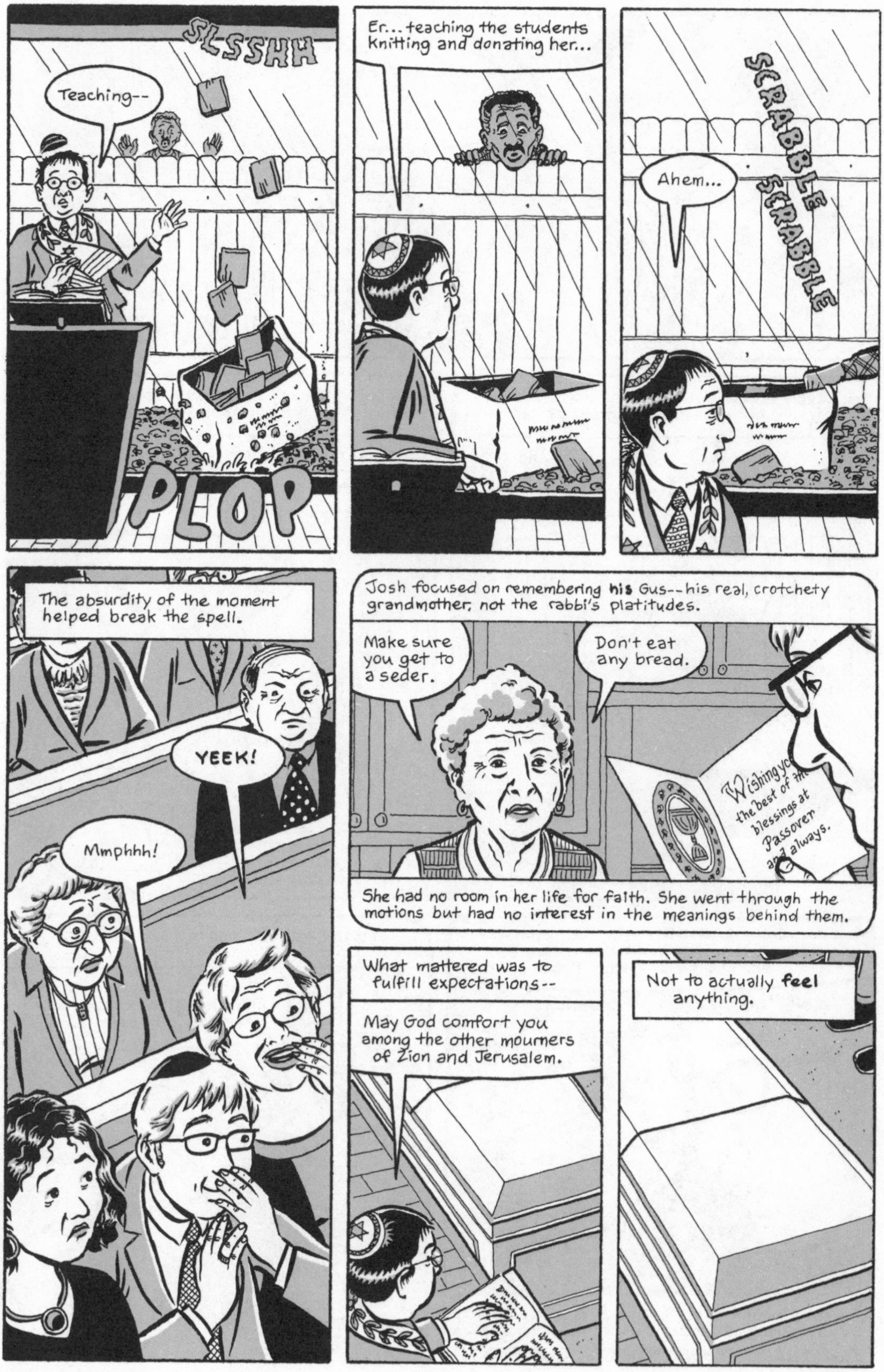
SLSSHH
Teaching--
PLOP
Er... teaching the students knitting and donating her...
SCRABBLE
SCRABBLE
SCRABBLE
Ahem...
The absurdity of the moment helped break the spell.
YEEK!
Mmphhh!
Josh focused on remembering **his** Gus--his real, crotchety grandmother, not the rabbi's platitudes.
Make sure you get to a seder.
Don't eat any bread.
Wishing you the best of the blessings at Passover and always.
She had no room in her life for faith. She went through the motions but had no interest in the meanings behind them.
What mattered was to fulfill expectations--
May God comfort you among the other mourners of Zion and Jerusalem.
Not to actually **feel** anything.

In the chapel after the ceremony, Josh saw his father, who had attended the service out of respect for his ex-wife's family.

Yeah...

But the strange trip was only in its second act, as everyone piled back into the limo...

Listening to the eulogy, I was thinking how people can be so different in different contexts and at different stages of their lives.

Gus obviously mellowed somewhat, but I can't imagine what your mother and her brother were thinking to hear their mother spoken of like that.

The rote service left Josh more confused than ever. He began to doubt whether he had ever really known his grandmother-- and now he never would.

...which followed the hearse to the Kings Highway Yeshiva.

A group of students was lined up, assembled to pay respects to an old woman most of them had probably never even seen.

The hearse's back door was opened to reveal the casket within.

It was a truly bizarre and uncomfortable moment--for all involved. And Josh felt strangely **guilty**, like a voyeur passing himself off as an invited guest.

You've got to be kidding me! For whose benefit **is** this?

Cremations, Cubicles, and Cant

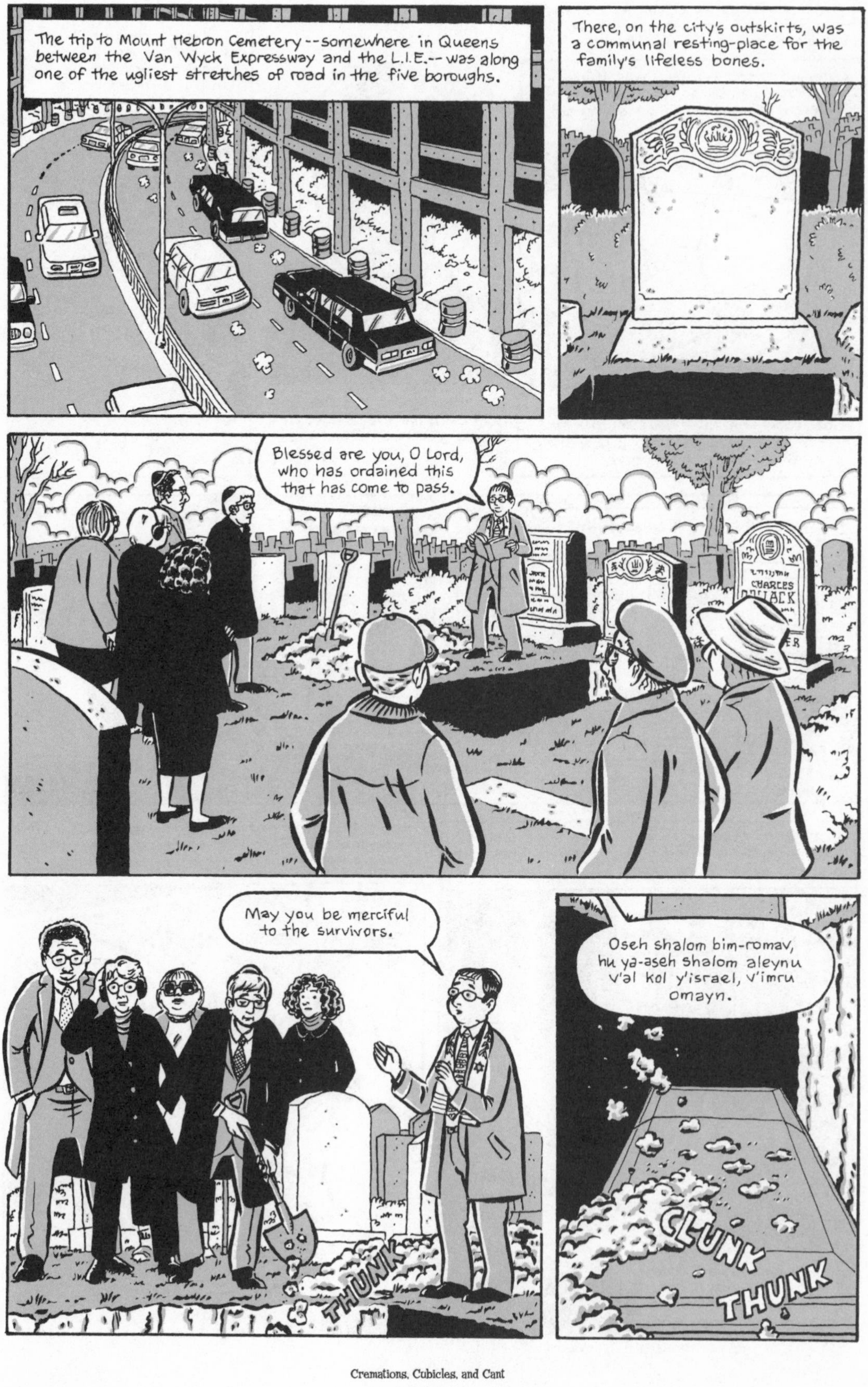
The trip to Mount Hebron Cemetery--somewhere in Queens between the Van Wyck Expressway and the L.I.E.--was along one of the ugliest stretches of road in the five boroughs.
There, on the city's outskirts, was a communal resting-place for the family's lifeless bones.
Blessed are you, O Lord, who has ordained this that has come to pass.
CHARLES
May you be merciful to the survivors.
THUNK
Oseh shalom bim-romav, hu ya-aseh shalom aleynu v'al kol y'israel, v'imru omayn.
CLUNK
THUNK

THAT evening, the family sat **shiva** in Gus's dingy apartment. The mirrors were turned to the wall, and Josh sat on a footstool.

Now tell me again why I'm not allowed to sit in a normal chair?

It's all part of the mandatory grieving process. For a week we're not supposed to work, or wash our hair or clothing. Just be as uncomfortable as possible.

Basically, not do anything but feel sorry for ourselves... and my mother.

And don't forget the other rules: no leather shoes, no shaving or haircuts, and you can't clip your toenails...

Though you can **bite** them off!

And no sex!

As visitors came and went, Josh found himself more emotionally alienated than ever.

I was her chiropodist for twenty years. A lady with feet like that—I thought she'd live forever...

The arcane codes of **shiva** only **widened** the gulf between Josh and his grandmother...

Gus was gone, but Josh hadn't yet said his own farewells.

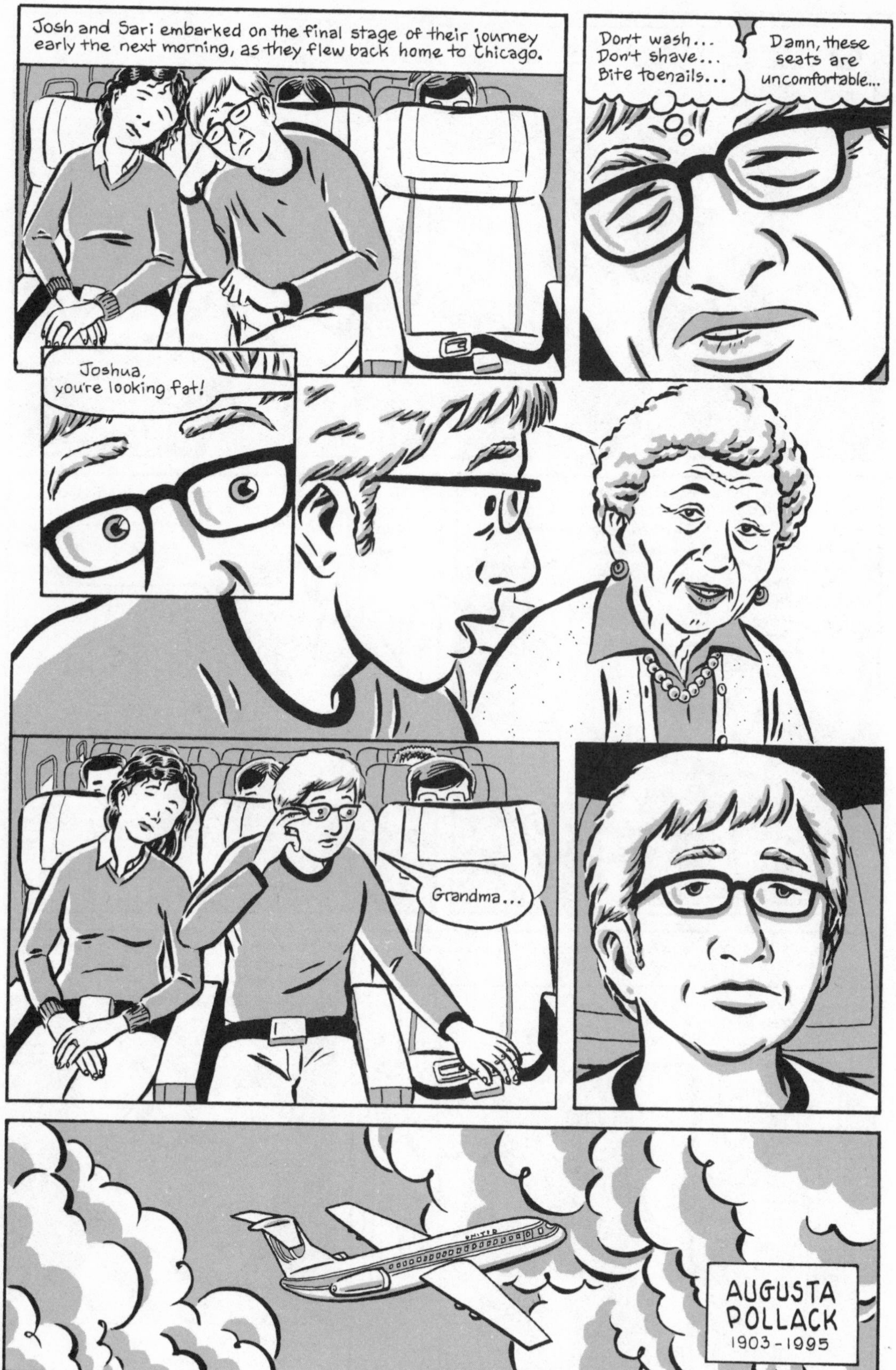
Josh and Sari embarked on the final stage of their journey early the next morning, as they flew back home to Chicago.
Don't wash... Don't shave... Bite toenails...
Damn, these seats are uncomfortable...
Joshua, you're looking fat!
Grandma...
AUGUSTA POLLACK 1903-1995

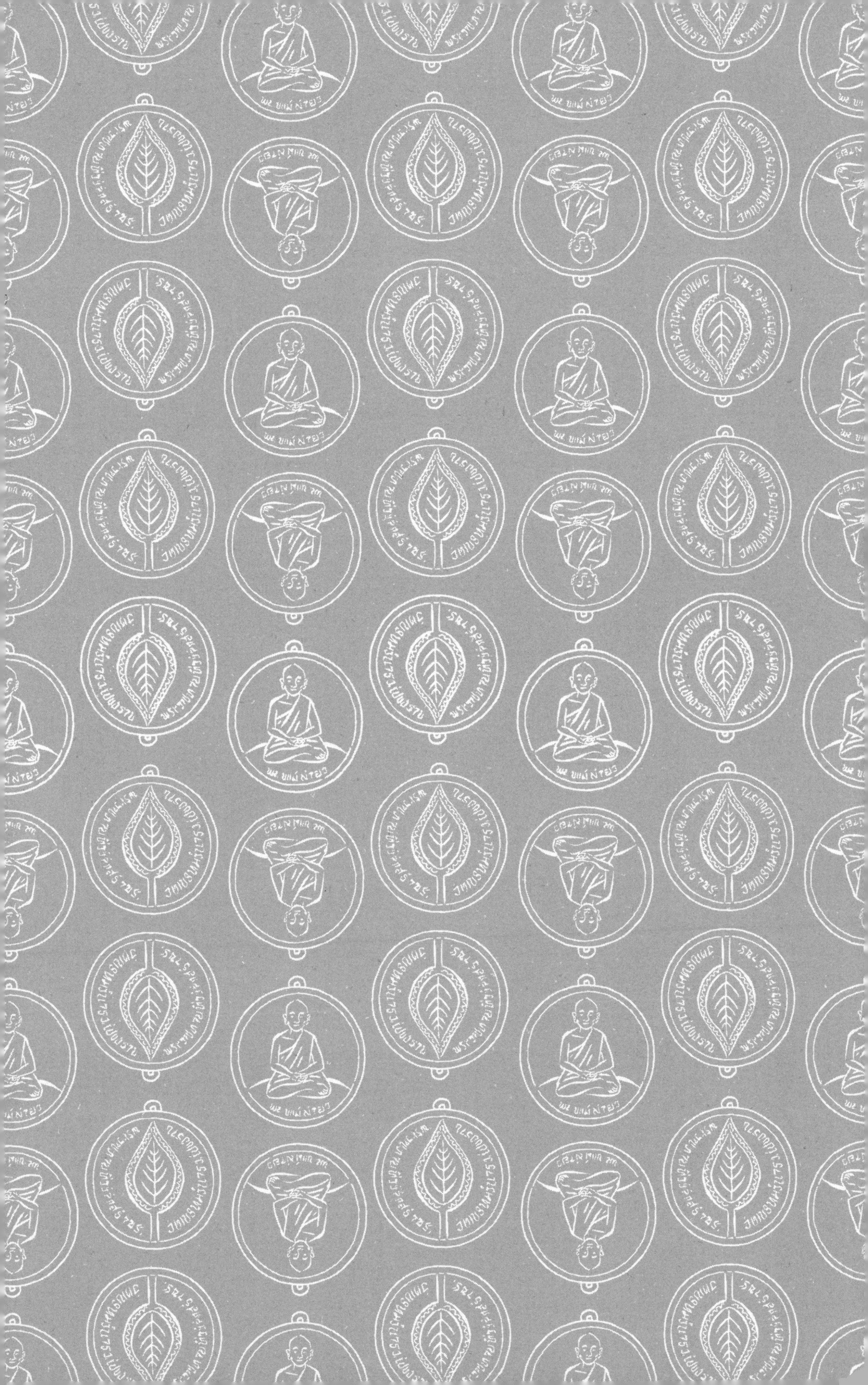

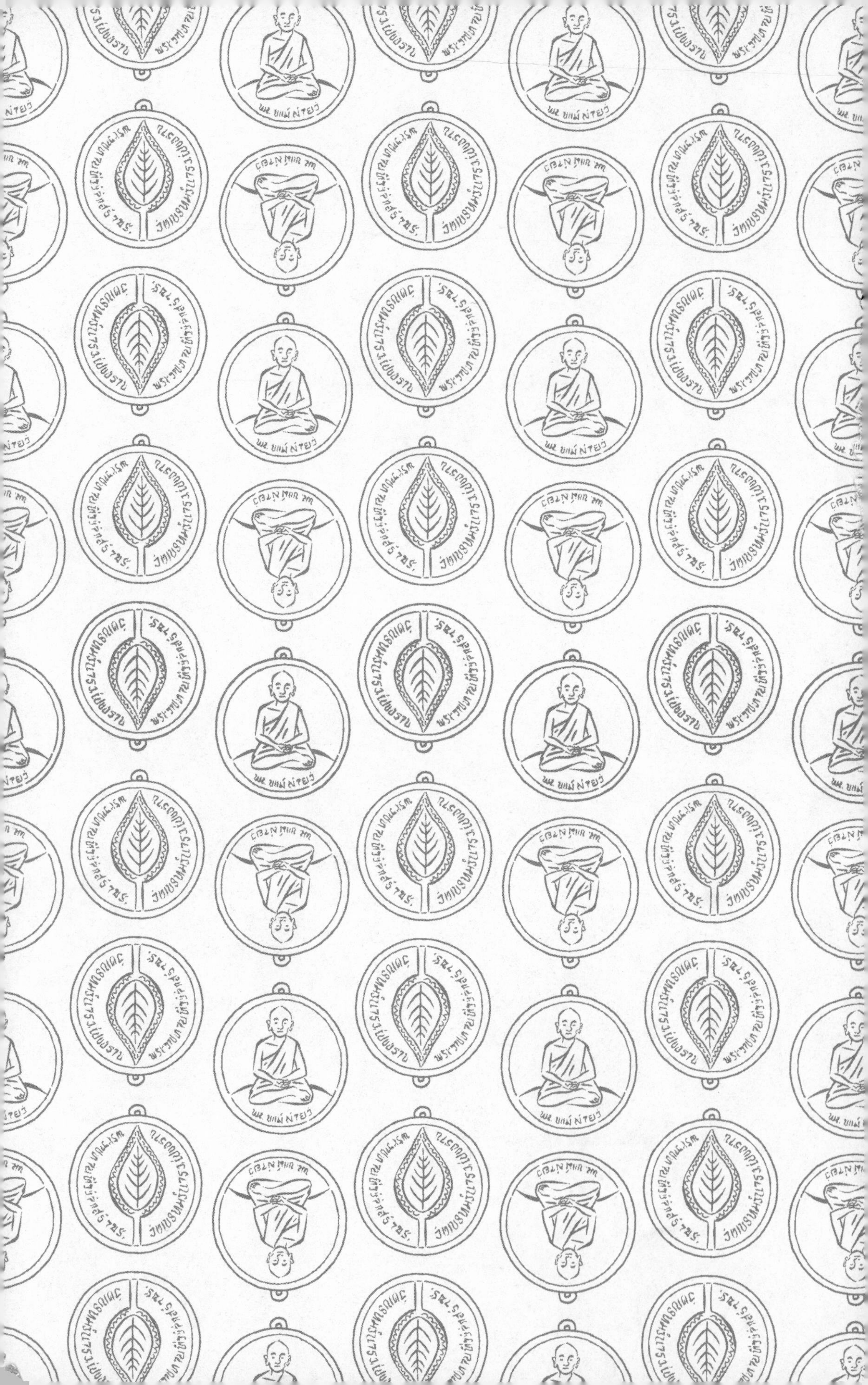